John Walsh

The Greyhound in 1864

John Walsh

The Greyhound in 1864

ISBN/EAN: 9783744678278

Printed in Europe, USA, Canada, Australia, Japan

Cover: Foto ©ninafisch / pixelio.de

More available books at **www.hansebooks.com**

THE GREYHOUND IN 1864:

BEING THE SECOND EDITION OF A TREATISE ON THE ART OF

BREEDING, REARING, AND TRAINING GREYHOUNDS

FOR PUBLIC RUNNING:

THEIR DISEASES AND TREATMENT.

CONTAINING ALSO

THE NATIONAL RULES FOR THE MANAGEMENT OF COURSING MEETINGS

AND FOR

THE DECISION OF COURSES.

BY

STONEHENGE,

WITH ILLUSTRATIONS.

LONDON:
LONGMAN, GREEN, LONGMAN, ROBERTS, & GREEN.
1864.

PREFACE

TO

THE SECOND EDITION.

DURING the eleven years which have elapsed since the first edition of this book was published, my opportunities of investigating the subject of which it treats have been largely increased. On nearly every Coursing ground in England, Wales, and Scotland, I have seen the various breeds of greyhounds tried against each other, and have been enabled to judge of their merits, as well as of the treatment adopted in rearing and training them throughout the different Coursing districts. The experience thus gained has enabled me, I hope, to correct many errors, and to develop some truths; in doing which I have been compelled to rewrite several chapters, and to introduce new matter into all. Without laying myself open to the charge of vanity, I think I may take credit to myself for having assisted the young Courser in learning how to manage his kennel; but this has been amply repaid by the knowledge which has been as freely imparted to me by the veterans of the leash, who, I rejoice to say, are at all times ready to assist their less experienced brethren, either directly or through the press. This unselfish spirit has, nevertheless, been coupled with as keen a rivalry as ever, and it has not been either from carelessness or contempt that any secrets of the kennel hitherto unknown have been permitted to escape. In the chapters relating to the rearing and kennel management of the greyhound, however, there will not be found any great additions to the directions given in the first edition, the chief ones relating to training and the choice of sires and dams—upon which the views put forth by me twelve years ago have been somewhat modified—and I have consequently entirely rewritten the chapters referring to those departments.

In the diagnosis and treatment of the diseases of the dog, some valuable additions to the directions given in the last edition have been made in the present one; foremost among which may be mentioned the German discoveries in regard to the natural history of the worms infecting his body, and to their prevention or removal. The recent researches of Küchenmeister and Von Siebold on this subject have been embodied, as far as is likely to be useful to the non-professional reader, and the most safe and trustworthy remedies suggested. There is still much to be learnt; but it is by gradual steps that any further progress is likely to be achieved, and these can only be gained by recording what is already known or surmised, as I have endeavoured to do.

It is a subject of great congratulation to myself and all admirers of Coursing, that, within the last ten years, the heavy betting which formerly attended it has almost entirely disappeared. With the exception of the Waterloo Cup, there is not a stake in the present day on which any considerable amount of gambling takes place, the investments being confined to such sums as can be well afforded by the owners of the dogs engaged and their friends. Partly as a consequence of this, and to some extent also from the careful supervision of the press, we no longer hear of the charges of fraud which used to be constantly made against the judges. That these officials do occasionally make mistakes is plain enough, but that they are caused by bribery is never supposed by the most suspicious. Contrasting this state of things with what used to occur meeting after meeting, and with the existing state of the turf, Coursers may well be satisfied with the progress of events in their own sport, and they may, I think, hug themselves with the conviction that it is conducted in as honest and sportsmanlike a manner as is consistent with human nature.

The formation of the National Coursing Club, and the new rules which have emanated from that body, have not a little aided in effecting this result. Having, in conjunction with the Earl of Sefton and Mr. C. Jardine, had the honour of drawing up those for the Decision of Courses, I may be naturally supposed to have a partiality for them; but putting this aside as far as is possible, they will, I think, be found more simple and more just than the old ones. To these I have appended the decisions of the Club on the several questions submitted to them since the organisation of that body by Mr. C. Jardine in 1858, and which must now be considered as precedents for future guidance.

It was my intention to have added the portraits of three of the most successful stallions of the last ten years, and an equal number of celebrated bitches, to the list included in the first

PREFACE TO THE SECOND EDITION.

edition. From some cause or other, however, I have been unable to obtain the photograph of 'Scotland Yet' from Mr. Campbell, although I had understood from that gentleman, in answer to my application, that it was at my service. This will account for the omission of this world-renowned brood bitch, and also for the non-substitution of another, as I depended upon the receipt of the photograph till the last moment, when it was no longer possible to replace it by another. The three sires I have selected were without dispute the best of their day,—'Bedlamite' being universally successful, 'David' distancing every competitor in the south, and 'Beacon' in the north of England and Scotland. Of the two bitches, 'Riot' stands unrivalled since the time of 'Mocking Bird' and 'Cerito,' with whom she never came in contact, and cannot therefore be compared. 'Chloe,' though not so generally successful, was the winner of the Waterloo Cup, and over Altcar has proved herself the best bitch since the time of 'Cerito.' These five portraits, all of which are extremely faithfully rendered, may therefore be considered as valuable additions to the previously existing series, and as bringing it down to the present day.

With these explanations of the nature of the additions to, and alterations in, the present edition of 'The Greyhound,' I lay it before the Coursing public, as a treatise on 'The Greyhound in 1864,' in the hope that it may be received as favourably as its predecessor.

STONEHENGE.

KENSINGTON SQUARE:
  Oct. 1864.

PREFACE

TO

THE FIRST EDITION.

From the very flattering reception which was given by the Coursing public to my letters on the Greyhound, which appeared in 'Bell's Life,' I have been induced to republish them with considerable additions and alterations. It will be found that I have entirely rewritten the chapters on breeding, and that I have gone much farther into that interesting subject than I had previously done. Much that is now put forth is theoretical, and as such must claim the indulgence of those who will perhaps dissent from my opinions on this abstruse subject. But I may state, that it is not to support a preconceived theory that my arguments are adduced, but, on the contrary, my theories are the result of facts which have been forced upon me, while utterly in the dark and working at random, in endeavouring to arrive at the truth.

The addition of the series of portraits will, I hope, give interest to the perusal of this book; and as they are, most of them faithful representations, the young Courser will be enabled to judge for himself whether the assertion be true, that 'the greyhound can run in all forms.' To those gentlemen who have either lent the portraits already in their possession, or have gone to the trouble and expense of procuring them expressly for me, I beg to tender my cordial thanks, whilst to those who have been disappointed in their expectations of seeing their favourites appear in my gallery, I must offer the apology, that it is evident there must be some limit. I have endeavoured to select the most characteristic forms and the most remarkable performers, but some of those I could wish to include were so badly painted as to be wholly valueless, and others, which had been well represented by the artist, were already engraved as parts of large subjects, and the copyright in the hands of those who denied me the privilege of extracting individual portraits. This was especially the case with 'Waterloo,' 'Heather Jock,' and other Scotch dogs, which I regret that I am not able to offer to my readers, from the above cause, although, through the kindness of Mr. Gibson, I had procured copies of them all from his celebrated Caledonian Picture by Ansdell. With these exceptions, however, I am enabled to offer one or more specimens of nearly every breed which has been more than commonly successful in public. Mr. H. Hall is so well known as an animal painter, that his name is a guarantee for the fidelity of the four portraits from his easel; nevertheless, I cannot help thinking that he has been led into a little flattery, in point of length, in each instance. Messrs. Ansdell, Barraud, and Calvert, also stand so high as to require no commendation from me. But I may be pardoned for drawing attention to the portrait of 'Sam' by Mr. Glass, and to the several productions of Mr. Wells, which I humbly think are of great value to those who care about the faithful portraiture of their favourites. I have the authority of Messrs. Sharpe, Temple, and Randell, for saying, that they consider those drawn by him for them most perfect representations of their respective animals; whilst 'Mocking Bird,' 'Miss Hannah,' and 'Vraye Foy,' have been seen by so many, that I must leave their portraits to speak for themselves, as, for want of time, they have not yet been submitted to their respective owners. The engravings on wood will, I think, be generally admitted to surpass anything which has ever yet appeared in this style—and Mr. Hacker has done full justice to the frontispiece on steel.

The unexpected delay in the publication of my remarks has arisen from the difficulty in getting the portraits of existing dogs well painted, and also in finding the requisite number of efficient engravers. This is a long process, and as there are few who can accomplish the task of engraving animals, in the style of those which I have the pleasure of offering to the public, the time which has been occupied has been necessarily long. That it may not be thought to have been misspent is the ardent hope of

STONEHENGE.

Oct. 1, 1853.

LIST OF
PORTRAITS ENGRAVED.

NAME OF DOG	PAINTER	DRAUGHTSMAN	ENGRAVER	PAGE
Blacklock	Calvert	Wells	Branston	1
War Eagle	Wells	Wells	Branston	11
Cerito	Ansdell	Branston	Branston	178
Mocking-Bird	Wells	Wells	Branston	183
Miss Hannah	Wells	Wells	Branston	185
Ruby	Wells	Wells	Branston	188
Dressmaker	Lawrence	Wells	Branston	191
Titania	Sent by Mr. Temple	Wells	Thompson	192
Tendresse	H. Hall	Branston	Thompson	193
Riot	Wells	Wells	Butterworth and Heath	197
Whiff	Goddard	W. Bagg	W. Bagg	201
Cactus	H. Hall	Branston	Branston	202
King Cob	Barraud	Branston	Branston	203
Figaro	H. Hall	Branston	Branston	214
Czar	H. Hall	Branston	Branston	219
Sam	Glass	Branston	Branston	225
Bedlamite	Photograph	Wells	Butterworth and Heath	227
Chloe	Roe	Wells	Butterworth and Heath	232
Deacon	Robertson	Wells	Butterworth and Heath	234
David	Wells	Wells	Butterworth and Heath	236
Monarch	Sent by Mr. Sharpe	Wells	Thompson	237
Hughie Graham	Photograph	Wells	Branston	238
Vraye Foy	Wells	Wells	Branston	246
Maid of Islay	Photograph	Wells	Branston	257

The whole of these Engravings are drawn to the above scale; and thus the measurements of any dog may be ascertained by a pair of compasses, and a reference to the scale.

CONTENTS.

CHAPTER I.
INTRODUCTORY REMARKS.

Distinction between public and private Coursing—Qualities desirable in a good Greyhound seldom combined in the same Individual and dependent upon Blood and Form—Definition of term 'Blood'—Dependent on the Brain and Nervous System—External Form not always indicative of the Qualities of the Animal—Examples of this—'War Eagle' compared with 'Blacklock'—Examples of Animals good in all Countries 1

CHAPTER II.
THE DESCRIPTIVE ANATOMY OF THE DOG.

In the Management of the Greyhound a Knowledge of his Diseases is necessary, to understand which the general Structure of the Frame must be explained—Anatomy of the Skeleton—Description of the Head and Neck—The Fore-Quarters—Hind-Quarter—Back—Measure of the various Points—Varieties of the Gallop—Best Size for the Greyhound—Form of Tail—Colour and Coat 18

CHAPTER III.
PHYSIOLOGICAL REMARKS.

Nervous System—Organs of Circulation and Respiration—The Digestive Organs—The Kidneys—Examination of the Dog when attacked with Disease—Forms in which Medicines should be given—Best mode of administering Remedies 44

CHAPTER IV.

DISEASES OF THE GREYHOUND.

1. *General Diseases, with increased Action of the Heart, &c.—Febrile Diseases.*

Ephemeral Fever, or common Catarrh—Influenza, or Epidemic Catarrh—Distemper or Typhus Fever—Rheumatic Fever (often ending in Palsy)—Small Pox 58

CHAPTER V.

DISEASES OF THE GREYHOUND—*continued.*

2.—*General Diseases, without increased Action of the Heart.*

Chronic Rheumatism—Chest-Founder—Chorea, or St. Vitus's Dance—Rickets — Enlarged Joints — Chronic general Dropsy from diseased Kidneys—Cancer and other Malignant Diseases—Epilepsy—Anæmia . 84

CHAPTER VI.

DISEASES OF THE GREYHOUND—*continued.*

3. *Local Diseases generally attended with Inflammation.*

Inflammation of the Brain (Tenatus, Turnside, Rabies, &c.)—Inflammation of the Eye and Ear—Inflammation of the Larynx and Throat (Blain)—Inflammation of the Lungs (Pneumonia, Pleurisy, Bronchitis, and Phthisis)—Inflammation of the Heart and Arteries—Inflammation of the Stomach (Poisoning, Indigestion)—Inflammation of the Intestines (Peritoneal, Mucous, and Muscular, or Colic, Diarrhœa, and Costiveness, Dropsy of Belly, Fistula in Ano)—Inflammation of the Liver (Jaundice, Torpid Liver)—Inflammation of the Kidney (Acute Dropsy)—Inflammation of the Bladder (Calculus, Rupture, Blennorrhagia, and Malignant Diseases)—Inflammation of the Skin (Mange, Blotch, Warts, Canker of the Ear, Surfeit, Eruption between the Toes, &c., &c.) 105

CHAPTER VII.

ACCIDENTS, ETC.

Cuts, Bites, and Tears—Fractures—Dislocations—Hæmorrhage—Ruptures 146

CHAPTER VIII.

WORMS AND OTHER PARASITES INFESTING THE DOG.

Natural History of Intestinal Worms—Prevention—Curative Agents—Other Internal Parasites—External Parasites—Fleas, Ticks, Lice—Mange Insect 152

CHAPTER VIII.*

Innocence of Public Coursing compared with Racing—Its suitability to the Man of limited Means—Advice to Young Coursers on the best means of obtaining a Stud of good Dogs—Selection of Brood Bitches—Examples of good and bad ones 178

CHAPTER IX.

General Principles of Breeding—Modern Theory of Generation—Remarks on the above—Instances of successful Stallions, not good Runners—Reason for this—Explanation of the Nature of what is called 'a Hit' 203

CHAPTER X.

PECULIAR CHARACTERISTICS OF VARIOUS STALLIONS.

Greyhounds divided into Newmarket, Wiltshire, Lancashire, Scotch and Yorkshire Varieties—Descriptions and examples of each—Summary . 219

CHAPTER XI.

Advantages or otherwise of the Bulldog Cross—Best Age of Sire and Dam—Table of the Ages of the Sires and Dams of the Winners and Runners up of the Six principal Stakes run in England during Ten Years—Duration of Pregnancy 246

CHAPTER XII.

In-and-in Breeding—Examples of Success in adopting the Practice—Best Time of the Year for Breeding—Management of the Brood Bitch—Foster Nurse 257

CHAPTER XIII.

Rearing the Whelps—Best time to choose them—Question as to Rearing at Home or 'at Walk'—Time and Mode of Feeding—Necessity for Change of Diet—After Twelve Months of Age, require only Feeding once a Day—The Evening the best time to Feed—Necessity for Daily Exercise — Plenty of Bones should be given — Table of the Weights at various Ages—Undue severity deprecated—Best Diet for the Greyhound—Flesh and Bread—Mode of making Bread without Barm—Other and cheaper Diets sometimes used—Removal of Dew Claws 269

CHAPTER XIV.

Leading—Accustoming to the Muzzle—Entering to his Game—Kennels —Kennel Management—Dressings for Fleas, &c.—Physic—Expenses of Rearing and Training 292

CHAPTER XV.

Maximum and Minimum of Work in Training—First Preparation of the Overfed Dog—Of the Bitch 'in Season'—Modes of reducing Fat— Directions for Feeding—Private Trials—Final Preparation—Management at Meetings and after Running—Concluding Remarks . . 309

CHAPTER XVI.

National Coursing Club—Precedents established by it—Constitution and Bye Laws—Rules for the Guidance of Coursing Meetings—Rules for the Guidance of Judges in their Decisions of Courses 342

APPENDIX.

Pedigrees of Bitches . . . 375
Pedigrees of Stallion Dogs . . 392

'BLACKLOCK.' *

CHAPTER I.

INTRODUCTORY REMARKS.

Distinction between Public and Private Coursing—Qualities desirable in a good Greyhound seldom combined in the same Individual, and dependent upon Blood and Form—Definition of the term 'Blood'—Dependent on the Brain and Nervous System—External Form not always indicative of the Qualities of the Animal—Examples of this—'War Eagle' compared with 'Blacklock'—Examples of Animals good in all Countries.

THE PURSUIT of the hare by means of the Greyhound may be conducted upon two very different principles; one of which is

* For pedigree &c. see Appendix.

usually adopted in private, the other in that more open display which is known as 'public coursing.' In the former of these sports, the destruction of the hare, *per fas et nefas,* seems too often the sole object of those engaged in it, and their only limitation consists in the number of the dogs, which no one but a decided 'pot hunter' allows to exceed a brace at a time. On the other hand, the public courser considers the hare as the only available means of testing the powers of his greyhounds, and these animals are not so much regarded by him as competing with the hare as with one another. It is true that there are many exceptions, some private coursers being as scrupulous in giving 'poor puss' every fair chance, and as watchful to detect every good point in their greyhounds, as the most ardent public courser can desire, but still they are the honourable exceptions; and the general run of private coursers care for little besides the kill, and to them a 'good killer' is the *ne plus ultra* of the greyhound. This defect is by no means necessarily attendant upon private coursing; but unless a judge of the course is always selected, I am afraid it will generally be the result, for without his watchful eye no one will admit the inferiority of his own dog, but all will rest satisfied that they have attained perfection, if they have got a dog which will stand the sole test of merit, from which there is no appeal, viz. the 'bagging of the hare.' Every other point may be disputed or explained away, but the kill is tangible and evident, and therefore it is always laid hold of and paraded by the greyhound-owner, where there is no appointed judge to put the various points at their proper level. The public courser will certainly desire the destruction of the hare when his own dog is engaged, because he knows that without blood occasionally the greyhound loses his courage and fire; but the spectators are often as much interested in the escape of a 'rare hare' as in the performance of the two dogs pursuing her. The consequence of this difference of circumstances is, that a good private dog is seldom of much use in public, because he has been practised so much in order to make him sure of his game, that he has learned to run cunning, and reserve his powers for their most advantageous display: in fact, he has found out that he and his partner, by each alternately pressing the hare, can beat her with little difficulty, whereas if they both do their best from first to last, the hare has a fair chance of escape. The case is just like that of three horses running together, and two of them belonging to the same stable, when by one of these two 'making the running' the powers of the other are reserved till the finish; by these unfair means, although really inferior to the third horse, he would often be able to beat him without difficulty, because the third has been obliged to keep pace with the horse making play, in order to prevent his getting too great a lead, whereas the horse in reserve has been husbanding his powers from the first. This is considered fair in the race-course, because it is open to all to do the like, and the same opinion is held among private coursers, but in public it is maintained that the greyhound's speed gives him sufficient advantage over the hare, without exercising his mental powers also. The axiom, therefore, has been laid down, that the greyhound is the best, which throughout the course does the most towards killing the hare, and not necessarily the one which kills her. On this principle every display of cunning leads to a certain loss, because it allows the other dog to do something in the meantime towards killing the hare, in other words, 'to score one or more points;' and consequently the contest is not between the two dogs on the one hand, and the hare on the other, but between the two dogs themselves, as to which shall really in the whole match do the most towards killing the hare. A little 'waiting' now and then is a point in favour of the dogs as against the hare, and is often encouraged in private; but is fatal, if the contest is in public, not only to the present success of the animal, but often to his further existence; for its display generally ensures his speedy death, unless it comes on after such an amount of work as to excuse its occurrence. Hence the first-rate public dog will often fail to please the private courser, because he will not kill as many hares as the more experienced private one, who would nevertheless, under the fiat of a competent judge, guided by public rules for the decision of courses, be easily beaten by his less sagacious antagonist.

This difference between the two modes of conducting the sport termed coursing no doubt exists pretty generally, but, as I have already hinted, by no means of necessity, since it is just as easy to run the greyhound in private under the rules for public coursing, as at the Amesbury or Waterloo meetings. But it requires the appointment of a judge, which is not always practicable, and when he is appointed it requires also implicit obedience to his *dicta*. With this arrangement the private coursing field may be, and sometimes is, made as interesting as the public one, and may then be considered as exactly of the same character. Without it, it degenerates into 'pot hunting,' and though it may suit the taste of many, it has no attractions for me. Still I have no wish to interfere with its enjoyment. Even in the public field I would scarcely care to see a course without some interest directly or indirectly in the particular dogs engaged. But it appears to me absurd to say that, viewed as a competition between dogs, a good day's coursing at Altcar or Amesbury is less interesting than a day's racing at Newmarket or Epsom. By many it has been alleged that its excitements are not to be compared with those of the race-course; but in the contest between two high-bred greyhounds, there are so many more points of interest than in the race between horses, that I cannot subscribe to this opinion. In the latter, speed is the only quality implicated, and though there is the difference between speed for half a mile, and speed for three or four, still it is, after all, that quality only which is concerned. In the course, on the contrary, there are many more points of interest to be considered, which every ardent courser congratulates himself upon understanding, and the attainment of which he is at great trouble to cultivate in his stud.

Now these desirable points, which we all endeavour to combine as much as possible in the same individual, are, not only the speed and stoutness of the race-horse, but also what are commonly called good working and killing powers, which imply mental as well as bodily tact, hardihood, and honesty; this last quality, when analysed, is mainly dependent upon the amount of jealousy possessed by the greyhound; for what is it, after all, but the desire to excel the competitor, from first to last, without reference to the final result? In the pointer always, and often even in the foxhound and harrier, a great degree of jealousy is injurious; and in them a mutual dependence is to be cultivated, but the moment this comes into play in the public greyhound he is not to be relied upon, and is said to 'be false' or 'to lurch,' because he displays a degree of cunning, leading him to allow his rival to do the work which, if more jealous of him, he would endeavour to do himself. It is, therefore, not only the simple desire to kill which is to be cultivated, but also the desire to anticipate the competitor in killing: many a false dog will run well and with great fire single-handed, but with an assistant he will not exert himself, unless he finds that he must do so, or lose all chance of his game.

But all the above-mentioned qualities are seldom combined in perfection in the same animal. As a rule, the very speedy dog must be of a different form from the very stout one. As well might the breeder of race-horses expect to combine the mile-horse and the four-miler in one, as the greyhound-breeder to get a flyer capable of staying as long as the small compact dog, which would be beaten ten lengths to the hare by his speedier antagonist. The same will apply to working powers; but there can be no reason whatever why the fast dog may not be bred as honest as the slow one. Still this is not often the case; but I hope to show the reason why it is not so. The grand point is, to ascertain, by experience, the shape and blood which *have* succeeded in defeating the greatest number of competitors in that country, which is to be the seat of the competition proposed to be carried on. The shape is, of course, tangible and open to the eye; but the nature of what is called blood is of a deeper character. Now, what is usually meant by 'blood'? Mr. Thacker, who has done so much to explain and improve the art of breeding the greyhound, was of opinion that there was really a difference in the shape of the globules of the blood of a high and low-bred greyhound; but this theory is now known to be fallacious. The microscope will measure the most minute difference in size or shape, but still it fails to discover any such deviation; and no test, except perhaps the nose, could detect any difference between the blood of the 'Flying Dutchman' and that of a cart-horse, or between the blood of a 'Mocking Bird' and that even of a sheep dog or lurcher. In the high-bred horse, as well as in the high-bred dog, the skin is thin and delicate, and the superficial veins are more readily seen; but these vessels are also really more numerous and capable of containing more blood; so that during the very severe struggles of a long-continued gallop the heart and lungs are relieved from the overwhelming quantity of fluid, which would otherwise be dangerous to the safety of the animal. Hence the blood has been taken as a test of high breeding, and has been supposed to differ in the form and composition of its globules, whilst the fact is, that the difference really lies in the vessels which contain it. But the chief distinction between the high-bred animal and his inferior consists in the brain and nervous system. It is true that we know little or nothing of the ultimate composition of the various parts of this system, but we judge by its manifestations that there is a difference, though we are unable to detect it. In the same way, we cannot, by the eye, easily distinguish between iron and steel, though we know that the qualities of the two are essentially different; and the difference between the nervous system of a high-bred race-horse and that of a common roadster is just as great. The one will cheerfully persevere till, exhausted by fatigue, he falls and dies; whilst the other will knock up and refuse to answer to the severest punishment which can be administered by the whip or spur. So it is with the greyhound. If well-bred, he runs till he can no longer stand, and, if not in condition, often dies from his exertion; while, if of low parentage, he will take care to stop long before he has injured himself by his efforts. But it may be said that this argument will apply equally to the blood, and so it would, but that we have strong reasons for believing that this fluid is really the same in all individuals of the same species; that is to say, as far as regards the composition and shape of its globules. But with regard to the nervous system we find a great variation in different individuals and families of the same species. If we compare the brain of the bull-dog with that of the poodle or sheep-dog, it will be seen at once that the volume of the former is much greater than that of the latter; yet the intelligence of the poodle is far greater than that of the bull-dog, indeed it is higher than any other of the canine race, and requires a considerable portion of brain for its development. Now (without descending into the disputed points of phrenology) there can be no question that the intellectual faculties depend upon the anterior, whilst the animal passions reside in the posterior part of the brain; and hence, while the poodle's brain is of the same width behind as before, the bulldog's is considerably wider and higher between the ears than behind the eyes. The consequence is that his animal passions are all carried to an inordinate pitch, beyond even his own power of control; and he will suffer himself to be cut to ribbons before he will quit his hold. In many cases the attachment to the master is forgotten or overruled, and he will, if excited, fasten upon him as readily as upon the object of his instinctive pursuit. Here, then, is apparently a cause and effect; there is an extraordinary development of an organ, and a corresponding increase of a faculty, which, no doubt, is intimately connected with that organ, and this entirely independent of any change of blood, as far as we know. The same will be found in man; the pugilist has the posterior part of his brain enlarged, whilst the forehead is often low and deficient in volume: again, the apparently delicate man, of high intellect and large brain, will often go through fatigues which would wear down an equally delicate frame, where the nervous organisation was of a less perfect character.

It may therefore, I think, be assumed that what is usually called 'good blood' is a highly perfect state or condition of all the organs of the body, depending upon the development of the brain or nervous system, and requiring that part of the brain to be large in which reside the qualities which are particularly desired in the individual: thus a race-horse of 'good blood' would require such an organisation of brain as would give him quickness and cleverness of stroke in his gallop, and also stoutness sufficient to continue it. A greyhound of 'good blood' would also require these properties even more fully than the horse, but in addition there would be demanded the following qualities—namely, tact, destructiveness, jealousy, and hardihood or impenetrability to injuries. Tact is wanted to enable the dog to command himself at his turns, and to prevent his overtaxing his energies in his efforts to carry out his purpose; this quality, in addition to those assigned to the race-horse, would render the greyhound *capable* of doing what is required; but, to make him *willing and anxious*, there must be superadded, destructiveness to induce him to endeavour to kill, jealousy to lead him to surpass his fellow if possible, and impenetrability to injury, to make him regardless of fatigue, injuries, and disappointments. With a brain manifesting these qualities, a comparatively bad frame will beat a very superior one, whose brain is deficient in the three last. At least such will be the result, if my theory is correct; but at all events we do know that there is some strange difference between two animals, similar in external form, by which the one shall be enabled to beat the other without allowing a point of merit in a long course, and this invisible difference in general language is called a difference in 'blood.' There seems to be less *essential* difference apparent in the greyhound than in the horse, between the slow form and the fast one. Any one conversant with race-horses could pick out certain animals, and positively decide that they *must* be slow, but no one can do this with the greyhound, for, though he might make a good guess, there would be no certainty in his conclusion. Who, for instance, looking at the form of Mr. Webb's 'War Eagle,' could suppose that he could have first-class pace? yet that such was the case will be generally admitted. Compared with his sister 'Well I Never,' he was in shape as a cart-horse to a race-horse; still, though she was as fast as most greyhounds, he could always lead her to the hare by several lengths.

'WAR EAGLE.'*

* For pedigree &c. see Appendix.

The engraving of 'War Eagle' is very like him, and should be carefully studied by those who think that the light and speedy-looking form of 'Mocking Bird,' 'Hughie Graham,' 'Titania,' or 'Blacklock,' is essential to produce great pace. Now 'War Eagle' has one of those heads, wide between the ears, which I believe give the three qualities I have named; but whether to the fullest extent of which the greyhound's brain is capable of being produced, I do not pretend to say, since the measurement of the whole does not afford any clue to the individual parts. But I believe that in almost all cases when you find a greyhound's head which, like his, measures nearly 15 inches in circumference, midway between the eyes and ears, there will be the three desired qualities developed; in varying proportions perhaps, but, as a whole, to a great extent. The same form of head I have never found to the same extent in others of his breed, though very visible in some, as for instance in 'Tendresse,' but it will be almost always seen in the 'Jason' family, where it may fairly be attributed to the bull-dog cross. How it came to 'War Eagle' and 'Tendresse' I am at a loss to know, but there it is; and those who have seen them run may judge of its correspondence with their performance better than myself, who have never seen either of them in the slips.

In order to enable my readers to make this comparison, a portrait of 'Blacklock' is given at the head of this chapter, which is said to be a faithful likeness of that wonderfully fast and successful dog. The back of his head is developed to a great extent, and in this point he resembles 'War

Eagle;' but it will at once be apparent that there is a great difference between the two forms in every other particular—the one being light and airy, the other thick and muscular.

There can be no doubt whatever that, *cæteris paribus*, the shape of 'War Eagle' is not that best calculated for speed; but the racing form so much desired by all must not be calculated from individual cases, and can only be ascertained by comparing a large number of fast dogs with a similar number of slow ones, and then we shall arrive at a frame much more open, generally more lengthy, and not of such massive proportions as his; and as a rule, as we lose this shape we lose speed in proportion; that is to say, the capability of going fast will be in a ratio with the length of the greyhound's limbs. But we also find that stoutness generally corresponds with the thick, muscular, compact form, and therefore we are led to believe that in proportion as we sacrifice the one of these forms to the other shall we lose its corresponding faculty. The portrait of 'War Eagle' must, however, convince the most sceptical, that speed is not inseparably connected with the opposite shape to his. And though there may be a difference of opinion as to his stoutness, yet his shape must show that we may hope to get that quality combined with pace in the same individual, because he has the form usually considered essential to stoutness, without the loss of speed.

Again, it has been supposed by many that speed to the hare is incompatible with working qualities, in combination with that venomous desire to kill, regardless of pain or injury, which characterises some breeds, and which is entirely distinct from the quality called stoutness. But let those who have seen the litter got by the 'Curler' out of 'Lucy,' run in 1852, say whether they did not combine great outgoing speed with all the other qualities I have enumerated. For though, as I have said, they possess first-class pace, they were as stout as steel, good workers and killers, and regardless of punishment. But, as I have already remarked, in the 'Jason' head inherited by the 'Curler,' and most of the other descendants of 'Jason,' will be found the same shape, or nearly so, which I have described in 'War Eagle,' and with this advantage, that it is almost always found in that family, and not, as in the 'Foremosts,' only occasionally, and I think there is less development of the forehead in the 'Jasons' than in the 'Foremosts.'* I have measured a great number of the descendants of 'Jason,' and have found in almost every instance the dimensions to exceed fourteen inches and a half, in some reaching to fifteen inches. The development is still greater between the ears, where it cannot be so well measured on account of the jaw not reaching so far back. Whether this form of head be inherited from the bull-dog or not, it is, I am sure, characteristic of this family; and as it does not appear in the portrait of Mr. Sharp's 'Monarch' (the grandsire of 'Jason,' and free from the bull-dog cross, which comes through 'Risk'), it may fairly be supposed to be derived from that strain.

* This form of head is seen in 'Mocking Bird,' though not in any other of her family. It therefore, most probably, comes through 'Frederica,' the dam of 'Foremost,' and granddam of 'Mocking Bird.' It is also well developed in 'Riot,' who is descended, though one stage more remotely, from 'Frederica,' being by 'Bedlamite,' son of 'Figaro,' and therefore a grandson of that bitch.

In the first edition of this book, the opinion which is expressed in the foregoing paragraph could only be supported by such examples as had appeared in public up to that time. But during the interval which has elapsed since its publication several greyhounds have lived and died, which confirm my belief still more strongly. Mr. Randell's 'Riot' is perhaps the most notable example, and her great rival in the south, Mr. Long's 'David,' is another almost equally strong, with whom may be coupled his son 'Patent,' a great winner in every country. Both 'Riot' and 'David' were fast enough for 'Altcar,' and though possibly not quite possessed of the flying speed of Mr. Gregson's 'Neville,' or Mr. C. Jardine's 'Mocking Bird,' nothing slower would lead them to the hare; and it is not capable of demonstration that they could have done so, as they never came together. Mr. Raxter's 'Romping Girl' might also be adduced as a case in point, but her stoutness was never so fairly tested on the Downs or at Newmarket or Cardington, though she was a winner in Scotland in the spring, where the trials are often nearly as severe as at the great southern meetings. To these examples might fairly be added Mr. Purser's 'Prizeflower,' and her daughter (now Mr. Bland's), 'Pride of the Village,' as well as Mr. Lister's 'Chloe,' winner of the Waterloo and Altcar cups, and also running well at Ashdown in her puppy season, when she went down to Lord Sefton's 'Sapphire' in the deciding course. This last-named bitch, together with her half-sister 'Sampler,' possessed all the qualities I have adduced in a high state of development; and though the blue never shone to advantage at Altcar, and her pace was not equal to that of the other greyhounds I have adduced, yet she was wonderfully stout and clever in proportion to it. Now, with the exception of 'Sampler,' all these fast, clever, and stout dogs were descended from 'King Cob,' and most of them possess a strain of 'Bugle,' which is manifested in 'Sampler,' who is also descended through 'Foremost' from 'Frederica' (dam also of 'Figaro'), to which bitch I have alluded in the foot-note at page 14. 'Mocking Bird's' wonderful powers I adduced in my first edition, as well as those of 'Miss Hannah' and the 'Bedlamite' litter, all possessing a combination of these qualities in the highest degree; but from the enormous stride of 'Mocking Bird,' she could not command a bad hare like 'Riot' or 'David,' who were nearly equally at home with a short running, or weak hare, and with a racing one. Many more instances could be given of greyhounds capable of competing successfully in all countries; and indeed the fact is now generally admitted, that it is not necessary to select different strains of blood for the Altcar plains and the south-country downs. The members of the Altcar Club have been extremely successful at Ashdown and Amesbury, whenever they have put in an appearance; and independently of Lord Sefton and Mr. Randell, who are constant supporters of down coursing, Mr. Thompson with 'Tirzah' and 'Truth,' Mr. Jefferson with 'Java' and 'Imperatrice,' Mr. Jones with 'Jael,' Lord Grey de Wilton with 'Gabriel,' 'Greek Fire,' and others, Mr. Brocklebank with 'Bindweed,' Mr. Hornby with 'Hunca Munca,' and Mr. Lister with 'Chloe,' 'Cockle Tom,' and 'Cheer Boys,' have distinguished themselves of late years.

The opinion that a slow clever dog, if he were only stout, could be depended on in severe countries, is now nearly exploded, and the combination of pace and cleverness, with as much stoutness as can be obtained, is the object of the courser's attention in breeding, let the country he runs in be what it may.

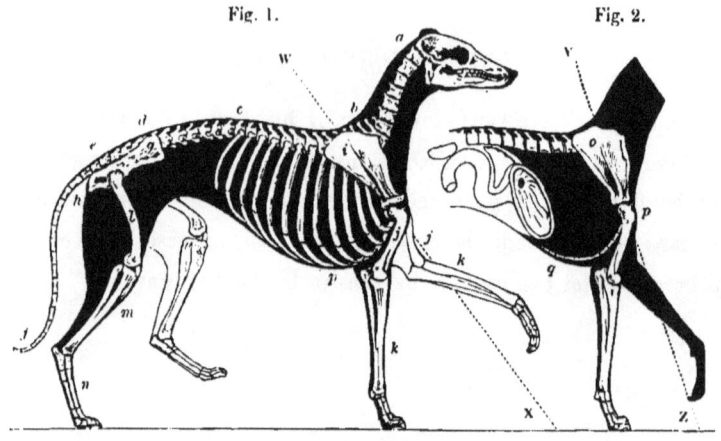

PLAN OF SKELETON.
Fig. 1. w, x, Axis of oblique Shoulder.   Fig. 2. y, z, Axis of upright Shoulder.

CHAPTER II.

THE DESCRIPTIVE ANATOMY OF THE DOG.

In the Management of the Greyhound a Knowledge of his Diseases is necessary, to understand which the general Structure of the Frame must be explained —Anatomy of the Skeleton—Description of the Head and Neck—The Fore-Quarters—Hind-Quarter—Back—Measure of the various Points— Varieties of the Gallop—Best Size for the Greyhound—Form of Tail— Colour and Coat.

EVERY COURSER must be aware that the rock upon which the greater proportion of his failures has been wrecked, was a disease of one kind or other. 'Distemper,' says one, 'has ruined my kennel, so that I have no good dog this year.' 'Ah! if such a dog had lived, I should have won the Waterloo Cup,' says another. The fact is, that a dog requires not only every care in maintaining his health, by good food, good exercise, and good lodging, but he also demands a thorough knowledge of his diseases, in order to prevent their encroachment on the health of his frame, by which his powers of body and mind (for he has a mind) are lost. It will, therefore, be my object to make my readers understand the nature of the diseases to which the dog, and more especially the greyhound, is subject, and to explain the best and simplest mode of treating them. But, in order to render my observations intelligible to my readers, I must commence by explaining the general structure of the animal which is to come under treatment, and this I hope to do in such terms as to be understood by the most ignorant (medically) of my readers.

The dog is an omnivorous animal by long habit, though probably originally carnivorous, as indicated by his teeth, of which the following is the formula:—

$$\text{Incisor } \frac{6}{6} \quad \text{Canine } \frac{1-1}{1-1} \quad \text{Molar } \frac{6-6}{7-7} = 42.$$

He belongs to the division in the animal kingdom Vertebrata, and the class Mammalia. His body, like all the mammalia, may be described as consisting of two sets of organs, one of which (the skeleton, with the muscles and nerves setting it in motion) serves to obtain the food of the individual, and to enable it to escape the attacks of other animals; whilst the other, composed of the various organs of respiration, circulation, digestion, and secretion, is intended to maintain the body in a state of repair, affording fresh materials when wanted, and at the same time purifying the whole by processes which are now becoming daily more and more intelligible.

THE SKELETON consists of the skull, trunk, and extremities. The skull is hollowed out to contain the brain, and also the eye, ear, nose, and tongue; it is attached to the trunk by the neck, which is the commencement of a series of hollow bones united together to form a canal extending from the head to the tail, and containing a continuation of the brain in the form of a compound nerve—the spinal marrow, as it is commonly called. The trunk is formed of this chain of bones called the spine (divided into the seven cervical, $a\ b$, thirteen dorsal, $b\ c$, and seven lumbar vertebræ, $c\ d$), and, extending backwards still further, of the sacrum or rump-bone $d\ e$, attached to which are the twenty bones of the tail $e\ f$, which are no longer hollow for the lodgment of the spinal marrow. Besides the spine, the trunk is composed of the thirteen ribs $b\ c\ h$, attached to the thirteen dorsal vertebræ by ligamentous bands, and forming, with the breast-bone (Fig. 2, q), the thorax or chest, for the protection of those important parts, the lungs and heart, and partially also the stomach and liver. To the sacrum, also, are attached by similar ligaments the hip-bones $g\ h$, for the purpose of affording protection to the bladder, and to the uterus, &c., in the female, and to give a firm fulcrum to the hind-legs, which are the main organs of propulsion. In the dog, as in the horse, there is no collar-bone, and the only attachment between the fore-legs and the body is muscular, so that the chest is as it were slung between the shoulder-blades on the fore-legs. By this arrangement there is not the shock which there would be in coming down after a leap if the arm were attached by means of a collar-bone to the chest, and there is also greater liberty in the shoulder, so that the stride is increased in length, to the great advantage of the animal's speed. The fore-leg is divided into the shoulder-blade i, the arm j, and the fore-arm k, to which the foot is attached by means of the pastern, answering to the palm of the hand in man, whilst the knee corresponds to his wrist. The hinder extremity again is divided into the stifle or true thigh m, the leg or lower thigh n, and the hind pastern, terminating in the foot. All these various bones are connected together by joints strengthened by strong ligaments, and are moved by muscles of various sizes and forms. It is unnecessary here, however, to go into the descriptive anatomy of these different parts; all that is required to be known is, that every movement is occasioned by the contraction of one or more muscles attached to two different bones, and by this pulley-like action bringing them towards one another. This mechanism of the skeleton, with its moving power, the muscles, constitutes, when invested by its skin, the general outline of the body as we see it, and by its proportions we judge of the capabilities of the animal which is submitted to our observation. Experience has convinced all coursers that a dog with plenty of length from his hip to his hock is likely to be speedy, because there is a greater than usual length of muscle to act upon the hock, and also a longer stride. The same unerring criterion has also led us to believe that a good back will give increase of power —in fact, that, *cæteris paribus*, size is power. But this law must not be taken without exceptions, since there must of necessity be a due proportion of parts, or else the successive actions necessary for speed will not take place in due order, and with the proper regularity of stroke, and also because, by a well-known mechanical law, what is gained in power is lost in speed or time. This framework, then, of bones and muscles, when obtained of good form and proportions, is so much gained towards our object; but still, without a good brain and nervous system to stimulate it to action, it is utterly useless, and without a good heart and lungs to carry on the circulation during its active employment, it will still fail us in our need. Again, even if all these organs are sound and formed of good proportions by nature, if mismanagement or other causes interrupt their proper nutrition by digestion and assimilation, the framework speedily falls away, and our hopes are irrecoverably wrecked.

THE HEAD.—I have already said that, in my opinion, the head should be large between the ears, and in a dog from twenty-five to twenty-six inches high should measure at least fourteen and a half inches in circumference midway between the eyes and ears. This point is one which is not usually insisted on, many coursers preferring the narrow and elegant head, which will easily allow the neck-strap to slip over it. My own conviction is so strong that I do not hesitate to advise the selection of the head with a wider back to it, and as narrow and low as it can be obtained between the eyes. Very little intelligence is required in the greyhound; and if it were possible to obtain the full development of the appetite for his game, the seat of which is, no doubt, in the back of the brain, without any corresponding increase of intellectual faculties, it would be desirable to do so. But unfortunately this is not attainable without some slight drawback; for, though it may be possible to select heads in which there is a very great increase in volume in the back of the head, in proportion to the enlargement of the forehead, still the latter part is more or less developed, and in these animals greater care is necessary in the rearing to prevent them from self-hunting, or from assisting the sheep-dog of the farm in finding and killing what rabbits and hares are in the neighbourhood. But when that care has been taken, this greyhound is really valuable; his courage is immense; no amount of injury or work seems to cow him (though he is not necessarily stout, for this quality, I believe, resides in the whole nervous system, and not in any part of it), and even the whip only subdues for a time his appetite for blood. The jaw can hardly be too lean, but the muscle should be full, and there should be little or no development of the nasal sinuses. I am not fond of long-nosed greyhounds, but I have seen good ones possessing that appendage in almost every variety of shape. The eye should be full and bright, giving the idea of high spirits and animation. As to the ears, there is a very great variety in the different breeds, from the large upstanding ones of the 'Heatherjock' variety to the small and elegantly-falling ear of most of our modern greyhounds. The bitch has always a neater and more compact head than her brothers, and there is generally a livelier look about the eye; but though the head is smaller, it is still in the same relative proportion to the whole body, which is more neat and elegant also. No courser should omit to examine the teeth, which require to be strong and long enough to hold the hare when taken.

The Neck of the greyhound, in the old rhyme, was compared to that of a drake, and of all the comparisons therein contained this is the nearest to the truth. It certainly is not so long or so round as a drake's, but sometimes approaches very nearly to it. This form will enable the greyhound to seize his game while in full stride, without losing his balance; but I have known many good killers with short necks, almost like that of a bull; still, as a rule, a long neck is of great importance, and should be well considered in selecting a cross. Too often the thick compact form has also the bull neck, but in some breeds, as in the 'Curler' and 'Vraye Foy' family, which are very muscular, the neck is proportionally long.

The points I have been considering are not immediately connected with speed; but now I have to describe the framework by which locomotion is effected. It must be apparent to any one who watches the gallop, that its perfection depends upon the power of extending the shoulders and fore-legs as far as possible, as well as of bringing the hind-legs rapidly forward to give the propulsive stroke. Upon the due relation between these two parts of the action everything depends; and if the one part is more perfect than the other—that is to say, if the hind-quarters are well brought into action, while the shoulders do not thrust the fore-legs well forward—the action is laboured and slow; whilst,

THE NECK AND FORE-QUARTERS.

on the contrary, if the shoulders do their duty, but the hind-legs are not brought well forward, or when they do not thrust the body onwards with sufficient force, the action may be elegant, but it is not powerful and rapid. For these various purposes, therefore, we require good shoulders, good thighs, a good back, and good legs; and lastly, for lodging the lungs and heart, whose actions are essential to the maintenance of speed, a well-formed and capacious chest.

IN THE FORE-QUARTERS, therefore, I repeat, the shoulders must be so formed as to thrust the fore-legs well forward, and to do this the shoulder-blade must be as oblique as possible. The reason for this is, that its muscles may be able to exert their full power upon the true arm j, in bringing it into a straight line with the axis of the shoulder-blade. It will be seen by the diagram at page 18, that the upright shoulder (Fig. 2, o), when it has raised the true arm p to a straight line with its own axis, has not thrown the end attached to the lower arm nearly so far forward, as the oblique shoulder-blade (Fig. 1, i) has been able to do by the same amount of muscular contraction. This alone is a great advantage; but, by the greater angle which it forms with the arm, it also enables the greyhound to bear the shock of a fall upon his legs in coming down from a leap without injury, which is another most important feature. An oblique shoulder is likewise usually accompanied by a longer true arm, because the point of the shoulder must be raised higher from the elbow to allow of the obliquity, and in proportion to the increased length will the fore-foot be extended forward; thus this form gives longer levers with greater power of leverage, and *more space for the lodgment of muscles*. If, then, we have this form, combined with good length from the elbow down to the knee, compared with that from the knee to the ground, and with a good development of bone and muscle in addition, perfection in this essential part of the frame is ensured. In this last point (from the elbow to the knee) there is a very great difference in greyhounds; but, by a careful measurement of various well-formed legs, I am inclined to think that from the elbow to the knee ought to be at least twice the length from the same point to the ground. In this measurement the dog should be standing on a level surface with his weight bearing upon both legs, and I think the measure should be taken in this way, and not from the base of the two middle nails, because in the stride the action is from the ball of the foot, and not from the end of the toes. In variously-formed feet there is a difference of nearly an inch in length of toes; and many a dog with short toes would measure from the ground nearly an inch less than another with long toes; which latter would, nevertheless, measure, from his toe-nails to his knee, nearly an inch more than the former.

Such are the general points of importance in the fore-quarter; the minor ones are, good, bony, and well-developed shoulder points, elbows neither turned in nor out, muscular arms, good bony knees, not too much bent back, large and strong pasterns, and well-formed feet. With regard to this last point much difference of opinion has arisen, and most coursers advocate the selection of the cat-like foot, as in ' War Eagle:' but I do not myself care for more than a moderately-short one, provided the knuckles are powerful and well up, and that the toes do not spread; and provided, also, that the sole is thick and covered with a good horny skin.

THE HIND-QUARTER is even of more importance than the fore-quarter, and is composed of three separate divisions, varying greatly in total and comparative length in different individuals; these three divisions are, the true thigh l, between the hip and stifle joints; the false or lower thigh m, answering to the leg of man, and situated between the stifle and hock; and lastly, the leg n, between the hock and foot. The two first of these divisions should be nearly equal in length; and in most well-proportioned greyhounds are each about one-fifth longer than the lower arm; whilst the leg from the hock to the ground should bear about the same relation to each of the thigh bones as the fore-pastern does to the arm; that is to say, it should be about one-half, generally rather more than less. Many good greyhounds vary much in these proportions, as will be seen by examining the accompanying series of portraits; and the stifle joint is often placed far from midway between the hip joint and the hock—generally it is a little nearer the hip—but I have seen it much lower than the mid-point, but never in a greyhound of good pace and performance. With a greyhound thus formed, having both the upper and lower thigh bone one-fifth longer than the lower arm, with the hock also placed a little above the level of the knee, and the top of the shoulder-blade only the length of the thigh bone above the elbow, it follows either that the top of the hind-quarter will be considerably higher than the fore, or that the hind-legs will be bent at the hock and stifle joint considerably out of the straight line. Either of these forms is conducive to speed; but the latter is the more elegant, and also appears to be the best calculated for preserving the equilibrium in the turn. If the hind-legs are straight, and yet the back is level, the fore-legs must be long, or else there can scarcely be sufficient speed. This form is, however, inferior to the bent hind-legs, and correspondingly short anterior extremities. The type of the best formation is seen in the hare, in which there is a still greater disproportion; and as the greyhound has to cope with her in speed and working, he must, to a certain extent, be formed upon the same model, and so he really is when the proportions are carefully examined in a skinned hare. In the portraits of Mr. Randell's 'Ruby,' and Mr. Brown's 'Bedlamite,' the best form of stifles may be seen. The latter dog himself possessed remarkably developed stifles, which have been transmitted to many of his descendants, and on which I believe much of their success has depended. This peculiarity consists in the stifles being set on wide apart, so that they can be brought well forward in the stride without any difficulty. Good bony stifles and powerful hocks are essentially requisite for the attachment and leverage of the various muscles, and unless these are large and powerful in the haunches and thighs no greyhound can be of first-class powers; this point is, however, so well known that it is scarcely necessary to insist upon it.

But in order to unite the hind and fore-quarters, and to assist in fixing the pelvis (Fig. 1, $d\ e\ g\ h$), from which the muscles composing the haunch take their fulcrum, a good BACK is required, and when of good form it has been compared to a beam. Now the back is composed of a series of vertebræ, having the ribs attached to the sides of the first thirteen, but, in those of the loins, depending alone upon the hip bones and lateral processes for the lodgment and attachment of muscles. It must be self-evident that every additional inch in length of back increases the stride by that amount exactly, and therefore if prolonged indefinitely it would be advantageous, till counterbalanced by the disadvantages inseparably connected with this form, in consequence of the diminished strength. The length of back should therefore be looked for between the neck and the last rib, rather than between the last rib and the hip bone; and this is a very important consideration too often neglected. In measuring a dog I should take only the following points, which should be nearly of the proportions here given in one of average size : —

PRINCIPAL POINTS:—

Height at the shoulder, 25 inches.

Length from shoulder point to apex of last rib, 15 inches.

Length from apex of last rib to back of buttock, 13 to 15 inches.

Length from front of thigh round buttock to front of other thigh, 21 inches.

But, to be more minute, it is as well to measure also the SUBORDINATE POINTS, as under : —

Circumference of head between eyes and ears, $14\frac{1}{2}$ to 15 inches.

Length of neck, 9 to 10 inches.

Circumference of chest, 28 to 30 inches in condition.

Length of arm, 9 inches.

Length from knee to the ground, 4½ inches.

Circumference of loin, 18 to 19 inches, in running condition.

Length of upper thigh 10½, lower thigh 11, and leg from hock to ground 5½ to 6 inches.

In taking these measurements, the fore-legs should, as nearly as possible, be perpendicular, and the hind ones only moderately extended backwards.

The back ribs should be well spread and deep, for unless they are in this form a sufficient attachment cannot be afforded to the muscles of the loins, which constitute the chief moving power in drawing the hind-legs forward, and in fixing the pelvis. The loins must therefore be broad, strong, and deep, and the measure of their strength must be a circular one. Breadth alone will not do, since the lower muscles require to be well developed as well as the upper, but a good measurement *round* the loin is a good test of power in that quarter. It was the fashion from 1840 to 1850 to select flat and straight backs, and these certainly are handsomer than the high-arched backs previously so much in vogue. Either form may be qualified to do its duty, if there is only the power of straightening the line in the arched back, but if permanently arched it becomes what is called the 'wheel back,' and the power of extension in the gallop is very much limited. Since the time of 'Bedlamite,' who was very drooping in his quarters, and possibly partly in consequence of the attention which I drew to this point, the very level back is not so much in fashion, and the arched loin, coupled with the Bedlamite' quarter, is much sought after. With regard to the *chest* there are two things to be considered, namely, capacity for the lodgment of the lungs and heart, and the attainment of that form most conducive to speed and working. It must not be too deep, or the animal is constantly striking it against obstacles; it must not be too wide, or the shoulders are unable to play smoothly upon it, as they must do in the action of this quarter; but it must be of sufficient capacity to lodge the heart and lungs. A just relation between these three counterbalancing essentials is therefore the best form, neither too small for good wind, nor too wide for speed, nor too deep to keep free from the irregularities of the ground, but that happy medium which we see in our best specimens, and which the portraits of most of our best dogs will exhibit to the eye of the courser.

But it is very remarkable that, in spite of all the talent and powers of observation which have been brought to bear upon the greyhound, and in spite of the various shapes which have been described so often and so well, no one has ever succeeded in prognosticating from the form of the individual the peculiar character of the gallop which that animal may inherit. It is true that we may easily guess, when we know the sire and dam, that the descendant will very probably gallop in the same style as they did before him; but without such information, and merely by looking at the form alone, no one, I believe, could often succeed in making a successful guess as to the action of a particular greyhound — something more, then, is requisite than mere shape, and most probably that something resides in the nervous system. But in order to understand this question, let us enter upon a consideration of the various styles of gallop to which I have alluded. Now, a careless observer might fancy that a gallop is a gallop, whether short and quick or long and dwelling; but, though himself unable to comprehend the difference, his more experienced friend would at once tell him that of two puppies submitted to his inspection the gallop of one would probably lead on to victory, whilst that of the other could only end in defeat. These various styles of going I shall divide into—

1stly. The short, quick, merry, and terrier-like gallop, well seen in the old Wiltshire greyhound. In this style there seems to be no labour at all; the fore-legs are not extended with an effort, nor do the hind-legs and stifles seem to be brought forward with any unusual power. Very high speed is never attained, but the gallop, such as it is, may be maintained for an immense time. There is a great power of stopping, turning, and starting without effort, and a middling hare has little chance; a fast Wiltshire hare will, however, often get away without a turn. Wiltshire ' Marquis ' and his descendants—' Critic ' and his stock — partake of this character. ' Cactus ' is a good specimen of the form.

2ndly. The true greyhound gallop, in which there is more or less effort apparent at every stroke, the shoulders and fore-legs are well carried forward, and the hind-legs seem constantly trying to overtake them. There is more or less elegance, but the stifles are always well brought forward. It, however, requires a good heart to keep up this style, which is somewhat fatiguing, but it ensures good speed, and is essential to its combination with working powers. It passes from the enormous stride of 'Cerito' and 'Mocking Bird,' through the 'King Cob' and 'Foremost' styles, down to that type of elegance and effect seen in most of the 'Bedlamites,' including more particularly 'Riot' and 'Romping Girl.'

'Cerito' may be taken as a good specimen of this gallop for the flat, but her stride was too overreaching for hilly ground, as was evinced in her course in Wiltshire, and in those at Broughton and Market Weighton; for though she won seven courses out of ten at the two latter places, still her performances there are not to be compared with those at Altcar, where the soft peaty soil exactly suited her. 'Miss Hannah,' on the contrary, is an example of this style in the opposite degree to that of 'Cerito,' being sharper and less overreaching, and consequently more adapted to hilly and hard ground. Were she as large as 'Cerito,' with her own style, she would be perfection itself; as it is, I should take my stand upon her *for all countries*, rather than upon her still more fortunate rival in public estimation. The 'King Cobs' partake of the 'Miss Hannah' style, but generally with rather less smartness, whilst the 'Foremosts' are more nearly approaching to that of 'Cerito.' Lastly, the 'Bedlamites' exhibit this kind of action in the most perfect manner, bringing their stifles well forward, and with less apparent effort than 'Cerito,' doing more execution in point of pace, with far more command of themselves.

3rdly. There is the defective gallop, which may occur either from a want of projecting the shoulder forward, or of getting the hind-legs and stifles under the body, or from both. Very often the dog seems to dwell in a position in which the fore-legs are raised, without the shoulders being at all moved, and the hind-legs are extended backwards to the utmost. This is wholly useless, though sometimes tolerably good speed is attained, but there is never good working power, and the dog is continually falling if sufficiently fast. Many examples of this defect might be adduced, but it could serve no purpose but to annoy the owners of the animals mentioned.

4thly. There is the heavy, dull, inanimate style, which may be inherent in either of the above, and which depends upon defective nervous organization; it is fatal to the individual possessing it, and ought to ensure his speedy departure from the kennel and the coursing field, by means of the cord or poison. In the puppy this is very difficult to detect as a permanent fault, since many first-rate dogs have retained this sluggishness to the end of their puppyhood; but the defects mentioned in the third division, when seen at the age of nine or ten months, are seldom wholly recovered from. There is no comparison in the value of two greyhounds, one possessing either of the two first styles, and the other either of the last; for whilst the two first are good in their different varieties, the two last can neither enable a dog to go fast, nor run stout, nor work, and he is only fit to look at when at rest. In this position he is often a perfect picture, and many is the purchaser, who has bought a dog at a sale from the beauty of his form, who has been disappointed by seeing him go as I have attempted to describe when let loose in the field. These various actions should be well considered, because I believe they are of great importance in selecting a good cross; for, however well the shape of the sire may suit the dam, still, if the action is totally different, I much doubt the success of the experiment. But this is a subject which will come better under the chapter devoted to the selection of a good cross for the female.

The best SIZE for the greyhound-form is a very difficult question to answer in a satisfactory manner, but I think that most coursers now consider the full-sized dog-greyhound of 70 or 75 lbs. as not likely to be so successful as one of 58 lbs. to 65 lbs. weight; of course there are exceptions to all rules, but this I believe to be the general impression upon the subject. In Wiltshire very small dogs, as well as bitches, have run well, but perhaps this will never happen again, as they were chiefly successful when pitted against large unwieldy animals, which are now seldom started in such a country. Within the last ten years the following dogs and bitches of full size have run well in Wiltshire: viz. ' Billy-go-by-'em,' of 70 lbs. weight; ' Agitation' and ' Regina Victoria,' of full size; ' Lord George,' 74 lbs. ; ' Czar,' 61 lbs.; ' Leeway,' 54 lbs. ; ' Ebb,' 53 lbs.; ' Puzzle-'em,' 63 lbs. ; ' Mocking Bird,' 61 lbs. ; ' Egypt,' ' Lopez,' ' Bedlamite,' and ' Merlin,' above 60 lbs., and that beautiful bitch ' Lizzie,' running about 57 or 58 lbs. This list must show that great weight and size are not objectionable even on the Wiltshire Downs, if united with a good heart and sufficient activity of form; but heaviness and lumpiness are to be avoided in all countries. Still we often see small bitches with a good turn of speed, of which ' Riot,' who weighed 47 lbs., is an excellent example, but, *cæteris paribus*, a moderately large dog, or bitch, not overgrown, will beat a small one at all points.

Besides the points of form which I have enumerated as really connected with the action of the animal, some others are usually selected as indications of the goodness of the breed; these are the TAIL, the COLOUR, and the fineness of the COAT. The tail ought, according to general belief, to be long and gently curved like a tobacco-pipe, large and strong at the root, then rapidly diminishing till it becomes in the bone as small as the little finger. But there should certainly, in my opinion, be some considerable quantity of hair towards the tip, not surrounding the tail, but forming a slight brush on the under side; this is often removed by a little resin in the hand, but in most of our best dogs it naturally exists. In puppies it is very much stronger than in old dogs, and it is a sign of hardness of constitution. Many of our best breeds have possessed more curl in their tail than I have described, but it is not to be admired, though it may be tolerated; still, as the form of the tail is not essential to speed or working powers, it should never be taken into consideration as a test of blood, because we have a better criterion of the goodness of the breed in the pedigree of the individual than in the shape of his tail, and few coursers now-a-days would be content to rear a puppy without knowing more of him than the shape of his tail, or his colour and conformation.

With regard to colour I confess to a strong prejudice in favour of self colours—of which black and red (especially with black muzzles) certainly are to me by far the most attractive. And this attraction is not only dependent upon the superior beauty to the eye, but upon the result of the examination of the pedigree-list published by Messrs. Thacker and Welsh from 1840 to 1852. In this list, ever since its commencement, these colours have been found much more frequently than any other; and therefore have a statistical claim upon our notice. Dogs of these colours also appear to be more hardy than the white with spots, or the lighter fawns, and I am inclined to believe that black and red are the true and original colours of the greyhound, from which all the others are derived. The white is no doubt the result of domestication, and is never found in any natural breed of dogs, even in the Arctic regions, in which the only examples of white quadrupeds occur in a wild state. Within the last ten years, however, the numerous milk-white descendants of Mr. Campbell's 'Scotland Yet,' who was herself a pure white, have altered the proportions greatly, and instead of a white greyhound being as it previously was a 'rara avis,' it is now so common that we often see, as in the last Waterloo Cup, eight or ten per cent. on that colour. But taking black, red, and white, as the three primitive colours of the domestic dog, we shall find that all the others may be, and I believe are, derived from their mixture, the only variation consisting in the intermediate shade, which is sometimes uniform, as in blue and fawn, sometimes spotted in large patches, or ticked in small ones, and sometimes striped, as in the brindle, and in the black (or blue) and tan. Thus a black dog put to a white bitch will most probably produce either black and white, or white and black, or blue, puppies; next, a black dog put to a red bitch will produce either black or red, like the father or mother, or else red with black muzzles and ears, or black and tan, or the black and red pie peculiar to the foxhound and harrier, or lastly a brindle, which is a black stripe on a red ground; and thirdly, there is the union of red and white, which will produce either white and red, or red and white, or fawn, puppies. But besides the mixture of these primitive colours, there is also that between black and fawn, and blue and fawn, producing in the first case black-muzzled fawn or fawn-brindled, and in the second, blue-muzzled fawn or blue-brindled. Nearly the same mixture of colours occurs in the cow and horse; in the former of which we have all the colours found in the dog, but in the horse the brindle and blue are absent; black and white producing piebald or grey, and black, white, and red, the various roans and strawberries.

In reference to the brindle it has been supposed by Mr. Thacker, Mr. Mundy, and some others, that it is due to the bull-dog cross; but if the above theory is correct, this opinion is erroneous; that it is so, is proved by the fact that several of those dogs which are clearly of bull-dog origin, are of different colours —as, for instance, 'Rapid,' and her brothers 'Rattler' and 'Rainbow,' in the pedigree of 'Jason,' which were black or blue; 'Effie Deans,' in the pedigree of the 'Czar,' a fawn bitch; and Mr. Fyson's 'Fancy-Boy,' red. Another argument in favour of the above cause of the brindle is the following:—if a *dark*-brindled bitch is put to a black dog, she will generally produce black puppies, but if put to a red dog she will more frequently throw red-brindled puppies; whereas a *light*-brindled bitch will produce more brindled puppies by a black than by a red or fawn dog, because it will take more black in this case to obliterate the brindle than of red or fawn, whereas in the dark brindle a very little additional black will make the whole skin uniformly of that colour. Of course in all these cases the colour of the *family* is to be taken into consideration, as well as that of the individual, and this holds good in all cases, whether of colour, form, or blood. As an instance of the above I will take Mr. Lawrence's 'Landgravine,' a dark-brindled bitch, and nearly all of a dark-brindled blood, being by 'Chieftain' *bd d* out of 'Ruby,' whose dam was also brindled. Now 'Landgravine' has been put to three dogs, producing litter the 1st: by 'Foremost,' *bk d*, all black; next, by 'Vraye Foy,' *r d*, all brindled; and thirdly, by 'Lopez,' *bk d*, part brindled and part black and white, 'Lopez' being himself partly of the blood of 'Westwind' *bd d*. I could easily produce other instances as strong or even stronger than the above, but of the fact I have satisfied myself, and any one else may easily ascertain for himself whether I am right or wrong.

As far as I know, the only instance of a true brindle occurring in any of the carnivorous mammalia, not subject to domestication by man, is in the tiger and some others of the cat genus; it would, therefore, be much more logical to assert that the brindled greyhound was derived from the cat than from the bull-dog; because we know that it is peculiar to the one and that it is not peculiar to the other; for we also know that there are as many red, black, and fawn bull-dogs, as there are of the brindled colour. In fact, there is every reason to believe with Mr. Goodlake that this despised colour occurred in the greyhound breed, long before the cross with the bull-dog was thought of, so that the colour in the latter may be derived from the former, for aught we know to the contrary. Indeed, so little is certain as to the origin of the different varieties of the dog, that the bull-dog himself *in toto* is just as likely to be a thickened greyhound, as the greyhound a lengthened bull-dog. Upon this abstruse question I do not, however, intend to dwell, because the arguments are purely hypothetical, and the result in consequence so very unsatisfactory. But I am quite entitled, from the present state of the argument, as admitted by naturalists, to infer that nothing is known of the primary root of the dog; and consequently that it is impossible to assign any particular colour as originally peculiar to any variety. At present we can assert that the brindle is confined to the bull-dog, mastiff, and greyhound, but then so is the black-muzzled red and fawn, which are, however, highly prized among greyhound-breeders; so that I think I am justified in asserting that the prejudice which we most of us entertain (myself among the rest) against the brindle is not founded on any real objection, but has arisen from Mr. Mundy's and Mr. Thacker's dislike, founded upon their supposition of its connection with the bull-dog. This theory of its origin was shown by Mr. Goodlake to be untrue; nor if true would it be a valid objection, since many of our best modern greyhounds are traced to this cross. And if my theory is correct, that the brindle is only the result of a cross between black and red, sometimes mixed with white, in the various shades of black, blue, red and fawn, it will follow that the brindle is only a consequence of such crossing. Let any breeder look over his book, and consider whether he has not sometimes had a brindled puppy thrown by one of his bitches, in which there was no cross of that colour as far as his knowledge of her pedigree went, nor in that of the sire. But in such a case it will, I believe, invariably happen that the sire and dam were of opposite colours, either in themselves or in their families; but generally in the individuals as well as in their predecessors. Indeed, wherever either in sire or dam the breed has been confined to one colour for many generations, the produce will almost invariably follow that colour, unless it so happens that the other parent is also bred to some particular colour, which is not often the case. This is well shown in the cases of 'Foremost,' 'King Cob,' and 'Jason.' In the progenitors of the first of these, there has been no mixture with the black except white, and the consequence has been that he has got scarcely any stock but of his own colour. In 'King Cob,' on the contrary, there was a mixture of white, brindled, and fawn, and consequently his stock have been of various colours, with a tendency to white. Again, in 'Jason,' the colours of his ancestors have been confined to red, blue, and black; the result of which has been that almost all his stock have been black-muzzled reds or fawns, and with very little white. Lastly, in 'Figaro' and 'Sam,' though both black themselves or nearly so, the stock have generally followed the dam's colour, because in both cases there was a mixture of colours in the stock from which the sires and dams of these dogs were descended. Now these facts being granted, it is useless to look back for a brindled ancestor, whenever such a colour comes out in the son or daughter of two greyhounds of a black or red colour, because their mixture alone will often produce it; but as there are few public pedigrees without a solitary instance of the stripe occurring in them, it is difficult to produce a case in which it has come solely by the mixture of red and black; and I know of no such case, for this simple reason, that I know of no public pedigree without its occurrence, except in those instances such as 'Foremost,' 'Bedlamite,' and 'Ranter,' where none but black puppies were got. In private breeding I have, however, known the brindle peep out without any trace of it for six or seven generations back, beyond which few private pedigrees can be accurately made out.

But though many good dogs have appeared of a brindled colour, yet it cannot be denied that it does not stand so high in general estimation as those I have mentioned: the same rule will, however, apply to colour as to tail—the pedigree alone ought to guide us; and it will lead us right, in spite of tails, colours, or coats. With all my prejudices, therefore, in favour of blacks and reds, I confess that I can give no reason for the preference, other than the fact that there are more winners of those colours than of any other. But to show that these are really the best colours, more than this is necessary, as we must prove that the proportion *of winners to losers* is greater in these colours than in others. This, however, is a task which I am not inclined to impose upon myself, but as a guess, I much doubt whether the result would coincide with the prevailing opinion, when the numerous recent successes of the descendants of 'Scotland Yet' are recollected.

Fineness of coat is also considered an indication of good blood, but many of our best breeds of late have been remarkably rough, and harsh in the hair, though still short, and far from the state of coat found upon the old rough greyhound. Among these the 'Foremosts' and 'Barrators' are very remarkable; but nevertheless their sides, thighs, and cheeks, are thinly covered with hair. Some of the Scotch varieties are also coarse in their coats; and, on the whole, I think fineness of coat can scarcely be relied on as a mark of breed.

Having now gone in detail into the various points of the greyhound, I would impress upon the young courser the importance of considering only those which really affect the usefulness of the animal. Let him only take care to get a good breed, without stain in the pedigree, and then by selecting those puppies of good form, regardless of colour and tail, he will be less likely to be disappointed than if he kept a pretty-coloured animal, with a faultless tail, and had discarded one of a less prized coat, and perhaps curly tail, but which yet had the form and style of going which would serve his purpose as a public courser.

CHAPTER III.

PHYSIOLOGICAL REMARKS.

Nervous System—Organs of Circulation and Respiration—The Digestive Organs—The Kidneys—Examination of the Dog when attacked with Disease—Forms in which Medicines should be given—Best mode of administering Remedies.

NERVOUS SYSTEM.—In these railroad days there is a good illustration of the office of this important organ, which may be compared to the electric telegraph. The brain is the central office with a manager (to represent the intelligence of the animal supposed to reside in his brain) always present. This central manager issues his orders to all parts by means of certain wires (corresponding to the nerves of motion), and is informed of any stoppage or accident, or other cause for interference on his part, by another set of wires (the nerves of sensation); while again every station has a means of communicating with every other station by a different system of wires (the nerves of organic life), which have their separate ganglia or the lesser station-masters. Here, then, you have a tolerably exact counterpart of the nervous system, and in fact nearly all which is known of the general action of the nerves is, that they *resemble* in their functions the galvanic battery. It is true that we are able to ascertain experimentally that, certain parts being gone, certain functions are destroyed, and that, by slicing off consecutive portions of the brain, certain faculties disappear; but of the ultimate essence of the nervous action we know much less than we do of the electrical phenomena which attend upon the action of the telegraph. However, to understand the effect of medicines as far as is known, and the cure of diseases, thus much of the nervous system is all that is necessary. Here, as in all other organs, size is power—the large brain will give increased intelligence, or increased appetites, according to the part which is developed—and in proportion to the tone of the nervous system will be the activity and liveliness of the individual.

ORGANS OF CIRCULATION AND RESPIRATION.—The bones, muscles, and nervous system, indeed, every part of the body, must be supplied with blood, and with warm blood, too, in order to the performance of the action which each part has to fulfil. Bones must be nourished, muscles must be nourished also, and be supplied with arterial blood before they can act, as must the brain and nervous system generally. All these organs are built up out of the blood at the time when it is circulating in the minutest arteries, which are termed the capillaries. The stronger and quicker the contraction of the muscles, and the more vigorous the action of the brain, so much the faster must the blood be furnished by the agency of the heart. Hence, it has become a general observation that a dog or horse which fails in his effort 'has a bad heart,' and so he often has. A weak heart is totally incapable of carrying on the circulation under distress, but becomes clogged, overwhelmed, and, as it were, drowned in its own blood. The heart is nothing more than a double forcing-pump of most beautiful construction, one half of which receives the blood from all parts of the body, and forces it into the lungs (through the most minute portions of which it passes), whilst the other half receives this blood after it has passed through the lungs, and then forces it into all parts of the body, supplying the wants of the nervous system, the muscles, bones, skin, and also all the organs of digestion, &c.; and being itself composed of muscular substance. The vessels or tubes conveying this blood are respectively called arteries and veins, having intervening between their extremities a network of vessels so minute as to be called capillaries—from *capillus*, a hair.

In this rough enumeration of the various organs, we must next consider the agency of the lungs, which has only lately been fully understood. By the researches of modern physiologists, it is now ascertained that these organs are chiefly intended to supply the heat which is required for the performance of all healthy functions. Without the lungs no warm-blooded animals could resist the cold even of an English winter, when exposed to its action without protection; but, by their agency, such a temperature is preserved as is required, and nothing in the animal economy is more beautiful than this process. Now, this heat-maintaining power is owing to the combination of the carbon and hydrogen in the blood with the oxygen of the air, forming respectively carbonic acid and water, and being effected in the lungs through the thin membranous walls of the capillary vessels at the time of the circulation

ORGANS OF CIRCULATION AND RESPIRATION.

of the blood through them. This union is a simple burning of carbon and hydrogen; that is, these gases each unite with oxygen, just as our coals and gas do in our own dwellings; and the lungs are as much a stove as any in our houses, the only difference being that the burning is more gradual, and, consequently, the temperature is not raised high enough to give out light, and a moderate heat. In a state of muscular repose, therefore, the only office of the lungs is to burn off the superfluous carbon, and thereby maintain the proper temperature of the whole body, by warming the blood which is then equally diffused, and this carbon is continually afforded either by the regular supplies of food, or, failing this, by the fat of the body. But, over and above this heat-maintaining process, they also serve to burn up the carbon which results from the wear and tear of the muscles, bones, &c., and which, during violent exercise, is poured into the blood in enormous quantities. It appears now to be well ascertained that every contraction of a muscle is accompanied by the loss of a part of its elements, large or small, according to the degree of its action—and the same is most probably the case with the brain and all other organs when in activity. The moment, therefore, the muscles are put into violent action, whether those of the limbs, or the trunk, or even the heart itself, increased quantities of carbon are poured into the blood. This fluid, thus as it were overflowing with carbon, circulates through the lungs and occasions the feeling of distress which instinctively calls for more air in order to burn it off, and thus keep the blood in a state of purity. The electric telegraph (the nerves of sensation) is set in motion, the brain, on receiving information of this excess of carbon, issues its mandate back again by means of the wires at its command (the nerves of motion supplying the respiratory muscles), and the breathing is accelerated in an exact ratio with the quantity of carbon given out into the blood by the wear and tear of the muscular system.

For this reason a greyhound must be possessed, not only of powerful muscles, but also of a powerful heart, to furnish them with blood, in order to keep up the supply of fresh materials required by their wear and tear; but he likewise requires a capacious chest, for this is a measure of the quantity of air which can be continually renewed by each act of breathing, and, in proportion to the quantity, will be the rapidity of the combination between the carbon in the blood and the oxygen contained in the air as one of its elements. Hence, the more capacious the chest, the less will be the distress occasioned to the animal under violent exertion; that is, provided the heart is capable of doing its duty, by circulating the blood as fast as the air is supplied. No dog can be of good wind without lungs of sufficient size; but a powerful heart is also required to fulfil the grand purpose of decarbonising the blood; and from the want of this arises the distress which we so often see in a badly-trained or badly-reared dog. For, if the heart is never called into active play by violent exercise during the period of growth, it is only formed of sufficient size and power to carry on the circulation in a state of repose, and then, when required for extraordinary exertions, 'it is not big enough for the place,' and is incapable of doing its duty—the blood, instead of being deprived of its carbon, retains it, continuing blue even in the arteries, and giving that colour to the lips and mouth. To such an extent is this failure sometimes carried, that the death of the animal ensues from the circulation of carbon to a poisonous excess in the brain.

Such, then, are all the processes carried on in the body, with the exception of the special organs of sight, hearing, smell, and touch, and also of those organs which supply the materials for the wear and tear of the various parts of the individual, and of the organs which are intended to carry on the species by the reproduction of others similar in their characteristics to the parent stem.

It is right, however, to remark, that there are other organs which assist the lungs in purifying the blood, which, in fact, carry off some of the carbon mixed with refuse matters in an unfit state for so delicate a texture as that of the lungs. These organs may be said to remove the smoke and cinders of the stove in the shape of fæces and urine, but, as they are intimately mixed up with them, I shall reserve their examination till we enter upon

THE DIGESTIVE ORGANS.—These organs consist of two separate and distinct sets, the first being one continuous alimentary canal, enlarged and contracted at intervals, which commences at the mouth and terminates at the anus; whilst the second comprises the assistant solid viscera, intended to serve various purposes, as the salivary glands, the liver, spleen, and pancreas, the small glands distributed along the intestines, and lastly the kidneys. In this short and hurried account of these important organs, which are the seat of most of the diseases to which the dog is subject, it is impossible to do more than glance at their various offices and structures; I shall, therefore, simply describe the alimentary canal as divided into the gullet, the stomach, and the small and the large intestines—all being lined with mucous membrane, which again is covered by muscular fibres for the purpose of propelling the contents of the stomach and intestines, and in the greater part of the course of the canal by a smooth serous membrane (the peritoneum) to allow the different viscera to roll easily one upon the other. Now it is highly important to remember these three general coats (as they are called), because their diseases are different, and require totally opposite treatment.

The food, being seized by the jaws of the dog, is, if of great bulk, rapidly torn into such pieces as can be swallowed, and, in the natural condition of the animal, prior to his domestication, such a process would exercise the jaws very considerably, so as to call upon the salivary glands to pour out their secretion in great quantities; but when the food is offered to him in a divided state, which prevents all necessity for using the jaws, some other means for procuring this necessary fluid must be provided, and this can only be done by the use of bones, for him to gnaw. The food, when swallowed, passes down the gullet into the stomach, which, in the dog, is of considerable size, and will in a large greyhound hold four or five pounds of food tolerably well; this organ, as is well known to everybody, is the main agent in digestion. Now, by digestion, we understand the reduction of food by the gastric juice (which is secreted by the stomach), so as to render it fit to be taken up by the absorbents and conveyed into the blood; this absorption is, however, effected chiefly in the intestines, with the assistance also of the bile and pancreatic juice. But the preparation of the food for absorption is not by any means completed in this first part of the alimentary canal; it is still to be submitted to the action of various fluids as it passes on through the long course of the intestines, which vary considerably in length in the higher animals. In the carnivora, living on food easily digested, the intestine is short, not being more than three times the length of the body, whilst in the sheep it is twenty-eight times as long. Again, in the omnivorous animals, as, for instance, man, the length is from five to six times that of his body, being intermediate between the two. The mucous membrane of the alimentary canal is everywhere studded with minute glands, which force out a fluid varying according to the particular part in which they are situated; but, in all parts, there are some which secrete mucus, that jelly-like fluid, a familiar specimen of which the lining membrane of our own noses compels us to take notice of, and to store in our pocket-handkerchiefs. In the stomach these glands principally secrete gastric juice—a strong solvent of animal and vegetable food. The whole surface of the mucous membrane is covered with what are called *villi*, and which resemble to the naked eye the pile of velvet. In these the proper absorbent vessels originate, and through them the prepared food is taken up and carried into a duct (the thoracic duct), which finally empties itself in one of the large veins near the heart. The food thus prepared by the action of the saliva and the gastric juice in the stomach is called *chyme*, and is then, after losing some small portions of its most simple materials through the *villi* of the stomach, passed on into the small intestines. Here the bile and pancreatic juice are at once mixed with it, and stimulate the muscular coat of the intestines to pass it on gradually towards the extreme orifice, the anus. During this passage the solution or digestion is completed, the *chyme* becomes *chyle*, a smooth pultaceous semi-fluid, from which all the materials useful for the support of the body are absorbed. The residue, being the particles of food which are unfit for digestion, is passed on into the large intestine, receiving in its course the addition of *the solid portions* of the materials of the body, which are no longer useful to the different organs of which they originally formed a part. I have said that the *chyme* receives the bile and pancreatic fluids, and is finally converted into *chyle*; the latter of these fluids seems solely to fulfil this office, but the pouring out of the bile by the liver is also a means of assisting the lungs in their office of purifying the blood. This is, indeed, a very material part of the functions of the liver, and it is found that when this organ is torpid and does not act, a very prejudicial effect is produced upon the whole body, but more especially upon the brain. In fact, the liver may be said to be the safety-valve of the system, carrying on the separation of the superfluous carbon and hydrogen, in the shape of bile, at the time when the lungs are not stimulated by exercise to burn them in sufficient quantity by combining them with oxygen. This organ, then, we shall find, when we examine into the diseases of the dog, is constantly liable to be affected by overfeeding and confinement. The lungs not being excited

THE DIGESTIVE ORGANS.

by exercise are only burning carbon enough to keep up the temperature of the animal, and consequently the blood is overcharged with this gas as well as with hydrogen, and the liver is called upon to do extra duty; but if neither liver nor lungs efficiently perform this important office, then the task is thrown upon the only parts yet undescribed, which are concerned in relieving the blood of its noxious elements—the used-up and waste materials which are no longer wanted in the animal economy.

These organs are THE KIDNEYS, whose office is to remove the *soluble* worn-out particles from the blood, and among them the saline materials. But their peculiar office is to carry off out of the blood the superfluous nitrogen, which has either been used in combination with carbon, hydrogen, and oxygen, in forming the muscles of the body, and afterwards, when no longer fit for use, poured into the blood, or which, not being required to supply the muscles, is in excess, and poisoning that fluid if existing in sufficient quantity. Hence, the greater the quantity of plastic or nitrogenous food, the more the kidneys are called upon, whether the animal is in a state of activity or rest, whilst the excess of carbonaceous food, in the shape of starch, sugar, or fat, is partly burned in the lungs, and partly carried into the bowels in the shape of bile. In all these excrementitious processes, with the exception of the production of the heat necessary to the existence of the animal, the grand object of nature seems to be to keep up the healthy constitution of the blood. This being the general food of all parts of the body—being, indeed, the very life

PHYSIOLOGICAL REMARKS.

of the individual—must be kept pure, and that purity is not left dependent upon one solitary organ, but nature has provided the lungs, liver, and kidneys to perform the office, and, in animals who perspire through the skin, that organ in addition. The dog, however, is not subject to perspiration (except from the limited surface of the tongue); his skin has no follicles for that purpose, and therefore it is more necessary that his lungs should be of good size. The horse, on the contrary, sweats to a wonderful degree, and is consequently capable of enduring exertion in hot climates to a much greater extent than the dog, which, on the other hand, bears a much lower degree of cold. This is also a chief reason of the many and obstinate skin diseases to which he is subject.

In this hasty sketch of the anatomy and physiology of the dog, I have endeavoured to explain all that is necessary to the comprehension of his various diseases; but when I come to speak of some particular affections I shall be obliged to be somewhat more minute in my descriptions. Of course it would be futile to attempt more than such an account as will enable the amateur to undertake their management, since a more elaborate treatise would take up valuable space, and would only confound and perplex those for whom this book is intended.

Before proceeding to the description of each particular disease, with its mode of treatment, it will be well to consider the best mode of examining the dog, when presented to us as a patient (and he is truly a patient), with humble, imploring eye, asking for relief, and ready to submit to any reasonable amount of pain in order to obtain it. The dog cannot answer our questions, however, and cannot by word of mouth tell us where the pain or inconvenience is felt, and hence there is sometimes great difficulty in detecting the seat of disease. Without the qualities of careful observation, tact, and patience, no good result is likely to follow. It is moreover desirable, that, like the good judge of a horse, who commences with the head, and goes regularly through the various parts of the body, so we should examine with a certain method and order; and in this examination all our senses must co-operate—sight, hearing, smell, and touch, must all be called to our aid. With their assistance we may hope to ascertain the actual condition of the dog which is to be treated, and, by a little care, the time will soon come when those signs will be understood which were previously hidden, or, if visible, yet not properly appreciated. On first visiting a sick dog you must be very careful not to alarm him; enter the kennel as if your object was anything but what it is; then, as if *impromptu*, take some slight notice of the dog, and carefully make your observations, without attracting his attention or alarming his fears. At this time observe the state of the eyes, and note the breathing, whether natural or quicker than usual, whether the dog lies on his side, or curled up, or sits up on his hind-legs. Note also if he sighs continually, or has hiccup, or expresses pain by whining or moaning, or suddenly darting his nose towards his flank, or chest, or any other part of his body. Mark also the state of the skin, whether the hair lies smoothly, or stares and is rough, or partly removed, or if there is any eruption visible. During this examination various questions may have been asked quietly of the attendant, and answered, relative to the urine, fæces, cough, appetite, &c.; after which the nose and ears should be gently examined with the hand, and then, patting the dog very gently on the head, place the hand on the region of the heart, behind the shoulder point, and ascertain whether it beats regularly, and at its usual velocity of from ninety to a hundred beats per minute. The ear or the stethoscope may then be applied to the chest, that by these means the examiner may ascertain whether the breathing is natural, or attended with an increase of mucus in the air-tubes. After this carry the hand quietly to the belly, and press gently to ascertain whether there is any hardness or tenderness, and more especially if the muscles leading from the chest to the pelvis on each side the navel have the cord-like feel which they assume in most of the abdominal affections. If, after this examination, you should have failed in detecting the seat of the disease, then persuade the dog to come out of his kennel, and you will probably find that there is palsy, or rheumatism of the limbs, which might easily have escaped your observation while quietly remaining in kennel.

Having, then, carefully made up your mind as to the nature of the malady, the next thing to be done is to proportion your treatment to the disease, always remembering that it is better to do too little than too much, and that the *médecine expectante* of the French, though often allowing the patient to die, is better than actually causing his death; and this, if true in the human subject, is still more true with dogs, where we have much less to guide us in our search. But every person who prescribes for a dog should take care that his prescription is properly given, and yet many of those who attend upon these animals are totally ignorant of the correct method. It is usual to administer remedies either in the form of a bolus, or, when liquid, as a drench. The ball may be given *without much fuss*, by simply opening the dog's mouth, and then, placing the ball well at the back of the throat behind the tongue, shutting the mouth, and keeping it closed with the hands, the ball must go down, whether the dog likes it or not. This is better than forcibly seizing the dog, and fixing him, as is necessary, for the purpose of giving him a drench, when the kennel man must bestride him, first getting him into a corner, to prevent his retreating, then placing a coarse cloth between the jaws, and bringing it under the lower jaw, the teeth of the dog prevent its slipping from the hand, and the lower jaw is well fixed. The upper jaw may then be raised with the other hand, whilst the assistant pours into the throat about enough for the dog to swallow at one gulp—that is, about an ounce, or rather more. If more than this is to be given, wait a few seconds, and then give the remainder in a similar manner, taking care to elevate the nose till all is swallowed. All balls which have much taste should be wrapped in silver paper and greased, or they are sure to be returned. Epsom salts will be taken voluntarily by many dogs, if mixed with broth, and most puppies will take castor oil in the same way.

CHAPTER IV.

DISEASES OF THE GREYHOUND.

1. GENERAL DISEASES, WITH INCREASED ACTION OF THE HEART, ETC.—
FEBRILE DISEASES.

Ephemeral Fever, or Common Catarrh—Influenza, or Epidemic Catarrh—
Distemper or Typhus Fever—Rheumatic Fever (often ending in Palsy)
—Small-pox.

EPHEMERAL FEVER.

I shall now proceed with the consideration of the first class, viz. Febrile Diseases, of which Ephemeral Fever, or Common Cold, is the first on the list, and may be taken as the ordinary type, though differing greatly in degree. Every one must be aware of the symptoms of this, which are thirst and chilliness, with loss of appetite, a little mucus at the corners of the eyes, which are dull and heavy, warm nose, listlessness, with loss of strength, and sometimes cough. This usually follows exposure to cold, and will get well of itself in two or three days, if the dog is kept warm, has a dose of castor oil and syrup of buckthorn, and no flesh, giving him porridge made with weak broth. It is very often confounded with distemper, the early stage of which it closely resembles, and from which it may be distinguished by the absence of rapid emaciation and loss of strength so peculiar to distemper.

INFLUENZA, OR EPIDEMIC CATARRHAL FEVER.

Should the above symptoms come on while an epidemic of the same nature is raging, it is commonly known as influenza or 'sniff,' which is not contagious, but caused by some peculiar state of the air, the exact nature of which is not known. Nothing is more common than for epidemic catarrhal fever to degenerate into distemper, or to end in inflammation of the lungs or bowels, but, unless either one or other of these complaints occur, it is better to trust to an emetic, and to mild diet, with abstinence from the usual exercise. Water may be allowed to any extent, but it is well to dissolve about one drachm of nitre in every quart, which acts beneficially as a febrifuge, and also, by its taste, prevents the dog from drinking an inordinate quantity. This simple treatment will generally suffice, unless, as I have before observed, some other affection supervenes, for which the observer should be upon his guard, as the dog is never safe from an inflammatory attack while the system is disturbed by fever, of however slight a character. The fæces should be watched, and if costive, but of good colour, then administer castor oil; if white, give five grains of blue pill the night before the oil; and if too relaxed, then give plenty of water in which good Carolina rice has been boiled, and also the rice itself as food, flavoured with jelly or broth.

THE DISTEMPER, OR TYPHUS FEVER.

At one time I was inclined to believe, from the numerous forms which distemper assumes, that there was really no such distinct disease, but that a variety of complaints had been ignorantly jumbled together, under a term, too, which affords no distinguishing mark by which to test its separate existence. But a closer observation has enabled me, I think, to seize the clue which explains all these apparent discrepancies, and also leads the way to the scientific treatment of this sometimes unmanageable disorder. I began my investigation by considering what symptoms invariably attend upon distemper, and certainly at first I was completely puzzled, for I found in one series of cases apparently nothing but cough and running at the nose and eyes; in another these signs were absent, and their place supplied by head-symptoms and fits; whilst again, in a third set, the dogs all suffered from diarrhœa, with discharges of blood, and had neither head nor chest-symptoms, in any stage of the disease. In all these cases, however, I observed that there was *fever*, and that of a particular kind—not like the ordinary inflammatory feverishness which dogs are subject to, and which attends upon almost all their acute attacks, but of a *low typhoid* nature, with great exhaustion, entire loss of appetite, and, in the latter stages, a collection of brown fur, or, as it is called in human medicine, *sordes*, about the teeth. 'Surely then,' I said, 'this is typhus fever,' and immediately the truth flashed across my mind, that in the ideas represented by that word typhus might be found the key to the anomalies so puzzling to all inquirers into the nature of the malady. But then I said to myself, 'Why did not Dr. Jenner, who was so close an observer, come to this simple conclusion?' To this I could only reply, that I should think, from the description of the disease given by him, that he was shown many cases as distemper which were simply inflammation of the lungs. It is notorious that his account does not tally with the experience of practical men, neither does the remedy which he has advised (vaccination) exert any power in preventing the occurrence of the malady. This is now the general opinion of those who have given the supposed preventive a trial, and I must fully confirm the truth of their conclusions. Every one, however, must recollect numerous instances in which a simple clue, once seized, will explain away all difficulties, except the one astonishing fact of this simple clue not having been previously detected. And just as marvellous it now appears to me that it should so long have eluded observation. The points of similarity between distemper in dogs and typhus fever in man are so strongly marked, that a treatise upon the latter is all that is wanted to enable any one who understands medical terms to treat the former with the greatest probability of success.

SYMPTOMS OF DISTEMPER.—I should define distemper in the dog as a fever of a nature similar to typhus, and always characterised by the following symptoms, which generally occur in the order in which they are mentioned:—There is first a dullness and restlessness, with partial loss of appetite, heat and dryness of the nose, rapid but feeble pulse, and dull eye, the white of which is generally streaked with dark-coloured blood-vessels. The dog seems extremely sensitive to cold, or to any other disagreeable sensation, as scolding, flogging, &c. The water is scanty and high-coloured, with thirst; and the motions either very costive or loose, and if the latter, often of a pitchy colour. *The strength and flesh fail in a remarkably rapid manner*, so that the dog is often unable to stand at the end of a few days or a week; the appetite is by that time entirely lost, and frequently the food which is given by force is returned, or speedily passes the bowels unchanged. The respiration generally becomes quicker than natural, though this symptom is not so universal as the others I have enumerated. In fact, all the processes of respiration, circulation, digestion, and secretion are disturbed in a remarkable manner; and in this, I believe, is the essence of the disease; and the healthy resumption of these functions is always attended by convalescence. The blood is no longer properly depurated by the agency of the lungs, liver, and kidneys, nor renewed by healthy materials, the result of good digestion; the circulation, consequently, is imperfectly carried on, and the brain is supplied with impure blood, which is full of matters acting as a poison to it, and, as a consequence, death often takes place at an early stage from a fit. Whatever secretions are effected are vitiated in quality, and altered in quantity, sometimes being almost stopped, occasioning the dry, husky cough, and constipation of the early stage; and sometimes in excess, when you have the profuse offensive discharge from the nose and bronchi, or the pitchy motions from the intestines which accompany the progress of the disease.

Such are the general and characteristic symptoms of distemper.

Those which I shall now enumerate may be considered as the local complications of the complaint.

1st. THE AFFECTIONS OF THE CHEST.—In accordance with the theory, that the essence of the disease consists in impurity of the blood, in consequence of the failure to act of its proper depurating organs, the lungs, liver, and kidneys, I should, à *priori*, expect that in the dog the lungs would be the most likely organs to be attacked, because they, with the tongue and nostrils, do their own duty, and also that performed by the skin in man and many other animals. They are, in fact, the main purifiers in the dog, and they may be expected to be the first attacked, and so they generally are, though in some epidemics the liver and stomach seem to suffer in a still greater proportion. As a general rule, therefore, you may expect, in the early stage of distemper, to meet with a short, dry, husky cough, with sneezing, or sniffing through the nostrils, the result of irritation and congestion of the mucous membrane of the nose and windpipe. This state goes on for some days, and occasionally lasts during the whole attack; but generally, at the end of a week, a thick yellow offensive discharge appears from the nose and eyes, and, after each fit of coughing, from the lungs also. The ear, applied to the chest, detects great rattling of mucus, and, on percussion, there is usually more dullness than natural. Respiration is somewhat quicker than in a state of health, but there is not generally that amount of distress in breathing which accompanies inflammation of the substance of the lungs, or pneumonia, as it is technically called. In some cases true pneumonia or else pleurisy supervenes, which may be detected by the peculiar symptoms hereafter to be described.

2nd. OF THE LIVER, STOMACH, AND BOWELS.—The liver, being next in importance to the lungs as a purifier of the blood, is also next in frequency of attack in distemper. Indeed, it is almost always more or less disturbed in its functions; and, so long as the motions continue of a good colour and consistence, you may rest contented that the attack will be a mild one. Usually, however, the flow of good bile is suspended, and a black pitchy fluid is poured out, which irritates the bowels and causes diarrhœa. The stomach is generally so upset as to reject food as soon as swallowed, or, if it is retained, the bowels pass it on without dissolving it, or extracting any nourishment from it. There is very commonly a discharge of blood, which may be looked upon as a most unfavourable symptom, and is almost always the result of ulceration of the mucous membrane of the colon or cæcum. JAUN-DICE, or 'the yellows,' as it is called, is a frequent complication of distemper, and it is a symptom of the attack chiefly falling upon the liver; it is usually fatal. It arises either from the liver ceasing to secrete bile at all, in consequence of congestion, or from its bile, after secretion, being pent up by mechanical obstruction.

3rd. THE KIDNEYS.—These organs, it may be recollected, purify the blood from those worn-out materials of the body which are saline or soluble in water. It is not to be expected, therefore, that they should participate in the disease to the same extent as the lungs and liver, because, as the distempered dog is not inclined to take exercise or food, the muscular fibres are not worn out to so great a degree as in health; they are therefore affected like all other secreting organs, but not to any marked extent.

4th. OF THE BRAIN AND NERVOUS SYSTEM.—This important set of organs is *primarily* affected with the others—in fact, it ceases to act with its usual vigour, and by such cessation lessens the activity of all other parts supplied with nerves. There is thus a complete circle of impaired functions, and it is difficult to say where the mischief begins; whether the nervous system is first affected, and so acts upon all parts connected with it, or whether it is only disturbed in common with the other organs of secretion in the first place; and, secondarily, from being supplied with impure and empoisoned blood. In any case, however, it is always more or less disturbed, occasioning fits of an epileptic nature, and, as a sequel to the disease, we frequently find what is called chorea, but which appears to be more like trembling palsy in its nature. There is often entire palsy of the posterior extremities, which is almost invariably fatal. Whenever the brain is much affected, there is likely to be ulceration of the cornea of the eye, which, however, is generally removed if the nervous system recovers its tone.

5th. OF THE SKIN.—In almost all cases of distemper there is more or less skin-eruption appearing under the flank and belly, and between the fore-legs. This eruption is sometimes in small vesicles, soon becoming full of pus, and at others in large blebs containing a bloody serum; the former is a favourable symptom, the latter quite the contrary. During the year 1853, distemper was very frequently complicated with an inflammatory œdema of the extremities. It commenced with swelling generally of one or both hind-legs, and then sometimes attacking the fore-legs—after a short time this went on to such an extent as to cause inflammation of the cellular membrane and a secretion of pus diffused throughout its whole extent. If this is not at once let out by incision, sloughing takes place, and the animal speedily sinks from exhaustion, but, by a judicious use of the knife and general support of the system, recovery may be expected. It proved fatal in many cases.

CAUSES.—The most common cause of distemper is, no doubt, infection, but it is occasionally epidemic, and then most probably depends upon some peculiar condition of the air. But it also seems to be the natural tendency of all debilitating diseases in young dogs to run on into this typhoid type. Whether the disease is common catarrh or influenza, or inflamed liver or lungs, or even the irritative fever of worms or teething, in all these cases the tendency seems to be, to put on the form of low typhus, and this is especially the case when dogs are ill-fed, or crowded together in ill-ventilated kennels; or, in fact, submitted to any of the ordinary predisposing causes of typhus fever in the human subject. And this disease, once established, soon spreads to all within reach of its influence. The infection seems to be carried with them by dogs after their convalescence. I have frequently known a most severe attack supervene upon the contact with a puppy in the slips, which was sufficiently recovered to run, though, of course, not in a fit state for such an exertion.

The kennel also seems to retain the infection for a long time, it being most probably absorbed with the urine, &c. The walls, &c., should therefore be well washed with chloride of lime, or

Sir W. Burnett's disinfecting fluid, after the dogs are removed, and some few days, or even weeks, should elapse before others are placed in them. Dogs seem to be peculiarly liable to distemper when approaching maturity, the greater number being attacked between nine and eighteen months old; but, as in the typhus fever of man, it is not confined to that age. The suckling and the old dog are also open to its attacks, though in a much less degree. As in the human being again, one attack generally, though not always, preserves the individual from a second. Indeed, the laws of contagion and the statistics of the two diseases are precisely identical, making allowance, of course, for the difference in the time of coming to maturity, and reckoning age in the dog by months, as in the man by years, so that a dog twenty-one months old may be considered as mature as a man of twenty-one years of age.

TIME OF INCUBATION.—The disease is generally, as in typhus fever, about ten days or a fortnight, after infection, before making its appearance.

DURATION.—Distemper varies in the length of the attack from a few days to two or three months; but the average period, like that of typhus fever, is twenty-one days.

DIAGNOSIS.—In its mildest form distemper is very often mistaken for ephemeral fever, or influenza, to which I have alluded at page 58. Severe distemper is most likely to be confounded with hydrophobia, from which it may be distinguished either by the absence of all aberration of intellect, or by the difference in the form of its manifestation. In distemper there is no restlessness, or, at all events, only a tendency to change the posture, whilst the hydrophobic dog is always on the watch, and eyes every one with a wildly-suspicious gaze. The distempered dog is nervous certainly, but only from fear, while the hydrophobic dog knows neither fear nor pain, and will resist to the death any threats or actual punishment. If the brain is much affected in distemper, there is almost always a fit or paralysis—neither of which occurs in hydrophobia—and lastly, the distempered dog eats nothing, whilst the hydrophobic animal has a depraved appetite, and devours fœces, wool, hair, or any other *extraordinary* matter which comes in his way. Distemper is also liable to be confounded with any of the inflammatory diseases which attack the brain, lungs, liver, stomach, or kidneys; but in the simple inflammation of those organs there is not that *excessive and rapid loss of strength* or appetite which occurs in distemper, nor is there such extreme and speedy emaciation as we meet with in that disease.

PROGNOSIS.—Under the absurd and empirical mode of treatment which has been adopted, viz. the use of the same remedy all through the course of the complaint, a very great mortality will necessarily ensue, but if treated properly, I believe the deaths ought not to exceed one in twenty cases — that is, supposing the animals were not predisposed to the disease by ill-feeding, over-crowding, &c., and that they are attended by a kennel-man who understands his business, and will carry out the instructions of a scientific professional man. But even with the assistance which these remarks may afford to a man of ordinary intelligence who is versed in the general management of dogs, I should confidently trust that the mortality would not be much greater than one in fifteen of those attacked.

LIABILITY TO A SECOND ATTACK.—It may, I think, be assumed that a dog once attacked by true distemper is not likely to suffer a second time, though such cases do sometimes occur. But I also fancy that if a *young* dog is seized with any severe disease, and it stops short of the typhoid stage, he will, *as long as he is well managed*, escape true distemper; but if he is subjected to a different treatment, he then becomes liable to the disease, either from infection, or as a result of any cold or other disorder. In other words, so long as the system is in a state of health, and not broken down by mismanagement, distemper or typhus fever can only be communicated to a dog peculiarly liable to it by natural constitution or 'breed.' And thus we see one or two puppies in a litter, though mixing with the others, escape the attack, and they are just as much protected as if they had gone through the disease, because their state of health, either by nature or good management, renders them proof against its influence; but let these very animals be afterwards neglected, and they take the disease readily enough. Hence experienced dog-owners, having remarked that a dog having any severe attack of catarrh or influenza is afterwards almost sure to escape death from distemper, have come to the conclusion that the catarrh or influenza was distemper itself in a mild form, and have certified that he has had the disease. But such a mistake is of little consequence in practice, because the dog is nearly as well protected by natural

DISEASES OF THE GREYHOUND.

strength of constitution as if he had passed through the disease, and quite as much so as the dog which is exposed to the influence of contagion without taking it.

The TREATMENT of typhus fever must vary with the stage of the malady, and will be best considered under the heads of—1st. The *incipient* period; 2nd. The period of *reaction*; 3rd. The *typhoid* period; and 4th. The period of *convalescence*.

1st. In the *incipient* period, I should recommend that a dose of calomel and jalap should be given as early as the disease can be clearly made out to be distemper. The dose should be as follows, according to the age of the puppy :—

At six weeks old . . .	Calomel 1 grain	. .	Jalap 4 grains
Three months old . .	,, 2 ,,	. .	,, 6 ,,
Six ,, ,, . .	,, 3 ,,	. .	,, 9 ,,
Nine ,, ,, . .	,, 4 ,,	. .	,, 12 ,,
Above nine months . .	,, 4 ,,	. .	,, 14 ,,

This dose should be made into a ball with linseed meal, and is chiefly useful in procuring a good flow of bile, and also in removing any lodgment in the bowels which puppies are so very liable to, from their habit of eating all sorts of filth coming in their way. After this has acted freely, which should be encouraged by warm broth, the puppy should be kept in an airy and warm box, and *never suffered to go out to exercise on any pretence whatever till quite free from disease*. This point, I am confident, is of the greatest possible importance. Plenty of water should be allowed for him to drink, in which is to be dissolved one drachm of nitre to each quart; and he should be fed upon light broth and jelly with a little oatmeal to thicken it. At this time the dog usually takes enough food of his own accord, but if he refuse it, a little should be given him with the spoon twice a day; and if the colour of the fæces is not tolerably healthy, two or three grains of mercury with chalk should be given every night.

From the time that any local symptoms begin to show themselves *the period of reaction* may be said to have commenced, and it is at this stage that the chief difficulty in treatment arises, since it requires some experience to decide upon the degree of inflammation or congestion present, and consequently upon the strength of the remedies required to combat the malady. I have said that the chief complications are those centred in, first, the *chest*, secondly the *abdomen*, and thirdly the *head*—the *skin* complications being of no importance, except as signs of the severity of the general attack.

1. THE CHEST.—When the chest *alone* is attacked (that is, uncomplicated with any affection of the bowels), tartar emetic and digitalis will always be the sheet-anchor. The dose for the puppy of nine months and upwards should be as follows, and for younger puppies in diminished proportions:—Take of tartar emetic and digitalis in powder of each ½ to 1 grain, nitre 6 grains; form a pill, to be given three times a day. If the inflammation of the lungs appears to run very high, and there is a hard firm pulse of 130 or 140 in the minute, then bleed to 8 or 10 ounces, and give prior to the above pills an emetic of calomel and tartar emetic of each 1½ to 3 grains. If this does not speedily reduce the

inflammation, then insert a seton, or apply a blister to the side of the chest. It must be borne in mind that the lungs are a vital organ, and that if much mischief is done, the dog is ruined for ever, though he may, nevertheless, survive the attack. The remedies should, therefore, be sufficiently active to reduce the disease *at once*. At the same time it is well to take care to do no more than is required; and, of course, some skill is necessary to hit the happy medium. If there is also diarrhœa, in addition to the chest symptoms, ipecacuanha may be substituted for the tartar emetic in the same doses, and one or two grains of solid opium with ten grains of chalk should be added, so as to check the looseness, which of itself is a highly dangerous symptom. Indeed, all through the course of distemper, it is most necessary to take care that the bowels are not too much relaxed. There is almost always accompanying the chest-affection more or less running at the eyes and nose; the latter is of little importance, it not being either a vital organ, or one of consequence to the greyhound; and the former will generally disappear as the dog recovers his strength. If otherwise, a drop of solution of nitrate of silver (six grains to one ounce of water) dropped in every day, will help to restore the healthy state of the organ. But there is sometimes a condition in which a young hand would be led to believe that there was great inflammation of the lungs or heart, and in which the above treatment would be speedily fatal. This is characterised by a rapid breathing, with slow laboured pulse, but without power, the number of respirations in some cases exceeding in frequency the beats of the heart. This is peculiar to distemper, and is a symptom of *weakness*, with congestion—not inflammation—of the vessels of the lungs and heart. Ammonia and other stimulants should be given freely, as in the typhoid stage, and plenty of good jelly, &c., should be forced down the throat with a spoon. The nose, ears, and feet, are generally icy cold, and, if the weather is severe, the dog should be put in a warm but well-ventilated room ; or, if that is inconvenient, should wear constantly a soft, warm cloth.

2ndly. If the ABDOMEN is the chief seat of the complaint, there may be either inflammation of the external coat of the bowels, which is not common, or inflammation and ulceration of the mucous coat and glands, which is one of the most usual forms in which the disease expends itself. In the first of these, called enteritis, there is great pain, tenderness, and swelling, with the cord-like lines on each side the navel, and constipation. In the second there is little pain, seldom any swelling or tenderness ; and there is more or less diarrhœa, the fæces being generally mixed with blood, and often, to all appearance, entirely composed of that fluid. In enteritis it will be necessary to give a grain of calomel, and the same amount of opium, three times a day; and in some severe cases, to bleed. If the swelling of the bowels is great, an injection should be thrown up, consisting of half an ounce of spirit of turpentine, and the same of castor oil, mixed in half a pint of warm gruel. If, on the other hand, the mucous membrane is attacked, and there is diarrhœa, then it must be checked with chalk-mixture and laudanum as often as the bowels are moved—and in sufficient doses to stop it, let those doses be ever so large.

If this fails, then give of diluted sulphuric acid 20 drops, and laudanum 1 drachm, in a little rice-water, every two hours. Rice boiled in milk or broth should be given as food, and rice-water as the only fluid to quench the thirst, which is always great. But in that very frequent complication attendant upon the distemper when attacking the abdomen, viz. inflammation or congestion of the liver, characterised by jaundice, and commonly known as 'the yellows,' medicine is of little avail, because there are no remedies which will act upon the liver sufficiently to relieve it, without at the same time producing such a degree of diarrhœa as will frequently prevent the recovery of the dog. However, it is right to try what can be done, and I think that the best chance will be afforded by giving five grains either of blue pill or of Plummer's pill three times a day, or the same quantity of mercury with chalk, taking care to support the strength by good nourishing food, and to regulate the bowels either by castor oil if costive, or opium and chalk if relaxed. If the inflammation appears to run high, with a full hard pulse, a good bleeding at the onset must be practised, but it is not often that the dog's strength rallies after this remedy is adopted, however necessary it may be to prevent a fatal termination. Nothing is more common than for the young dog attacked with distemper to have worms passing from him, which, of course, increase the irritation of the bowels. There is no objection to a dose or two of powdered glass, given as will be hereafter described; but any stronger worm medicines are too lowering to be administered in such a disease as distemper. It is better, therefore, to wait, rather than to attempt too much, for the irritation of the

DISTEMPER.

remedy will do more harm than that arising from the presence of the worms.

There is often, also, great irritability of the stomach, which I have found give way to one drop of creosote and one or two grains of opium, in the form of a pill, once or twice a day, or sometimes to two or three drops of dilute hydrocyanic acid, in a little clear trotter jelly, once or twice a day. This latter remedy requires care, as it lowers the action of the heart very rapidly in the dog, though its effect soon goes off.

3rdly. When the head is the seat of the complication, a seton should immediately be inserted behind the ears; and if the symptoms run very high, it is better, after making the opening, to insert a red-hot iron before putting in the tape. Some people have advised the opening to be made with a red-hot iron, but it is easier, and I think less painful to the dog, to do it as I advise. If put in in the usual way, take care to smear some blistering ointment on the tape before inserting it, in order speedily to produce a plentiful discharge. If the head feels hot to the hand, and the eyes are very bright and red, keep the head sponged with very cold water, or, what is still better, fix on it a bladder containing pounded ice, which may be easily done by covering all with a linen cap. Unless there is diarrhœa also, give the calomel and jalap in the dose ordered in the first period, and follow it up with the mercury and chalk. If there is diarrhœa present, give instead ten grains of nitre and one of digitalis, three or four times a day. There is often considerable swelling of the glands about the throat, which generally ends in the formation of matter. An opening should be made pretty freely in the most depending part as soon as fluctuation can be distinctly felt. In this stage the dog often suffers from fits, but as these are of no importance in themselves, and only mark the seat of the disease to be in the brain, it is unnecessary to do more than carry out the remedies directed for that complication; if, however, they occur early in the attack, they indicate active inflammation of the brain, and generally require bleeding and a calomel and jalap purge. Chorea or St. Vitus's dance is also a very frequent consequence of head-mischief, and must be combated by three or four grains of the sulphate of zinc, or half a grain of the nitrate of silver, twice a day, made up into a pill with linseed-meal or bread-crumb; but a more particular description of this disease and its treatment will be given under its separate heading.

4thly. The eruption of the skin requires no particular remedy, as it will soon go off if the dog recovers his strength and health.

TYPHOID STAGE.—As soon as the violence of the local attacks has subsided, if the disease is at all severe, the *typhoid* stage is almost sure to be developed; the dog is then often unable to stand, and is emaciated to a terrible extent. It is this stage which I believe indicates the essence of the disease known as distemper, and without which (unless the dog has been evidently submitted to the contagion) it cannot be pronounced to have 'had the distemper.'

In the typhoid stage good nourishment is essentially required, and therefore a small teacupful of beef tea or soup, thickened with arrow-root, should be forced down the throat every four hours, unless the dog will take it voluntarily, which is not often the case. The following mixture should also be given three times a day : — Take of tincture of cardamoms and sal volatile, of each 1 drachm ; decoction of yellow bark, 1 ounce. If the dog is very much exhausted, a spoonful of port wine should be added to the beef tea once or twice a day, and the skin should be kept warm by clothing or artificial warmth. In this stage diarrhœa must be carefully guarded against, and if present, laudanum must be added to the above mixture, in doses increasing from a teaspoonful upwards till the desired effect is produced. Starch and laudanum injections (two drachms of the former to an ounce of the latter) may also be tried, but they are of no use unless pressure is afterwards kept up upon the anus with a dry sponge for some time, to prevent their return. In this stage, if the chorea continues, the seton must still be kept in, in spite of its debilitating effect ; but as soon as the chorea disappears the seton may be withdrawn, and reintroduced if necessary. It is useless to expect healthy fæces in this stage, and we must therefore be contented with letting the bowels alone unless too costive or too loose. As the stomach recovers its tone digestion is restored, flesh and strength are gained little by little, and the secretions become more and more healthy.

CONVALESCENCE.—In the stage of *convalescence* great care should be taken not to cause the dog to exert himself in any way, and the mere act of jumping off or on a bench will often cause a relapse. He should never be allowed to take exercise until he is able to walk strongly, and even then he should be led for the first few times, for fear of his galloping before his strength will bear the exertion. The neglect of this precaution is one of the most frequent causes of a relapse, and the kennel-man should be especially cautioned on the subject. In feeding, also, he must be very much on his guard against giving too great a quantity at once, but should feed often with small quantities of highly nourishing broth and jellies.

RHEUMATIC FEVER OR ACUTE RHEUMATISM.

Rheumatism is one of the most common diseases to which the dog is subject, but in the acute form it is not nearly so commonly met with as in the chronic; still it is not unusual in the greyhound, which is accustomed to artificial heat in his kennel, to find on the day after exposure to bad weather the following symptoms come on:—There is first of all a general soreness of the body, increased on moving,—this is attended with fever; full, hard, and quick pulse; dry hot nose; and constipation. On the next day the soreness increases, and the dog seems *incapable* of moving; there is intense tenderness of the muscles, especially in general of the back and shoulders, the fever runs very high, and the bowels are obstinately costive. Sometimes there is inflammation of one or more joints, but usually the muscular system is the seat of inflammation, and the disease, unlike its namesake in man, does not shift from one part to another, but expends itself upon the part first attacked. If the treatment adopted is sufficiently prompt, these symptoms disappear in a few days, leaving nothing but temporary weakness behind; but if the animal is neglected, the inflammation of the muscles goes to such an extent as to destroy their power, and the dog is incapable of using them. In this state he is said to have palsy of the hind-legs, though I think erroneously. True palsy is a loss of power owing to a disease of some portion of the nervous system supplying the part affected, whereas I believe that the loss of power following rheumatism is seated in the muscle itself, and has nothing to do with the nervous system. Palsy will arise sometimes from rheumatic inflammation of the spinal marrow, but very rarely indeed except as a consequence of an accident, and when it does come on, it is almost sure to last many weeks, if not during the whole life of the dog. But the spurious palsy following rheumatism, if properly treated, often disappears in a week or ten days, and, unlike true palsy, may almost always be, in a great measure, dispelled for the time being, by any stimulus which is sufficient to frighten the animal out of his propriety, such as the whip. One form of chest-founder is an instance of this spurious palsy, and is nothing more than the consequence of inflammation of the broad flat muscle which slings the dog between the two shoulder-blades. It is, however, more commonly the result of *chronic* inflammation of the same muscle, which I shall describe under the proper head.

TREATMENT.—Whenever a dog is seized with the above symptoms to any severe degree, and the pulse will bear depletion, I should advise the loss of a few ounces of blood from the neck vein. I should then give five grains of calomel and two of opium, and on the next morning from an ounce to an ounce and a half of castor oil, with half an ounce of syrup of poppies and thirty drops of sulphuric ether. The disease extends to the *muscular* coat of the bowels, and requires the stimulus of the opium and ether to cause them to act. If this dose does not freely purge the dog in six or eight hours, then throw up a clyster of half a pint of gruel with two or three drachms of spirit of turpentine and half an ounce of castor oil. Nothing is more likely to be effectual in obstinate constipation, occurring in rheumatic fever, than the warm bath used three or four hours after the exhibition of the oil. The water should be as warm as the human arm will bear it — that is, about 100° of Fahrenheit—and the dog should be kept in 20 or 30 minutes; then take him out, place him before a good fire, and rapidly dry him by rubbing with warm cloths. This often produces a copious action of the bowels. But should all these means fail, then give one drop of croton oil and one grain of opium every six hours till it operates. As soon as the bowels are moved give the following pill every six hours :—

Take of Ipecacuanha	1 grain
Opium	1½ grain
Calomel	½ grain
Venice turpentine	2 grains: mix.

As soon as the soreness is somewhat diminished, rub the back and shoulders with the following liniment twice a day, before a good fire, taking care to rub it well in, and not to leave the hair saturated with it :—

Take of Liquor Ammoniæ,
Spirits of Turpentine,
Tincture of Opium,
Olive Oil, of each 1 ounce : mix to form a liniment.

By the adoption of these measures, and the repetition of the castor oil without the calomel, if necessary, the muscles generally recover their power in a few days. All animal food should be withdrawn, and the dog fed upon oatmeal porridge, flavoured with a little milk. Sometimes his appetite is entirely gone, but seldom for more than a day or two, and, unlike distemper, it is better to leave the stomach alone, and not attempt to force the dog to swallow food against his will.

SMALL-POX.

Of this disease I have only seen one well-marked set of cases, which occurred to some pointers of mine, and I shall therefore simply transcribe Mr. Youatt's account. It appears to be of modern origin, having only been noticed since 1809 :—

'The essential symptoms of small-pox in dogs succeed each other in the following order :—The skin of the belly, the groin, and the inside of the fore-arm becomes of a redder colour than in its natural state, and sprinkled with small red spots irregularly rounded ; they are sometimes isolated, sometimes clustered together.

The near approach of this eruption is announced by an increase of fever.

'On the second day the spots are larger, and the integument is slightly tumefied at the centre of each. On the third day the spots are generally enlarged, and the skin is still more prominent at the centre. On the fourth day the summit of the tumour is yet more prominent. Towards the end of that day the redness of the centre begins to assume a somewhat grey colour. On the following days the pustules take on their peculiar characteristic appearance, and cannot be confounded with any other eruption. On the summit is a white circular point, corresponding with a certain quantity of nearly transparent fluid which it contains, and covered by a thin and transparent pellicle. This fluid becomes less and less transparent, until it acquires the colour and consistence of pus. The pustule during its serous state is of a rounded form. It is flattened when the fluid acquires a purulent character, and even slightly depressed towards the close of the period of suppuration, and when that of desiccation is about to commence, which ordinarily happens about the ninth or tenth day of the eruption. The desiccation and the desquamation occupy an exceedingly variable length of time; and so, indeed, do all the different periods of the disease.'

Mr. Youatt advises the ordinary treatment for febrile disease, viz., a warm, airy, loose box, and protection from any sudden change of temperature, which he says is almost invariably fatal. As in the human subject, pneumonia is a very common complication of small-pox, and must be treated by bleeding, &c., vigorously, or the animal inevitably dies. The eruption in the cases which occurred in my kennel extended into the throat, and most probably throughout the whole of the alimentary canal. They all recovered without any further treatment than rest, fresh air, and an occasional dose of oil.

CHAPTER V.

DISEASES OF THE GREYHOUND—*continued*.

2. GENERAL DISEASES, WITHOUT INCREASED ACTION OF THE HEART.

Chronic Rheumatism— Chest-founder— Kennel-lameness— Chorea, or St. Vitus's Dance—Rickets—Enlarged Joints—Chronic general Dropsy: from diseased Kidneys — Cancer and other Malignant Diseases — Epilepsy— Anæmia.

CHRONIC RHEUMATISM (CHEST-FOUNDER, KENNEL-LAMENESS).

CHRONIC RHEUMATISM in the dog is, as far as my experience goes, almost entirely confined to the muscular system, and does not often attack the joints as in the human subject, except in very old and worn-out dogs, which have done much hard work, such as pointers and setters, &c. It may be either the sequel of the *acute* form, or it may arise independently of it, and in that case is very insidious in its approaches. In either case it interferes with the usefulness of the animal, but in the latter condition it is even more likely to lead to that state which is often called palsy, than when it follows upon an attack of rheumatic fever as a consequence of cold. Chest-founder and kennel-lameness are the two most common varieties of chronic rheumatism, and are both confined to the muscles of the shoulder and the chest. In chest-founder the chief seat of the disease is the serratus magnus muscle, which is a broad sheet of muscular fibres attached below to the lower ends of the ribs, and above to the upper edge of the shoulder-blade. This muscle, one on each side the body, suspends the chest to the shoulder-blade, and is exposed to great strains either in coming down from a leap, or in stopping the dog in his turns, particularly down hill. There is no other connection of any importance, either ligamentous or bony, which may serve to attach the shoulder to the body, and though this broad muscle is said to be aided by certain bands of cellular fibres, they can scarcely be considered as of much use in any but the ordinary movements of the body. When, therefore, the dog has been exposed to the severe cold and wet which he often experiences in the slips, and then has a trying course, killing his hare perhaps down a steep bank or the side of a hill, it cannot be wondered at that this muscle should suffer. The attack arises partly from the sprain, but also from the rheumatic inflammation consequent upon the exposure to cold settling in that muscle which has been most exposed to injury from the shocks of the course. If the chest-founder is at once attended to, there is every probability of its entire removal, but if it is neglected in the early stage it is a most intractable disease. The dog goes well up hill, and can often play and gallop in a straightforward direction as well as ever, but he loses his power of turning, or stopping himself down hill—and often falls when making a rush at his game.

DISEASES OF THE GREYHOUND.

THE BEST REMEDY, in the early stage, is the warm bath every day, at a temperature of 100° Fahrenheit, and with five or six pounds of salt in every gallon of water. After coming out of this the dog should be rubbed quite dry, and then should be well rubbed with the liniment, as recommended for acute rheumatism. I have also found great benefit from the Mistura Guaiaci in ounce doses twice a day, and in severe cases it is well, after giving up the warm bath, to put a seton behind and above the elbow, taking care to keep a muzzle on the dog, which is better than any bandage; indeed, I know of none which a dog will allow to remain on if he has the free use of his teeth.

KENNEL-LAMENESS is a very similar complaint with regard to its seat, but has an entirely different origin. It, however, is not confined to the serratus, but appears to attack all the muscles of the shoulder-blade, some more than others in one case, and the reverse in other attacks, though apparently arising from the same cause. This disease is chiefly confined to hounds, greyhounds, pointers, and setters, and is, no doubt, produced by the chill caused by putting them in a cold, damp kennel after they are worn down by fatigue. Still, some dogs get the disease when entirely confined to their kennels, but this is the exception rather than the rule; and I should hope that now-a-days few masters would allow their dogs to be so much confined as to show whether kennel-lameness can be produced irrespective of fatigue. It may be known from chest-founder by the dogs coming out of kennel lame and stiff, and by their being unable or unwilling to run at all, much less to gallop. In severe cases there is such a degree of lameness that the dog does not appear willing to leave his bed, though, after being compelled to do so, he is able to scramble along somehow or other. Sometimes the disease is confined to one shoulder, but more frequently it extends to both.

THE TREATMENT should be conducted on the same principles as for chest-founder; but *preventive* are much better than *curative* measures. A dog once seized with chronic rheumatism in any part is ever after subject to a return; and therefore it is highly desirable to avoid the cause which is known to produce it. This cause is, dampness in the kennel; and I shall, hereafter, advise their construction in such a way as to avoid this defect. The high bench, I am satisfied, is of great importance; and the clay substratum, I am inclined to believe, is an undoubted advantage. A very common cause is the quarrelsome and domineering disposition of the master-dog in the kennel, who drives the others down, and compels them to lie upon the floor. This should be guarded against carefully, and the dog changed to another kennel, or, if this is impracticable, he must be muzzled for a time, till he will permit his companions to rest quietly on the bench. I have tried to avoid this by putting up two benches on separate sides; but the dog is of so domineering a temper, that he will often persecute one or more of his fellows by following him backwards and forwards till he is tired of trying to get on the bench for fear of punishment. This is especially the case when there happens to be a mixture of the sexes.

A remedy for either of these rheumatic attacks has within the last few years been suggested, which I have known succeed in many cases. It consists of a red herring, into which has been rubbed a mixture of two drachms of nitre and one drachm of camphor. This should be given two or three times a week till the disease is cured. The dog should be starved till he will eat the herring, but if there is much reluctance shown to it, the nitre may be dissolved in his water, and the camphor only rubbed into the herring. The remedy has been successful in so many cases, that there can be no doubt of its potency, though, of course, like almost all others, it cannot be relied on as a certain and specific cure for this intractable disease.

CHRONIC RHEUMATISM attacks the loins and thighs, and also the muscles of the abdomen; but these affections have received no separate names in canine pathology. The same treatment as for kennel-lameness is equally efficacious in the early stage, and equally useless after the lapse of time which is too frequently allowed by the kennel-man before he acquaints his master with the extent of the mischief. I have already alluded to the common idea that this affection ends in *palsy*, and to my disbelief in the truth of the supposition. It is entirely contrary to analogical reasoning, and is opposed to my practical experience. Among the numerous cases which I have seen, of what has been described to me as *palsy*, coming on after rheumatism, I have never seen one which could be considered as anything more than the loss of power which results from the wasting of the muscular fibre in consequence of rheumatism. I have certainly seen palsy arising from inflammation of the spinal marrow in a rheumatic dog, but in every case I could trace the mischief to a strain or blow occasioning internal mischief, and thus pressing upon the nervous fibres contained within the canal. In the greyhound this would be a hopeless case; for though by strychnine, given in small doses and for some time, the tone of the nerves might possibly be in some measure restored, yet the animal never could serve any useful purpose, and had much better be put out of its misery by a dose of prussic acid or a few inches of cord.

CHOREA, OR ST. VITUS'S DANCE.

This is a very frequent sequel to distemper, and generally sets in by slight convulsive movements of one of the fore-legs, which gradually increase in severity till they attack one side of the body or even the whole frame. These convulsive twitchings are most evident when the animal is at rest, and often disappear when he walks or trots, returning as soon as he attempts to stand still; one fore-leg is then generally raised, and the animal keeps ducking his head, and twitching his leg at the same time, in a way which, once seen, cannot fail to be ever after easily recognised. This disease is essentially the result of weakness, whether caused by distemper, or worms, or improper diet. In either case there is irritation of the nervous system, conjoined with such a low and depressed state of the whole body, that the cause of the irritation cannot be shaken off. We know little or nothing of the mode in which irritants act upon the nerves, but we do know, by experience, that it is only in a state of depression that any permanent impression can be produced upon the nervous system. Hence in a strong, healthy, young dog, worms will scarcely produce any effect at all, but let the same animal be subjected to any lowering disease (distemper or influenza, or what not), and the irritation speedily produces chorea, which will not be removed till the worms themselves are got rid of. True chorea often goes on to shaking palsy, which is only another symptom of the same disease, but which is distinguished from it by its persisting during sleep, while chorea always disappears during that state of repose of the brain and nervous system.

THE TREATMENT should consist in the removal of the cause by appropriate remedies, and in the restoration of tone to the nervous system by tonics, generally of a metallic nature. Now the causes of chorea are various. In the first place, the mischief is often in the brain and spinal cord, in consequence of the congestion of that organ in distemper. For this a seton should be inserted in the neck, and the shower-bath applied to the head daily by means of the rose of a watering-pot, of course taking care to dry the skin afterwards, and to protect the body during its application by a waterproof cloth. If worms are the cause, they must first be got rid of by the remedies hereafter to be described, and should bad food, or any indigestible substance in particular, be suspected as the fountain of evil, then a simple dose of calomel, jalap, and rhubarb will be the appropriate remedy. As soon as the original cause is removed one step only is gained, for we must not expect the

THE TREATMENT.

disease to stop, but simply to lie at our mercy, which it would not be, so long as the exciting cause was still keeping up the mischief. As far as possible, the two courses should be pursued together; that is to say, we should give tonics, &c., at the same time that we are endeavouring to remove the cause. By this plan the immediate weakening effect of the seton, or worm medicines, is counteracted, and after they cease to lower the dog, the tonic medicines act still further in bracing the nervous system. For this disease the sulphate of zinc is, I think, the most effectual remedy, and rarely fails if the irritating cause is effectually removed. It is especially useful in the chorea of distemper, and should be given in three or four-grain doses to a full-grown puppy, twice a day, made up into a pill with crumb of bread. The nitrate of silver, in half-grain doses for a full-sized dog, I have found succeed in several cases where it has been tried, but in two cases, though persisted in to my knowledge for several weeks, it failed, and afterwards the zinc effected the cure. Should the cause be attributable to worms, iron is the best remedy, and the best form for giving it is the carbonate in scruple doses, mixed into a bolus with linseed meal and boiling water; of course this is not to be given till the worms are removed. When the disease becomes so violent as to degenerate into shaking palsy, the best thing to be done is to destroy the dog. In chorea fresh country air and good nourishing food are of the greatest importance, and without them there is little chance of a favourable termination. An occasional dose of castor oil is also desirable.

RICKETS.—ENLARGED JOINTS.

This disease is also a frequent source of annoyance in the puppy-kennel, and yet little or nothing has been written on the subject. Every large breeder must have met with numerous cases of puppies which have been returned to him at twelve months old, or earlier, with one or two of their joints so enlarged as to lame the animal, but with *all* of them more or less increased in size. Sometimes the stifle is as large as an orange, being exactly in a similar condition to the white swelling of the human knee. The disease arises partly from hereditary weakness of constitution, but chiefly from bad rearing, and confinement in an unhealthy and close kennel: either from a deficient supply of phosphate of lime, or from the stomach and bowels being so weakened as to be incapable of absorbing it, the bones are imperfectly formed. In proportion to the phosphate of lime too much gelatine is deposited, especially at the ends of the bones forming the joints, and the consequence is that they assume the large appearance so characteristic of the disease. Many even experienced coursers are proud of a puppy with large joints; but I am quite sure that, though the enlargement often disappears with increasing age and strength, yet that a well-reared puppy should never have his joints larger in proportion than the shafts of the bones. I am fond of seeing in young dogs plenty of bone, large hocks, and good knees, but I also like to see a corresponding development of the shafts of the bones of the forearm and thigh, as well as the shank bone. This, I am fully aware, is altogether heterodox, but I felt so strongly the truth of my opinion, that I am bound to maintain it. I would not condemn a puppy because he has good bony joints, nor even if rather lumpy, but if in the intervals between the joints there is a manifest falling off, with a tendency to distortion, by bowing out or in, or sometimes forwards, I should certainly avoid him, as likely only to lead to disappointment from a broken leg, or an inflamed or dislocated joint. For not only are the shafts of the bones weak and liable to fracture, but the ligaments of the joints are also small and delicate, and dislocation is almost sure to occur, after the useless outlay of time, money, and temper, to which I have an especial objection. To make myself clearly understood upon this subject, I must render myself liable to the charge of repetition, perhaps *usque ad nauseam*, but, nevertheless, I believe the importance is such that I cannot avoid dwelling somewhat on a point which is not sufficiently attended to. It is a well-known axiom that nature does nothing in vain, and that she only has recourse to any subsidiary process as the best means of supplying an accidental deficiency; consequently, when the joints are enlarged by the deposit of soft gelatinous matter to a greater extent than natural, it is only because it requires more of the second-best material (gelatine) than of the best (lime) to give the joints firmness enough to withstand the shocks even of the puppy's gallop. I do not mean here the puppy of two or three months old, but of seven, eight, or nine months of age. Prior to this age the ends of the bones are cartilaginous in all cases, with the exception of a small central nucleus of bone, and have little shock to withstand, from the want of speed in the puppy, and his great natural and instinctive objection to jump either up or down. When, therefore, after eight months in the bitch, or nine in the dog puppy, the joints continue very lumpy and enlarged, I consider it a sign of natural weakness of constitution, or of the imperfect supply of food containing the phosphate of lime, such as wheat or oat flour. The use of salt is also a great aid to the formation of bone, from its increasing the digestive powers, and from the general stimulus to secretion which it affords. If not previously used, therefore, it is well to supply it on detecting the existence of rickets or a tendency to it. A grain of the sulphate of iron, combined with the same quantity of sulphate of quinine, will also tend to strengthen the constitution, and increase the deposit of lime, as well as relieve the tendency to inflammation of the joints, which often goes on to irreparable destruction and deformity. But if puppies are reared on the principles I have endeavoured to explain, these enlargements will very seldom occur, except as a sequel to distemper in very obstinate and severe cases. So long as actual deformity is avoided, I would never despair till the dog is arrived at maturity, as, by careful feeding and the use of the above remedies, I have known astonishing cases of recovery from enlarged and rickety joints; but, alas, these recoveries are too often only to the eye. The texture of the bone is too soft to stand the severe trials of the course, and a fracture takes place at a time when, perhaps, a large sum of money is invested on the success or failure of the pet of the kennel. Every dog is liable to accidents, and may break his leg from a twist or blow without imputation upon his blood or *bone*; but if a fracture takes place by the mere power of the muscles, as in starting from the slips, depend upon it, such a case, except in old age, is from disease, and that disease is rickets.

CHRONIC GENERAL DROPSY FROM DISEASED KIDNEYS.

This intractable disease is technically called anasarca, and is an oozing out of the serum of the blood into the loose cellular membrane of the body and limbs; it is known by the swelling ' pitting ' on pressure by the finger—that is to say, the finger leaves a pit in the flesh just as it would in dough, and the depression is not filled for a minute or two—whereas fat leaves no such pit, but is elastic enough to return to its natural surface as soon as the pressure is removed. It is essentially a disease of old dogs, though in some rare cases I have seen it come on after distemper. In the healthy condition of the body the kidneys remove the watery or serous part of the blood as fast as is necessary; but when they become diseased in consequence of want of exercise, forcing diet, or other causes, they no longer do their duty, and then the minute vessels often give way, and the serum oozes out into the cellular membrane. One of the most frequent causes of the disease is the injurious and dishonest practice adopted by the owners of stallion dogs, of giving over-stimulating food to restore their exhausted powers. This plan may be compared to the old fable of killing the goose who laid golden eggs in order to get at her interior; for though the stimulus succeeds for a short time, yet in the long run the dog is rendered incapable of doing his duty long before he otherwise would, and this injurious effect comes on, even if he remains tolerably healthy, and of course if diseased he is *hors de combat* at once, making the proceeding still more unprofitable to the owner. All that these gentlemen seem to think necessary is the restoration of the powers of the system after each act to the state which shall enable the dog to repeat the performance for the next comer, who may make her appearance at any short notice; but they do not consider that the quality of the stock is impoverished, nor that the health of their own property also suffers. It is from this cause that few public favourites as stallions continue healthy themselves, or get healthy stock for many years together. They are taken from a state of active exercise to comparative idleness, and to much stronger and more stimulating food than they have been accustomed to; and from this cause diseased liver or kidneys, or both, is sure to arise, and, as a consequence, the disease in question. Let me, therefore, implore all stallion-owners, as they value *their own* property (to say nothing of the interests of those who send their bitches to them), to avoid every kind of stimulus, and to give only such an amount of good flesh and meal (and for them barley meal is the best) as shall keep them in good condition. Let them also allow them an hour or two's exercise daily, and they will find them healthy and strong for a dozen years, so that they will in the end be gainers by their honesty, though they may lose a few bitches in some one year, or even in each year of their being at the service of the public. Greyhound bitches are not nearly so liable to the disease, because they are not subject to the same treatment, but among pet lap-dogs, &c., one sex is just as likely to be affected with anasarca as the other; and this is especially the case with those fat, overfed, and ill-exercised spaniels which are petted by old ladies, and taken out in carriages for an airing.

In the TREATMENT of this disease it is important to detect the cause. If the kidneys are in fault, the urine will be scanty and high-coloured, and generally very rank-smelling; whereas, if the liver is at the bottom of the mischief, although the urine may be high-coloured, yet it is *yellow*, not *brown*, being tinged with bile, and it is also not so scanty. The fæces in liver-affections also are pale and clay-coloured, often like barm or perhaps perfectly white. The liver may also often be felt enlarged and hardened. In either case, if the disease is permanent, the greyhound is good for nothing, being of course unfit for breeding purposes, but, if the attack has only recently come on, it may possibly be removed by diuretics if the kidneys are at fault, or by calomel and jalap if the liver is congested only, and not organically affected. The best diuretic for this purpose is nitre and digitalis, from six to twelve grains of the former and one of the latter, with perhaps half a grain of calomel, if necessary, formed into a bolus, and given twice a day. If these remedies do not entirely relieve the complaint in a week or two, it is useless to persevere, except for the purpose of gratifying some particular fancy for a great favourite, and, as I cannot speak from experience, I have nothing to recommend in such a case. Here, as in most other cases, I am anxious to enforce preventive rather than curative means, as I have no faith in the strength of constitution for either running or breeding purposes of a dog which has been subjected to a long course of medicine for any disease. I have been told that the wet sheet packing, as used in hydropathic establishments, is very efficacious in anasarca, but I have never tried it, and can only give the evidence of a friend, who speaks highly of its power of producing an increased flow of urine.

CANCER AND OTHER MALIGNANT DISEASES.
FUNGUS HÆMATODES.

This incurable class of diseases is undoubtedly constitutional in its origin, and though when showing itself externally, either in the mammæ or in any other part, it may be removed by the knife, yet the remedy is only temporary, and the disease either reappears in the same part, or in some internal and most probably vital organ. The most common seat of cancer is the female mamma, and it generally occurs in bitches which have been kept from the dog, though I have seen it several times in terrier bitches which have had two litters a year for several years together. For the purposes to which the greyhound is put it is quite useless to attempt removal, as the animal is not likely to be sound enough internally, to run, and for breeding purposes should be carefully avoided, since the disease is no doubt hereditary. In the early stage cancer shows itself by one or more lumps, as hard as marbles, and generally more or less nodulated. Sometimes these little tumours feel no larger than peas, and occasionally are clustered together. As long as they remain quiescent, and do not rapidly enlarge, the best thing to be done is to leave them alone, and use the bitch for running, if her constitutional state will permit it. This is often the case; for the poison as often shows itself *first* outside as in, and so long as the vital organs are not implicated, training may be carried on with success, and the bitch is able to go through sufficiently severe work to enable her to win a stake. But when the tumours begin to enlarge rapidly, it is better to destroy the animal at once. If removal by the knife is ever of service, it is in the very early stage, while the tumours are still hard, and are not yet inflamed or tender; but, as the only object can be to get as much out of the animal as possible, I am satisfied that it is far better to get what you can at once, and then to destroy her. If, on the other hand, you attempt to remove the disease, you are obliged to lower the bitch by preparatory physic, and then keep her out of work whilst the sore occasioned by the knife is healing. Much precious time is thus lost, and when you do begin to train again, the chances are that the internal mischief has been in the meantime set up, and that you will find all power of standing work for ever gone.

FUNGUS HÆMATODES is another malignant disease which is perfectly incurable, and even if the tumour is removed by the knife, it will, like cancer, almost invariably return. It most frequently shows itself in the eye, or in the glands of the throat, forming a *soft* spongy and bleeding *fungous* tumour. By its softness it may be readily distinguished from cancer, which is of a stony hardness, and there is also a much quicker growth in *fungus hæmatodes* and a greater tendency to bleed. Bitches are subject to its attack on the organs of generation, and they are then almost invariably barren, though, from the constant irritation of the diseased mass, they will take the dog nearly at any time. There is at first no external appearance of disease, and the only symptom of its presence is the frequent return of the signs of 'heat.' In a few months, however, there is a swelling around the orifice of the vagina, which indicates the exact nature of the disease. Nothing can be done in these cases, and the bitch should at once be put out of pain.

EPILEPSY.

This may arise from irritation of various kinds, which can often be specifically ascertained to exist, such as worms, dentition, or the congestion of the brain accompanying distemper; but it may also occur from some unknown cause throughout the whole life of the animal. This last is genuine *idiopathic* epilepsy, and, when firml established, is very little under the control of medicine—the attack is not ushered in by any premonitory

EPILEPSY. 101

warnings, the dog appears in perfect health, and, if a greyhound, runs his hare as well or better than usual, or, if a pointer or foxhound, performs his accustomed work with his usual amount of *gusto*. Suddenly, however, the dog foams at the mouth, becomes convulsed, and falls on his side, where he remains with starting eyes, champing and foaming at the mouth, and blue at the lips, for an uncertain period, averaging, perhaps, a quarter of an hour. After the lapse of this time he gradually becomes still, and then rises on his legs, with some little difficulty, looks stupidly about him, and in a few minutes resumes his usual appearance, being, however, a little more dull than before. The fit is very likely to be produced while at his ordinary work, especially if more severe than usual. All cases of epileptic fits are tolerably alike in their symptoms, and no doubt all have a cause of some kind or other; and in the above kind of epilepsy that cause is supposed to exist in the brain. This is, however, only because the brain is the centre of the nervous system, of which we know less than any other, and hence is the most likely to be the seat of mischief. When, therefore, a dog is afflicted with epilepsy, and it cannot be traced to worms, or indigestible food, or distemper, or difficult dentition, or suppressed mange, or, in a suckling bitch, to the too great drag of a large litter of puppies, it is usual to conceal our ignorance by calling the disease cerebral or idiopathic epilepsy. The higher the breed of the animal the more prone he is to epilepsy, and this appears to be especially the case with those animals bred 'in and in.' The nervous system in them is much more irritable, and the slightest irritation will produce a fit. It is also peculiarly prone to attack some breeds, most probably from some mismanagement of the original stock, either in breeding or rearing them. Sometimes the mischief can be traced to a blow on the head, occasioning even a fracture and depression of the skull, but this is not often the case, and has been remedied by trephining in one or two instances.

DIAGNOSIS.—Epilepsy can only be confounded with hydrophobia by ignorant people, and may easily be distinguished by the suddenness of the attack, by the champing and foaming, with *blueness* of the mouth, and by the speedy recovery. It may also be known from chorea by the loss of sensibility during the fit, and by the entire remission of symptoms during the intervals.

PROGNOSIS.—If the cause can easily be traced and removed, the disease will generally disappear, but in the cerebral epilepsy the chances are very great against an entire recovery. In the course of years the cause seems to disappear in some cases, or the constitution to be so accustomed to it as to bear its presence with impunity—at all events the fits gradually disappear, and we can only conjecture the reason. Anatomy reveals no alteration of structure, and therefore it is impossible to detect the exact reason why such an amelioration occurs.

TREATMENT.—This should be conducted differently according to circumstances, but, in all cases, the cause, if known, should be removed. In distemper, I have already said that epilepsy may be disregarded, except as a symptom of mischief in the brain; in all other cases it is well to remove the exciting cause as soon as practicable, by appropriate treatment, as, for instance, in worms, by worm medicines suited to the nature of the parasite which infests the intestines, or, in indigestion, by an emetic and purgative, &c. When these precautions have been taken, and the fits still continue at intervals, the same treatment may be tried in all cases. In the first place I would give a calomel and jalap purge, and repeat it once or twice a week according to the strength of the individual; next I would administer the shower-bath to the head every morning; and perhaps it would be advisable, in a strong hearty dog, to use it by holding the head and neck under a water-cock for a few seconds. The dog should, of course, be rubbed dry, and taken out for exercise at once. The exercise should be slow, but continued for at least two or three hours a day, and in the cool of the morning if in the summer. The food should be light but nourishing. As to medicine, if the food is not properly digested, I should give a pill twice a day containing extract of gentian and dandelion, of each five or six grains, and one grain of ginger. But if the digestive powers are strong, then I should try the effect of the nitrate of silver, given in quarter-grain doses, and persisted in for at least six weeks or two months. Should the dog be weakly, I should, prior to this, give the sulphate of quinine and iron, a grain of each twice a day. Such is the only treatment I know of likely to be beneficial. I have succeeded in curing epilepsy on this plan, when caused by any of the above irritants; but I confess that I never was able to remove confirmed or cerebral epilepsy, though I have been able to diminish the frequency and severity of the attack. I own others may be more successful, and perhaps more persevering; for myself, I dislike a diseased dog so much, that I have little patience when I fancy the cure as uncertain or remote as in the disease in question.

ANÆMIA.

This is the result of imperfect nutrition, and is that state of the system in which the blood-vessels contain too little blood, and that of a thinner consistence and paler colour than natural. The dog looks half-starved, and his lips and tongue are almost the colour of human skin; the hair is weak, and without lustre, and there is often a slight swelling, without pitting, of the cellular membrane of the lower part of the legs and of the feet. It generally occurs in young dogs which have been reared in confined situations, such as the back yard of a town-house, or even in the country, where the pure air and light are excluded, as in any dark hayloft, or similar place. This state of the blood may be got rid of by pure country air and good food, especially with the addition of steel, in the form of carbonate of iron, ten grains twice a day. If the appetite is very bad, it is better to unite the sulphates of iron and quinine in grain doses; but in the greyhound the injury to the constitution is generally irreparable. Worms are often at the bottom of the disease, or, at all events, they aggravate it so much, that they must be removed before any remedies can be expected to succeed. A spoonful of cod-liver oil mixed with five drops of vinum ferri, and given twice a day, has often effected a cure in apparently hopeless cases.

105

CHAPTER VI.

DISEASES OF THE GREYHOUND—*continued*.

3. LOCAL DISEASES GENERALLY ATTENDED WITH INFLAMMATION.

Inflammation of the Brain (Tetanus, Turnside, Phrenitis, Rabies, &c.)—Inflammation of the Eye and Ear—Inflammation of the Larynx and Throat (Blain)—Inflammation of the Lungs (Pneumonia, Pleurisy, Bronchitis, and Phthisis)—Inflammation of the Heart and Arteries—Inflammation of the Stomach (Poisoning, Indigestion)—Inflammation of the Intestines (Peritoneal, Mucous, and Muscular, or Colic, Diarrhœa, and Costiveness, Dropsy of Belly, Fistula in Ano)—Inflammation of the Liver (Jaundice, Torpid Liver)—Inflammation of the Kidney (Acute Dropsy)—Inflammation of the Bladder (Calculus, Rupture, Blennorrhagia, and Malignant Diseases)—Inflammation of the Skin (Mange, Blotch, Warts, Canker of the Ear, Surfeit, Eruption between the Toes, &c., &c.).

SIGNS OF INFLAMMATION.

IN this group of diseases I have classed together all distinctly local affections attended with more or less inflammation and constitutional disturbance, but in which the constitutional affection is subordinate to the local disease. Thus, in distemper there may be inflammation of the lungs, bowels, or brain, but always occurring subsequently to the peculiar symptoms of the complaint, such as the loss of appetite and strength. But in *simple* inflammation of

DISEASES OF THE GREYHOUND.

the lungs the dog has not, *at first*, these symptoms, but appears well and hearty in himself, though breathing with pain and difficulty, and with a rapid and powerful pulse. Now the signs of inflammation, wherever seated, are the same, namely, increased heat and redness, swelling and pain—but the proportions of these symptoms to one another vary considerably, and in some cases one or other may be almost totally absent. The *heat* exceeds that of the surrounding parts, but is never higher than that of the blood. The *redness* is caused by the greater supply of red blood than usual, in the minute vessels especially. The *swelling* is owing to the same cause, and, in addition, to the effusion of some product of the blood into the cellular membrane; and the *pain* is due to the pressure of the swelled adjacent parts upon the minute nerves, especially when circumscribed by unyielding walls, as is the case in the chest and skull. The *effusion* varies according to the structure of the part inflamed—and for this purpose it is well to divide the whole body into, first, the glandular system, as the liver, kidneys, brain, &c.; secondly, the membranous system, again subdivided into the mucous (including its continuation the skin), serous, and cellular membranes; and thirdly, the fibrous system, including the muscular and ligamentous tissues. Inflammation of the glandular system ends either by what is called *resolution*, which is merely disappearance, or by the effusion of *pus*, or by softening. In inflammation of mucous membrane there may be merely an excess of the ordinary secretion of mucus, or there may be pus or fibrine thrown out, sometimes attended with ulceration and gangrene, or in the skin there may be an eruption in any of the numerous forms which are met with. In inflammation of serous membranes there may also be an excess of serum, constituting dropsy; or, again, pus may be thrown out, or fibrine, with adhesion between the two surfaces, as in pleurisy or peritonitis. In cellular inflammation, again, the serum of the blood may ooze out, forming anasarca or œdema, or there may be a deposit of pus, constituting cellular abscess. The inflammation of the fibrous system has already been explained under rheumatic fever and chronic rheumatism.

The terms *acute* and *chronic*, as applied to inflammation, merely mark the rapidity with which it attacks the individual, and can scarcely be defined, since the limits can hardly be fixed where the one ends and the other begins. Every one, however, will readily understand the two extremes, and must supply the line of demarcation by taking the point intermediate between the two.

THE TREATMENT required will depend upon the organ attacked, for if this is of vital importance, it is necessary to take care that irreparable injury is not done. In such cases, however, the attack of inflammation receives a specific name, such as Pneumonia, or Phrenitis, under which heads its treatment will be described. As a general rule, it may be laid down that wherever inflammation shows itself in an organ not vital, it may be left to nature, unless matter forms in the shape of *abscess*, when it should immediately be let out by making a free opening in a depending position with a lancet. Some little knowledge of anatomy is necessary to perform this operation safely, as without it important vessels or nerves may be divided; but serious hæmorrhage is so rare in the dog, that little fear need be felt on this score.

TETANUS.

After the above summary of the signs of inflammation, I shall now proceed to the description of *tetanus*, which is so rare in the dog as scarcely to demand a lengthened description. I have only seen one case, which was the result of a severe laceration occasioned by a badger. In this instance the foot had been literally smashed by the teeth of the badger. Intense inflammation came on, and on the third or fourth day the jaw of the dog became rigid, the neck was bent to one side, and in spite of large doses of opium, &c., he died on the sixth or seventh day from the bite. Chloroform appears to exert great influence over the nervous system in tetanus, when occurring to man, and it would be worth while to try its effect in the dog, using the cold douche to the head and spine at the same time. The inhalation may be easily managed by holding a sponge with chloroform on it to the nose of the dog till his spasms are relaxed, and then applying ice or the cold douche to the head and spine. In a valuable greyhound, suffering from tetanus occasioned by an accident, this plan would deserve a trial, as the dog, if he recovered, would not be permanently injured. Indian hemp is also said to exert great power over tetanus, and might be tried in ten-grain doses every four hours.

TURNSIDE.

TURNSIDE is a disease of one side of the brain only, so that the animal has a tendency to wander in a circle, like the gidd of sheep. I have never had an opportunity of examining the brain of a dog attacked by the disease, and I never saw but one case, and from that the recovery was perfect, though slow. The remedies were, a seton, purgatives, and finally nitrate of silver in quarter-grain doses. The dog was a large white setter three or four years of age, and the disease appeared after a very severe week's work in hot weather early in September. There was no fever, and the dog fed well enough, though taking very little at a time, and soon leaving the food to pursue his circles; but, on presenting it again to him, he would eat three or four mouthfuls ravenously, and thus, by a little management, he was easily induced to take his proper allowance.

PHRENITIS OR SIMPLE INFLAMMATION OF THE BRAIN.

I have already alluded to the inflammation of the brain which frequently comes on as a complication of distemper, but there is also sometimes an attack of that organ without the presence of that disease. It generally occurs in very hot weather, and is so closely allied to hydrophobia, that it is very difficult to distinguish the two; nor is it quite clear that they really are distinct affections. One thing is, however, clear, namely, that dogs are sometimes attacked by brain symptoms resembling those of rabies, and yet seem incapable of propagating the disease by salivary inoculation. Where, therefore, it is pretty clear that the dog attacked cannot have been previously bitten, it is well to hope that the inflammation is not of a specific character. This is the only guide with which I am acquainted, and indeed, after all, is generally a very fallacious one; but among greyhounds which are constantly supervised phrenitis is more easily diagnosed than in other dogs. It must, however, be remembered that hydrophobia is sometimes developed spontaneously, as we shall presently see.

RABIES, HYDROPHOBIA, OR CANINE MADNESS.

The first and last of these terms can only be considered correct, for the second leads to erroneous ideas of the nature of the disease, which is not attended with any 'fear of water,' but, on the contrary, with an insatiable craving for it. This should be generally known, for the sake of the human as well as the canine race, for on the correct diagnosis depends the fate of the dog supposed to be mad, and in great measure also the safety of any man, woman, or child bitten by him—since there is no doubt that the fear of the disease is as fatal as the disease itself.

Rabies is essentially a disease of the blood, occasioned by the presence of a poison, either introduced into it by inoculation, or developed in it from some unknown cause. Now it is a law in the economy of all animals, as far as we know, that when a poison is introduced or developed in the blood there is a tendency to get rid of it by some excessive secretion. Thus the poison of small-pox occasions the eruption which relieves the blood, by separating the enormous quantity of matter contained in the pustules spread over the body. Thus, also, in scarlet fever, there is a new cuticle formed on the skin, and also a new epithelium or lining of the mucous membrane of the stomach and intestines. The same holds good with the bites of venomous snakes, in which a discharge of serum, large or small according to the virulence of the snake, takes place into the cellular membrane of the limb bitten, sometimes extending to the whole body. Cholera, again, is an example of a similar natural attempt at the removal of a poison, and is most fatal when the shock is so great as to prevent entirely the discharge of serum. We find the same, again, with typhus fever, which is severe in proportion to the cessation of all the natural secretions.

I believe, therefore, that in rabies the disease is so fatal, because there is so little natural attempt to remove the poison, and because man, generally in self-defence, prevents one of the chief means of effecting the removal. Now, what are these means? My belief is, that they consist in an immense secretion of saliva, which is well known and admitted to exist, but also in an increase of muscular irritability, by which the dog is impelled to travel blindly forward somewhere, he cares not where. This muscular exertion calls for a great waste of muscular fibre, and by consequence an immense secretion of new matter to supply its place. This new matter is, of course, obtained from the blood, and the secretion calls upon the kidneys to do their part of the work, as is always the case when waste muscular fibre is carried rapidly off. Now it is this part of nature's handiwork which is generally prevented by man—the mad dog's travelling tendency is put an end to, and one of the chief means of carrying off the poison is at once interfered with. Of course this is no more than right, because a mad dog not only wants to use his legs but his jaws also, and therefore he is not safe to be trusted to his own natural instinct, and if allowed to live, he is confined to the narrow limits of his chain, and consequently is unable to wear down his muscles beyond the slight amount of exertion which his owner permits. In Egypt, where dogs are swarming, but are allowed to run at large, madness is almost unknown, and the same is the case with the dogs of the Esquimaux and Greenlanders.

The SYMPTOMS of rabies may be divided into two sets, viz. the premonitory, and the confirmed. In the former state the dog is sullen, and somewhat more careless of his master's caresses than usual. He will feed to a certain extent, but is not particular as to the nature of his food, always, however, preferring articles of strong taste, such as urine, horsedung, old dirty wool or hair, or stinking meat, and, in some cases, rotten eggs or fish. He soon becomes restless in the extreme, getting up and changing his position every five minutes or oftener, and appearing dissatisfied with his bed, which he will scratch continually, and often in a rage tear all to pieces. As the disease advances he becomes so irritable as to be indifferent to everything about him which usually would engage his attention, and is constantly occupied in watching some fancied enemy, which he often snaps at, and is evidently annoyed at missing. The eye looks wild and suspicious, but in this stage is not more red than usual. The mouth is generally frothy, and soon runs with saliva, though in some few cases it is dry and parched. There is not, however, so much saliva as in epileptic fits, but there is more than usual, and generally enough to show at the corners of the mouth when shut. *There is insatiable thirst always,* and this should be known to everyone, since, as I before remarked, the fear of water is often ignorantly supposed to indicate rabies, and the absence of this symptom consequently leads to an unsafe confidence in the sanity of the dog. These premonitory symptoms are found in all dogs which are becoming rabid. The confirmed disease shows itself either in violent raging and unmanageable mania, or in what is called dumb madness, in which paralysis of the muscles of the lower jaw, coming on early in the attack, prevents the employment of the only offensive weapon which the dog possesses, viz. his mouth. There is in both kinds, however, the same tendency to keep trotting on somewhere, and to attack everything which interferes with this instinct. From the earliest appearance of violence there is a loss of sensibility, so that the dog does not feel the slightest pain on being stabbed with a pitchfork, or burnt with a red-hot poker, which, indeed, a rabid dog will seize on and hold, though his lips and tongue are scorched to a cinder. When in confinement, there is almost always a peculiar howl; but I have never heard of a dog at large barking or howling, and I am inclined to think that this is an instinctive effort to use the only muscular exertion in the power of the animal. The howl is very remarkable, and is often strangely mixed up with the bark,. being unlike the ordinary voice of the dog, and sonorous and melancholy in the highest degree. The bowels are generally costive throughout, but the urine is often good in quantity, though thick, and dark-coloured. As the disease advances, the paralysis of sensation is followed by loss of power and motion, partial at first, but finally complete. This is particularly the case with the hind legs, the dog showing an unsteady gait, and often balancing himself from side to side. At last he falls; but, soon getting up, he continues his task of running forward, only to stagger and fall again, till he becomes convulsed and dies. This termination, it is true, is not often witnessed, because the bystanders most frequently destroy either the life or the liberty of the individual; and when confined the paralysis is not so obvious, but the death always takes place with convulsions.

The disease runs its course in the dog in from three to six days. I once had a case which terminated fatally in two days. I had bought a Newfoundland dog from the huntsman of a pack of foxhounds, by whom he had been allowed to mix with the pack in kennel, or, at all events, at exercise. Ten days after my purchase arrived, during the whole of which time he was tied up, he one morning began to show slight symptoms of rabies, refusing to take a bone from my servant's hand, but gnawing it voraciously when thrown to him. On attempting to approach him, an inmate of my family was bitten slightly in the hand, but, immediately sucking it, no injurious consequences followed. The symptoms rapidly ran on, till by the afternoon he was undoubtedly rabid, and I removed him by means of a noose run through a ring at the end of a long mop-stick, to a small and safe box. Here I was able to watch the development of the disease, and supply water as often as wanted. The dog was constantly jumping up at the hole through which the water was lowered, and would upset the vessel containing it time after time. On the second day the violence was intense; everything which came within reach was torn to pieces; but towards evening he was unable to reach the hole, which was in the top of a common-sized door; and late at night I left him lying on his side, paralysed and slightly convulsed—the next morning he was dead and cold. The eyes had been very prominent, and the whites were injected with red blood to such an extent, as to raise the conjunctiva into a distinct fold at the edge of the cornea. The saliva ran freely to the last, and the thirst continued apparently till death —at all events as long as water was supplied; but, after the morning of the second day, it was impossibly to get it down to the ground before it was upset by the violence of the dog.

PATHOLOGICAL ANATOMY.—There appears to be in all cases intense inflammation of the brain and spinal marrow, ending in loss of function, as is the case in all inflamed glands. The glandular system throughout is also more or less affected, especially the salivary glands; but the mucous glands of the stomach and bowels, the liver, pancreas, and kidneys, are all more or less injected with blood. Indeed, reckoning the brain as a gland, which no doubt it is, the glandular system seems to be the only part of the body affected, as far as anatomical examination allows us to detect alterations of structure. The poison itself is beyond the ken of the microscope or the analysis of the chemist, and can only be known by its effects. The common saliva of a dog out of health, which is somewhat viscid and frothy, could not be distinguished, by any known tests, from that of a rabid dog; but introduce the latter into one or more abrasions, in man or any of the domestic animals, and though the wound heals, yet a leaven has been introduced into the blood, which, by a process apparently similar to ordinary fermentation, soon converts other and healthy particles into its own likeness, and rapidly pervades the whole system. The brain, as the most vital organ among the glands of the body, becomes the most speedily inflamed, and its inflammation produces the series of symptoms which we recognise as rabies, masking and overwhelming all the others, except the flow of saliva. This being patent to the eye, and also the cause of its propagation by means of the bite, has been always the subject of remark, but otherwise it does not deserve the notice which it has received. There is reason for believing that the mucus poured out by the stomach, or the lining membrane of the lungs, would, if introduced into a wound, act in the same way as the saliva; but as this latter fluid is the only one which the bite will carry into the part bitten, so it has become the sole object of our fears and observations. It is very remarkable that carnivorous animals only have the power of producing the disease in another animal; the dog, cat, wolf, and fox can each be shown to have infected others of their own species, and also sheep, horses, cows, and man himself. But the latter have never, as far as we know, carried on the contagion, though there are many instances of mad horses biting their fellows, and their grooms besides, but without any ulterior bad effect. Why this should be so is not known, and though the difference of the salivary apparatus in the ruminating animals has been adduced as a reason, yet this will not extend to horses, and still less to man, in whom the salivary glands and stomach are so closely allied to those of the dog. The effects of the bite usually manifest themselves between the 30th and 60th day—usually about the 40th—and, in the meantime, the wound generally heals, but often reopens on the appearance of the attack.

ORIGINAL CAUSE.—This has been attributed by different authors to bad and putrid food, hunger, thirst, confinement, suppressed salacity, heat, cold, violence, hydatid under the tongue, worms, and epidemic, or self-generated poison without bite. But none of these causes can be traced throughout a series of cases, with the exception of confinement; for, in spite of Mr. Youatt's assertion to the contrary, I am inclined to believe that a greater number of pampered house dogs, which are confined to a limited range, and also of kennelled dogs, are attacked, than of the dogs of the poor which are always at liberty. We are also told by M. Clot Bey, the eminent French surgeon residing in Egypt, that the half-wild dogs of warm climates are almost exempt; and if this be true there is some reason for the belief that the disease is sometimes self-generated, that is to say, if it occurs most frequently in those dogs which are least likely to be bitten, namely, the well-cared-for and pampered house-pet, and the kennelled hound, or pointer. It must be obviously impossible to prove the spontaneous origin of the disease, unless some time could be fixed beyond which the period of incubation cannot extend. Thus, if the question could be settled by the occurrence of a case of rabies in a dog which had been secluded from his fellows for sixty or eighty days, the case might be argued perhaps in favour of the spontaneous origin, but the advocates of the other side would immediately maintain that the period must be extended to four, five, six, or even eight months. The only argument, therefore, which can be relied on is the one above given; and if the premises are as correct as I believe them to be, it is, I think, incontrovertible, when taken in connection with a large number of cases.

PROPORTION OF NUMBER ATTACKED TO THOSE BITTEN.—This is very difficult to determine, but the chances in the dog are so great against his escape that I should strongly advise the destruction of every one, let him be ever so valuable, which can be proved to have been bitten by a rabid dog. No one is justified in risking human life for the sake of the value of the dog, either real or imaginary;

and therefore we should never run the risk which the occurrence of any case of rabies inevitably causes to the attendants upon the dog, but at once do everything in our power to prevent so dire a calamity as the communication to a fellow-creature. Even though the risk be only as one to twenty-one of those bitten, as supposed by John Hunter, or as one to twenty-five, as given by Dr. Hamilton, still that risk must not be incurred. But this proportion is now considered too small, and in one well-ascertained case of seventeen persons bitten by a wolf at Brive in France, ten died of rabies.

DIAGNOSIS.— From the peculiar nature of the symptoms detailed above, it must be clear that rabies can scarcely be mistaken for any other disease, except in the very early stage. I have already dilated upon the difference between it and distemper, and, except tetanus and simple phrenitis of the latter really exists, there is no other affection which resembles it at all; but if the slightest suspicion exists, it is better to call in the aid of the best authority in the neighbourhood, and act by his advice and assistance.

TREATMENT.—This is out of the question in the canine race. There is every reason for supposing that it would be totally nugatory, but it is so utterly impossible to carry out any remedial measures without risk to the attendant, which nothing can justify, that it is better to abandon all hope, even when the dog can be allowed to remain in a safe and secluded asylum. A few cases of recovery are recorded, and therefore perhaps there may be some encouragement to leave the dog to his fate, supplying him only with water and food, when this can be done with safety; but in spite of all precautions, there is great risk. Boys will be boys, and will rush into danger, merely for its own sake. Bites have taken place by animals apparently so safely confined as to lull all fears of such an unfortunate result. The best plan, therefore, is the safest, and also the most humane for the dog, namely, to shoot him at once, and put him out of a miserable existence, for the disease is a very painful one in most cases.

PREVENTIVE MEASURES IN MAN.—As all greyhound proprietors are liable to have the disease in their kennel, they are of course subject to the bite of a rabid dog. In such a case I should strongly recommend them to suck the wound, if possible, *and if they have reason to believe that they have sound gums, and no crack or ulceration of the mouth.* A very easy way of ascertaining this point is to take some common salt into the mouth, and if no smarting occurs, then the surface is sure to be sound; and, on washing out the mouth, the sucking of the wound may be safely commenced, taking care to spit out the saliva, and to wash the mouth out with warm water immediately afterwards. As soon as this is done, I should advise recourse to be had to the nearest surgeon, who should be requested to excise the part immediately, if possible, and then to apply the nitrate of silver freely. Mr. Youatt is of opinion that excision does more harm than good, but his experience is opposed to that of the whole medical profession in Great Britain and the Continent.

The above short and hurried account of rabies is all that is necessary for the owner of the greyhound. I have, however, endeavoured to give sufficient explanations to enable my readers to know how to act if unfortunately they should be visited by so terrible a disease; but I have chiefly directed my attention to the most important part of all—the recognition of the disease itself.

INFLAMMATION OF THE EYE AND EAR.

I have already alluded to the *inflammation of the eye*, accompanying distemper and to malignant disease of the organ, and therefore I may omit their consideration at present. But, besides these conditions, we find occasionally the following states of this necessary part of the greyhound's structure. The most common form is *simple ophthalmia*, arising from cold, in which the white eye of the eye becomes red and swollen, and there are often red lines crossing the transparent cornea, which is more or less white and opaque, with or without ulceration. When an ulcer occurs it often eats through the cornea, and the contents of the eye escape, with total loss of sight. It is, therefore, highly necessary to guard against so fatal an accident. There is generally a good deal of mucus between the lids, and considerable intolerance of light.

THE TREATMENT should be conducted with a due regard to the severity of the attack. Where the animal is in high condition, and the symptoms are very severe, it is necessary to take blood from the neck, and to follow this up with 5 grains of calomel and

15 of jalap. If the inflammation still continues, give calomel and opium, of each a grain, three times a day; and if an ulcer exists, use one or other of the following drops every night, viz., wine of opium, or a solution of nitrate of silver, ten grains to the ounce.

This, generally, in a healthy dog, will succeed, but sometimes in a weak, badly reared, young dog, the inflammation, instead of assuming the above healthy character, puts on a more chronic form. The intolerance of light is greater, the white of the eye is more blue, the ulcerations are not so deep, indeed they are often pustules rather than ulcers, and the inflammation may be called *strumous ophthalmia*. The discharge is also more watery than in ordinary ophthalmia, and the lids very frequently are red and fleshy. For this state of things the lowering treatment above advocated would be highly prejudicial; and, on the contrary, a grain of quinine and three of hemlock-extract should be given three times a day. The same drops may, however, be used if ulceration is present, but the strength of the solution often requires a considerable increase. In the former of these states the diet should be very low, whilst in the latter condition the dog should be allowed as much nourishment as his stomach will bear.

OPHTHALMIA sometimes appears to assume a *rheumatic* character: in this affection the symptoms are intermediate in severity between ordinary and strumous ophthalmia. The redness is not so vivid as in the first, and the enlarged vessels appear *deeper under the surface*. They are, in fact, beneath the conjunctiva or

INFLAMMATION OF THE EYE—TREATMENT. 123

outer membrane and in the sclerotic. The intolerance of light is not so great, but the dog is heavy and dull, and, if not cured, is unfit for any useful purpose. A calomel and jalap purge should be given, as above ordered, and repeated twice a week; a seton should also be inserted in the back of the neck, and moderate nourishment given without flesh. No drops are here of the slightest use, indeed they are very prejudicial. This is a disease seldom found in dogs less than two years old.

ALL KINDS OF DOGS are very liable to *cataract*, which is an opacity of the crystalline lens occupying the centre of the ball of the eye. It may easily be known by the white pupil with transparent cornea, and may be distinguished from the white cloudiness or film of the cornea by the clear and defined lines which surround the white. In fact the lens lies behind the circular hole in the iris called the pupil, and therefore, as this is not implicated in the alteration of structure, the opening is as perfect as ever, but is white, instead of appearing black or nearly so. It is often the result of accident, as a blow or thorn, but also arises from hereditary tendency, as in horses and man. In neither case can anything be done, for though by an operation the opacity might be removed, as in the cataract of the human eye, yet as the dog would not consent to wear glasses, the sight would be indistinct, and no adequate advantage would be gained. The inflammation attendant upon a puncture or blow is often very severe, and requires the strongest remedies to counteract it, especially if the iris is injured. Sometimes a small portion of this beautiful structure escapes through the wound, but it is better to let matters alone, and there is scarcely the slightest chance of saving the eye. If, however, in a day or two, the eye maintains its colour and shape, and you find on examination that a small portion of the iris after its escape has become attached to the healed edge of the wound, forming a slight projection, or *hernia*, as it is called, it is better to touch it with the fine point of a stick of lunar caustic till removed.

SOMETIMES there is in old dogs a *dropsy of the eye*, in which it swells to a great extent, and finally bursts, discharging clear water. For this nothing can be done. There is also a disease of the nerve of the eye, which is nearly as incurable, and which is called *amaurosis*. Here there is total or partial blindness, without any very apparent alteration of the shape or colour of any of the structures; but the pupil, instead of contracting on the sudden exposure of the eye to light, continues permanently larger than natural, which is the chief means of distinguishing the complaint. A seton is the only remedy likely to be of service, and, if very recent, an active dose of calomel and jalap. When the disease is brought on by a severe course, which is often the case, these remedies will sometimes succeed, and, if partially successful, may be followed up by one-sixteenth of a grain of strychnine in a pill, three times a day, gradually increased up to a quarter of a grain, unless the peculiar symptoms brought on by strychnine are developed, when the remedy may be stopped for a few days, and then recommenced with the lesser dose. These symptoms are a twitching of the muscles of the body, amounting, in well-marked cases, to decided spasms. The dog cannot lie still, and the state is so marked as to be easily recognised.

INFLAMMATION OF THE EAR: INTERNAL CANKER.—Greyhounds are not very subject to this troublesome complaint: but, when it does occur, it interferes with their rest, and prevents their reaching that high state of health which is the object of the courser's desire. Sometimes, however, after severe weather, to which the dog has been exposed, he is seen to be annoyed with something about the head; he is evidently in pain, and shakes his ears, but not violently. On examining the interior of the ear it is seen to be highly inflamed, and, in a day or two after, a thick matter frequently makes its appearance from the passage. The redness often extends to the inside of the outer ear. After a time the pain becomes less, but the dog is always scratching or shaking his ears, and can take no rest. From the constant shaking the tips of the ears become sore and cracked; and this is often thought to be the seat of the disease, whereas it is only the effect. Attention is consequently paid to get rid of the ulceration, and the ears are even confined by a cap: all this is useless. The only remedies likely to be useful are general lowering measures, as starvation and purging, in the early stage, and, if the attack continues, a seton. The nitrate of silver solution (ten grains to the ounce) should be carefully introduced into the passage every day, previously washing away with tepid water by means of a syringe any pus or mucus which may have accumulated.

EXTERNAL CANKER is an eruption on the tips of the ears, like that attending the internal inflammation, but without that complication. It requires the same general treatment, but no application to the internal passage.

POLYPI sometimes occur in the ear, and can only be removed by extraction with the forceps.

INFLAMMATION OF THE LARYNX AND THROAT. BLAIN.

BLAIN is said to attack the dog as well as the cow and horse, but I have never seen or known of a case. It appears to be a vesicular disease of the mucous membrane of the mouth, stomach, and intestines, and shows itself chiefly under the tongue. Mr. Youatt recommends the vesicles to be freely opened, and the mouth washed with a solution of chloride of lime. Stomachic medicines and nourishing diet are also recommended by him.

SIMPLE INFLAMMATION OF THE LARYNX is a very common complaint in the dog, and can only be known from bronchitis or pneumonia by the use of the ear or stethoscope. If there is quick and painful breathing, especially if there is some little noise accompanying it, as if the dog was breathing through a sponge, suspicion should be aroused, and the ear applied to the chest; when, if no unusual sounds can be distinguished, we may be pretty certain the disease is confined to the larynx and windpipe. When acute, large bleedings are necessary, followed by a blister to the throat, and an active calomel purge. After this, nauseating doses of antimony and digitalis, with nitre, should be given every two hours in severe cases, or even oftener, if the symptoms are urgent. The disease runs its course very rapidly; and in a few hours so much mischief may be done as to cause death, or irretrievable injury is effected by the permanent thickening of the mucous membrane, in the same manner as in the 'roaring' horse.

INFLAMMATION OF THE LUNGS.

PNEUMONIA, PLEURISY, BRONCHITIS, AND PHTHISIS. The three first are almost always active in their character; and though considered as separate diseases, yet they often coexist in the same subject The lungs are composed of an internal mucous membrane, which is the seat of bronchitis; of a middle cellular membrane, the seat of pneumonia; and of an external serous membrane, which is the seat of pleurisy. But pneumonia seldom occurs without some degree of bronchitis; on the other hand, bronchitis very frequently runs its course, without any mischief to the cellular membrane. It is very difficult to detect the distinguishing marks of these three diseases, without the use of the stethoscope or placing the ear on the chest, which is quite as serviceable. They are all attended with increased frequency and hardness of pulse, with quick breathing, cough, anxiety of countenance, bloodshot eyes, and dislike to lying down. The latter symptoms are only seen in bad cases of bronchitis, but generally attend upon all cases of pneumonia and pleurisy—the chief distinguishing marks are the following:—

1. BRONCHITIS.—Cough incessant, not so painful, expectoration frothy, and white or yellowish, wheezing, and bubbling sounds heard by auscultation; percussion gives considerable resonance, though not so great as in a state of health; dog lies down, except in very bad cases.

2. PNEUMONIA.—Cough present and painful, but generally not incessant—expectoration rusty and stringy, seldom frothy; a crackling sound by placing the ear on the chest (auscultation) in the early stage, and afterwards no sound heard, and the inflamed side sounding dull on percussion owing to solidification of the lung, breath feels hotter than natural, anxiety great.

3. PLEURISY.—Cough slight, dry, short, and very painful; no expectoration, no wheezing or crackling sound, but a dry grating sound heard in the early stage, and pain felt on tapping the side with the fingers. In the early stage the breathing heard naturally; after effusion of water, only heard when that fluid gravitates so as to leave the upper part of the lung floating against that part of the chest.

The *treatment* for all these must be conducted upon nearly the same principles but with some considerable variations. Blood should be taken freely in pneumonia or pleurisy, and in severe cases of bronchitis. Blisters are useful in pneumonia and bronchitis, but do harm in pleurisy. In pneumonia and pleurisy, tartar emetic, calomel, and opium are the chief remedies with or without digitalis, according to the power and frequency of the pulse. In bronchitis, opium, ipecacuanha, and rhubarb are the most beneficial, in the doses I have already given. My limits will not allow me to go further into this section of the diseases of the dog, which, to be well and minutely described, would take ten times the space that can be afforded.

PHTHISIS in the dog is exactly similar to its corresponding disease in man. It comes on usually with slight cough, often unattended with feverishness; and with this there is evidently a want of stamina and power, so that the dog, though, perhaps, feeding well, is fatigued much sooner than usual. The cough is sometimes subdued for a time, but soon returns, and the expectoration is yellow and lumpy, and sometimes tinged with blood. This goes on frequently for months or years, until the constitution is worn down or hemorrhage takes place and the dog dies from exhaustion. It is one of the most common causes of the bursting of a blood-vessel in a course, and this is sometimes the first warning which the owner of a dog has of any disease, though when death takes place the lungs are found studded with tubercles, some one or more of which have softened, and thus destroyed the walls of the blood-vessel, which has given way. The disease is so incurable and so hereditary that it is scarcely worth while to enter upon any curative measure. In slight cases for a temporary purpose it would perhaps be desirable to try the effect of cod-liver oil, which, no doubt, would postpone the termination for some months, or longer, in the same way as in man. But as the object of every courser ought to be to have healthy dogs or none, it is better to destroy one which is evidently phthisical. On no account should a phthisical subject be used for breeding purposes, since there is not the slightest question as to the transmission of this disease from parent (whether male or female) to offspring.

INFLAMMATION OF THE STOMACH.

WILFUL POISONING; INDIGESTION.—I have already described the process of digestion and the coats of the stomach, and it is unnecessary for me again to allude to them. Inflammation of the stomach is only caused by improper food or poisons, or by neglect of exercise. It is seldom that this inflammation becomes acute, unless poison has been given, because the irritability of the dog's stomach is so great that he rejects the improper food by vomiting, if of so crude a nature as to produce active mischief. Poisons, however, are sometimes of such a character as to cling to the mucous membrane of the stomach, in spite of the most powerful efforts of the muscular coat to reject them by vomiting. When, therefore, incessant vomiting, without constipation, occurs in the dog, straining him severely for hours together, there may be a fair presumption that poison has been administered, either purposely or by mistake. But if death takes place, and the interior of the stomach is thick-

INFLAMMATION OF THE STOMACH.

ened with patches of red or black, and covered with thick tenacious mucus, the whole, with its contents, should be analysed by some competent chemist, if the proprietor is anxious to arrive at a degree of certainty which no other means can afford him.

Supposing these symptoms lead to the suspicion that poison has been administered, the best remedy is very thin gruel, with a spoonful of salt in each pint, which is to be forced down the dog's throat by drenching him with a spoonful at a time. A soda-water bottle is a good instrument, as it does not allow the gruel to come out fast enough to choke the dog. The liquid soon returns by vomiting, and should be repeated again and again, till it may be presumed that the stomach is effectually washed out. As soon as the vomiting has ceased, a small dose of castor oil may be tried, for though it frequently appears to return, yet some generally remains down and carries off any remaining particles. These directions will apply to any mineral poison, such as arsenic, corrosive sublimate, or oxalic acid; but if there is any reason to suppose corrosive sublimate has been used, which is not very likely, some eggs should immediately be given, for albumen has the property of decomposing this active poison. Arsenic, however, is almost invariably used where the poisoning is wilful, unless strychnine can be obtained, and fortunately this is not often at the service of those low rascals who alone resort to such measures. Strychnine acts on the nervous system, producing death, accompanied by violent convulsions, and its effects, therefore, cannot be confounded with those of arsenic. One of the most common consequences of attempted poisoning by arsenic, is the partial loss of the hair for a time; it comes off in patches, especially about the head and sides, without eruption of any kind. The only other probable cause of acute inflammation of the stomach is the presence of a sharp bone, or other foreign body, swallowed with the food, which, from its shape, will not obey the efforts of the stomach to dislodge it. This object, however, is generally assisted by an emetic of salt and water, given in large quantity, say a spoonful in a quart of water or thin gruel. Chronic inflammation of the stomach may be either the result of the improper quantity or quality of food, assuming the form of indigestion, or it may be owing to the presence of worms. If the former, attention should be paid to the diet and exercise—an aperient, consisting of 3 grains of calomel and 10 each of jalap and rhubarb should be given, and afterwards, if the fæces are of good colour, showing evidences of the proper secretion of bile, a bolus, consisting of 5 grains of extract of gentian, with 2 or 3 of ginger, should be given twice a day. If the stomach is very much out of order, I have found a warm mixture like the following answer better than pills :—

Take of Bicarbonate of Soda	1 drachm
Tincture of Cardamoms . . .	1 ounce
Infusion of Rhubarb	2 ounces
Infusion of Gentian	5 ounces

Mix, and give 2 tablespoonfuls for a dose, twice or thrice a day.

When the liver does not act, this mixture may be given with two or three grains of blue pill every night or every night and morning, according to circumstances. Sometimes, when the liver and stomach are sadly out of order, the following ball has been found of service, especially where the constitution has been upset by a long confinement in kennel, and *all* the secretions are sluggish :—

Take of Sulphur	12	drachms
Nitro	4	,,
Æthiops Mineral	2	,,
Linseed Meal	4	,,

Palm Oil enough to form 20 balls; one of which should be given every night.

This I have found answer much better as an alterative than Benbow's mixture.

INFLAMMATION OF THE INTESTINES.

Dogs are very subject to all the causes which produce inflammations of the several tissues entering into the composition of the bowels, which tissues are the same as I have already described as forming the stomach. The serous or peritoneal coat is often inflamed after exposure to cold; and this may be conjectured from the evident and constant pain which the dog suffers, and which is greatly increased on pressure. The pulse is very quick, hard, and small, and there is some feverishness, with a dry hot nose. There is great thirst—and generally a costive state of the bowels. The inflammation may be confined to the serous coat of the intestines (*enteritis*), or to that lining the cavity of the abdomen (*peritonitis*), or may comprehend both. But no amount of practice can do more than enable us to guess, by the severity of the attack, as to the precise seat of the disease. Of course the larger the extent of surface inflamed, the more severe, *cæteris paribus*, will be the symptoms. For this disease large bleedings are requisite, and they should be carried to fainting; after this, calomel and opium in grain doses may be given every three hours, and, if there are conveniences for the purpose, a warm bath will be beneficial, using every precaution to prevent cold afterwards. After giving the calomel and opium for twelve, twenty-four, or thirty-six hours, if the pain continues, the bleeding must be repeated, or, if it is relieved, a dose of castor oil may be given. If the rectum is full of impacted fæces, which may easily be detected by examining the flank, an injection should be thrown up.

In colic, which is a spasm of the muscular coat of the bowels, the pain is intense, but intermits; there is little fever or alteration of pulse, but the bowels are obstinately costive. The pain is so intense as to cause the dog to cry out when it comes on, but in the intervals he will come out of his bed and appear much as usual. A very common consequence of colic is *intussusception*, which arises from the irregular contractions of a portion of the intestine, by which it is forced on into the expanded, or rather the uncontracted, part immediately below it. Sometimes I have seen ten or eleven inches of intestine thus doubled by its own peristaltic action. No symptoms during life will serve to distinguish this accidental accompaniment of colic, for constipation is

INFLAMMATION OF THE INTESTINES.

the attendant of both ; and I am not sure that the use of drastic purgatives will not produce the intussusception as often as prevent it. If it could be recognised, there would be no great danger to the dog in opening the abdomen and drawing out the intestine; and in a very obstinate case of colic I should be inclined to try the experiment, when all other means have failed. The dog bears operations so well about the abdomen, that I should have no fear of any increase of mischief from the operation. The best remedies in colic that I know of are croton oil and opium, one drop of the oil to two or three grains of opium every six hours. Two hours after their exhibition the dog should be put into warm water at 98° Fahr., and, *while there*, with an enema syringe, should be pumped, *per anum*, as full of the water in which he is placed as he will bear without using dangerous force. This remedy is very efficacious, and will often remove the colic in slight cases, without the croton oil and opium. But when the disease is very severe, the two should be combined; as soon as there is a free evacuation, the danger generally disappears at once.

In DIARRHŒA and DYSENTERY, which are both the results of inflammation of the mucous coat of the bowels, there is great looseness of the bowels, with the passing of quantities of mucus, often tinged with blood. The distinctions between the two are variously given by different writers, but the most common distinction is merely one of degree. Thus, diarrhœa is merely a loose state of bowels owing to errors in diet or mismanagement of some kind, while dysentery is accompanied with mucus or blood, or both, and is often epidemic, or dependent upon some generally bad state of the system, as in distemper. In ordinary diarrhœa, the best remedy is a tablespoonful of castor oil, with a dessert-spoonful each of tincture of rhubarb and syrup of poppies. This carries off the offending matter which has caused the diarrhœa, and generally puts a stop to the purging. But, if unsuccessful, then

Take of prepared Chalk	2 drachms
Aromatic confection	1 drachm
Syrup of Poppies and Tincture of Catechu, of each	½ ounce
Water	7 ounces

Mix, and give two tablespoonfuls after each loose motion, with as much laudanum as may be necessary to produce the desired effect, varying from 30 drops to 2 drachms, according to the urgency of the case.

If there is reason to suppose that the dysentery is owing to an epidemic, and is not caused by any improper food, the above mixture may be given at the onset, without having recourse to the oil. Rice-water to drink, and rice or arrowroot as food, should also be given.

FISTULA IN ANO constantly occurs in old kenneled dogs, which are subject to prolonged constipation, and is simply the result of abscesses caused by the straining to get rid of impacted fæces. It generally goes on year after year, sometimes better and sometimes worse, and can only be cured by an operation, which consists in slitting up the wall of the bowel between it and the fistulous opening. It is very difficult to get the dog to submit to this operation without the use of chloroform, but with its assistance it may very readily be performed.

INFLAMMATION OF THE LIVER

Is another constant sequel of exposure to cold, especially after the use of calomel as an aperient. The symptoms are very similar to those of peritonitis, but the white or clayey motions and the yellow colour of the eyes soon lead to the conclusion that the liver is the seat of the mischief. I have already described this disease as occurring in distemper, and, when coming on independently, its character and treatment are nearly the same. In this case, however, the remedies may be carried to a greater extent, for there is not the same danger from the prostration of strength which comes on in the former case.

TORPID LIVER happens either as a consequence of active inflammation, or of overfeeding or want of exercise. In either case it may be known by the dullness of the dog, and by the whiteness of the motions. For this state a pill, composed of a grain or two of blue pill, and five grains of the compound rhubarb pill, every night, or night and morning, is the best remedy; or, if the weather is very severe, or the dog in training, then give the rhubarb pill, with half a grain or a grain of powdered ipecacuanha instead.

THE YELLOWS is a symptom of obstruction in the excretion of bile, and is easily recognised by the deep yellow colour of the skin and eyes. It is often a complication of distemper, but it sometimes occurs independently of that affection altogether. In any case it is a very fatal disease, and requires active treatment to procure an immediate flow of bile. Where the dog is not already much reduced in strength an emetic consisting of fifteen grains of ipecacuanha and three grains of tartar emetic will be the best remedy, followed as soon as the stomach is quiet by four or five grains of blue pill repeated every four hours. Sometimes a warm bath will aid the blue pill, but if it is used great care should be taken to give it hot enough, and to dry the dog well afterwards.

INFLAMMATION OF THE KIDNEY.

ACUTE DROPSY.—This disease seldom occurs in the dog except from the improper use of turpentine as a vermifuge, or of other stimulating remedies given for the purpose of rousing the generative powers. Sometimes a calculus forms in the kidney, and then severe work will produce inflammation—but generally the disease is the result of the above causes. If it goes on to any extent the secretion of urine is suspended partially or entirely, and as a consequence dropsy in some form shows itself. If recent, small bleedings are the most effectual remedy, followed by small doses of calomel and digitalis, about a quarter or half a grain of each three times a day.

INFLAMMATION OF THE BLADDER.

CALCULUS: RUPTURE, BLENNORRHAGIA AND MALIGNANT DISEASE. The dog is very subject to these various complaints, but, as so very little can be done for their relief, it is scarcely worth while to occupy the time of my readers by any elaborate account of the symptoms of each. One of these, however, is so very common that I may just describe it in few words. This is blennorrhagia, or a discharge of mucus from the urethra of the male. It arises from various causes, some of which I can scarcely describe, in decent language. For this I have found Venice turpentine in 5-grain doses as a pill, a very effectual remedy, or from 15 to 20 drops of the balsam of copaiba made into an emulsion with mucilage, and either of them given three times a day. The medicine must be perseveringly used for at least three or four weeks, or the disease will assuredly return. *Malignant disease* of the bladder can only be *suspected* during life, and, if discovered, is without remedy.

INFLAMMATION OF THE SKIN.

MANGE, BLOTCH, WARTS, CANKER OF THE EAR, SURFEIT, ERUPTION BETWEEN THE TOES, &c.—The various eruptions of dogs are, I believe, little understood, and in my own kennel I am happy to say that I have had little opportunity of studying them, but of late years I have seen and healed almost every variety. True *mange*, being undoubtedly contagious, as well as most probably hereditary, will sometimes intrude into the best-regulated kennels. It is usually divided into the scabby and the red mange, but if the subject were carefully studied, it would be found that there are several distinct eruptions, which are confounded together under the head of scabby mange. In one kind of the former, we have an eruption which is most probably produced by a vegetation similar to that found in the human scald head. In this form the disease is highly contagious and not constitutional, and the eruption consists of numerous pustules, at first distinct, but afterwards coalescing, and forming one or more large scabs. The hair does not at first fall of, but ultimately gets thin by degrees, until at last it disappears. This eruption is very troublesome to cure, and none but applications containing poisonous ingredients are of the least benefit. Their use, therefore, is attended with considerable danger to the dog, unless mixed with some article which he will not lick; but the itching is so violent, that he can scarcely be prevented from biting himself, even by the most disagreeable application. It is better to put on a muzzle of wire or pierced leather, and to keep it on while the remedies are being used, except at feeding time. The constitutional treatment should depend on the state of the dog: if too high in condition, he should be purged and kept low in diet; and if, as is generally the case, reduced in flesh and strength, then the contrary treatment by tonics and nourishing diet should be tried. No applica-

INFLAMMATION OF THE SKIN.

tion is so successful in this complaint as corrosive sublimate in solution, but it is very liable to produce salivation, and sometimes has been known to destroy the dog even when a muzzle has been constantly used, being absorbed into the system through the skin. It may be applied in solution simply, or combined with lime water in the form known as 'yellow wash.' The simple solution should be very carefully brushed into the roots of the scabs, and should be used of the strength of 3 grains to the ounce, and not more than once a week, using the 'yellow wash' daily and freely in the same way. This treatment generally suffices, but after its failure I have found, in several bad cases, the *yellow* iodide of mercury (in the form of an ointment of the strength of 1 drachm to an ounce of lard) succeed in curing the disease. In the other kind of scabby mange, caused by an insect parasite, described hereafter, little hard pimples may be found at the extremity of fissures, and here by careful exploration the insect may be found. These fissures or insect galleries are the distinguishing marks of the two forms of eruption, but as the treatment of them varies little, the diagnosis is not very important. The same remedies would succeed here, no doubt, as in the vegetative form; but sulphur is equal to the cure, and is much less injurious to the constitution. The *compound* sulphur ointment of the shops is the best preparation, and should be well rubbed in every night for a week, using here the muzzle to prevent the dog removing the application, more than from any fear of injury to him. It should be mixed with equal quantities of train oil and spirit of turpentine, the latter being very destructive to the insect, but, if used at full strength, it irritates the skin of the dog most unmercifully. A very successful but dangerous remedy for either of the above eruptions is the following:—

    Take of Decoction of White Hellebore
        Decoction of Tobacco, of each .   .   4 ounces
        Corrosive Sublimate .   .   .   .   8 grains
        Aloes in Powder   .   .   .   .   2 drachms
                Mix while hot.

The aloes is intended, from its bitter taste, to prevent the dog licking off the remedy; but I should never trust such an application without a muzzle.

Red mange is a peculiar eruption, which attacks the roots of the hair, of which it changes the colour to that of brick-dust. The hair does not fall off, except from the friction arising from scratching. It is no doubt produced by a vegetable fungus. The best remedy is a mixture of blue mercurial ointment, and the compound sulphur ointment, which should be well rubbed in every other day. When this eruption occurs in white dogs, and the dirty look of this ointment is objected to, one made with 1 drachm of white precipitate to an ounce of lard may be used with advantage.

In both scabby and red mange the blood is often contaminated, and internal medicine must be given to restore it to a state of health. For this purpose no remedy has so much power as arsenic, and if given with care there is not the slightest danger in administering it. The dose is from 5 to 8 drops of the liquor arsenicalis, which should be mixed with the food, and never given on an empty stomach. The object is not to irritate that organ, but, on the contrary, to avoid this effect, and to cause the absorption of the arsenic into the blood, where it exerts its peculiar power. What this is I do not at all understand, but the effect is undoubted, and, as practice is better than theory, our ignorance of the *modus operandi* is not very much to be deplored.

BLOTCH is an eruption depending entirely upon the excessive fullness and impurity of the blood, owing to want of exercise, and high feeding. It generally attacks the greyhound either when he is rested after severe work without altering his food, or when too highly fed throughout the summer season. It comes on by a discharge of thick serum among the hair, and is first detected by the appearance as if some gum or starch had been dropped upon the coat, and had matted the hair together. In a few days this falls or is scratched off, and the skin shows itself red and deprived of its cuticle, and continuing to discharge the same serum, which is, however, constantly licked off by the dog's tongue. No external remedies are here required, and the treatment should be by a dose or two of calomel and jalap, or the alterative balls daily, with an ounce of Epsom salts twice or thrice a week. The food should be considerably reduced, and some green vegetables or turnips should be mixed with it occasionally; the eruption seldom lasts more than ten days.

WARTS do not often occasion much inconvenience in the dog; but if they do, they may either be removed by the knife, or by rubbing in a little corrosive sublimate in powder, then wetting the wart, and after a few minutes washing all off. This produces the death of the wart, and it drops off in a few days.

CANKER OF THE EAR I have already described in the form in which it is produced by irritation of the internal ear occasioning a constant shaking of the head; but sometimes mange or surfeit attacks the ear as well as other parts, and, in that case, if the internal ear is perfectly free from disease, the same applications will be useful as to other parts. Here a cap tied over the head is sometimes useful in preventing the dog from scratching himself.

SURFEIT is a general eruption produced either by improper food or exposure to the sun, and is very different in its nature, though often confounded with mange. The chief points of difference are, the acuteness of the attack and the degree of fever which accompanies surfeit, and also the watery nature of the discharge. It requires only a few days' low diet and a dose of Epsom salts to set all to rights, unless the dog is much out of health; in which case he should be treated according to circumstances. It closely resembles blotch, from which it can only be distinguished by the discharge being more watery, and the patches running into one another.

AN ERUPTION BETWEEN THE TOES is a constant source of annoyance to the greyhound trainer, often coming on during severe work, and laming the dog, quite independently of the soreness occasioned by the friction of the road. On examining the foot it will be seen that there is considerable redness, and some little discharge between the toes, and often round the roots of the nails. This is owing, like the 'blotch,' to overfeeding, and disappears by the same method of treatment. When, however, the inflammation round the nails has gone so far as to produce ulceration, a little blue-stone or solution of nitrate of silver should be applied daily, which will soon dry up the discharge, and heal the ulcerations, if the constitutional treatment is at the same time properly attended to. After applying the blue-stone, a very little pitch ointment should be smeared gently over the sore places, or, if this seems to irritate, the common zinc ointment of the shops.

CHAPTER VII.

ACCIDENTS, ETC.

Cuts, Bites, and Tears—Fractures—Dislocations—Hæmorrhage—Ruptures.

CUTS, BITES, AND TEARS.

THE PRESENT division of my subject is that comprising *the accidents to which the dog is subject*. Of these, cuts, bites, and tears are better left alone, unless the separation of the two edges of the skin is so great as to occasion deformity in healing. In such a case, a few stitches may be put in, not with a view to procure what in human surgery is called 'union by the first intention,' but to enable the two surfaces to unite by granulation. It is a curious fact, that this 'union by the first intention' is peculiar to man, and therefore the treatment of cuts, &c., in the dog, must be conducted upon different principles to those which are most serviceable in human surgery. When these accidents occur about the legs, it is better to avoid using any stimulating application, but to insert the ligatures, if necessary, and then put on a bandage, which may be kept wet if there is much inflammation. But in every case, when the ligature or bandage is required, the muzzle is called for constantly, till firm union is established. Where cuts occur in public running, and the dog has to appear in the slips the next day, the bandages should be kept constantly wet with lukewarm water, and then, on removing them, just before running, apply some friar's balsam, or, what is far better, some collodion. This last remedy acts both as a stimulus, producing smarting at the time, but making the nerves of the part afterwards more insensible to pain, and as a shield against the ground, as long as it remains on. It should be thickly and boldly applied with a brush, taking care not to touch it, after putting it on, for some minutes, as, while setting, it is tender, and liable to be easily disturbed from its adhesions. Half an hour after its application, it will stand for some time the stretching, &c., which the mere walking in the slips will give it, but comes off in the course, not, however, till it has served the useful purpose of enabling the dog to put his foot to the ground, and thereby wear off some of the stiffness occasioned by the injury; it should always accompany the courser in flinty countries. When the cut is severe, as, for instance, at the root of 'the stopper,' a piece of sheet India-rubber may be firmly fixed round by means of the proper solution, which is easily procured at the Mackintosh shops. Canada balsam spread on leather is also a very convenient application where the cut occurs during a meeting and requires guarding.

FRACTURES.

FRACTURES in the dog, if simple, and occurring in the long bones, may be treated by wooden splints and bandages. Here also a muzzle is required. If near the hip, it is better to leave the case to nature, taking the precaution to confine the dog to his kennel for a fortnight or three weeks, after which time a moderate degree of exercise is advantageous rather than otherwise. A new joint is formed in most cases, and the lameness is never quite got over, but in a brood bitch or stallion sufficient exercise may be taken to keep up the health of the dog. If a toe is the seat of fracture, the best plan is to place a small ball of India-rubber in the cleft between the pads, and bandage the whole foot. The object of this is to prevent the bones uniting in such a way as to destroy the arch of the foot, which is essential to the proper action of the tendons of the toes, and consequently to the elasticity of the dog's action. Such a case, however, requires a practised hand, without which it is better left to nature.

DISLOCATIONS.

OF THE VARIOUS JOINTS, the knee is the most frequently dislocated, and if simple (that is, not complicated with a wound of the skin), may be easily reduced by a little steady extension. After the reduction, it is safer to put on a bandage of an elastic nature, crossing it behind the knee in the figure of 8, so as to prevent the foot from being put to the ground. When the hip is dislocated, considerable and long-continued force is required to effect the reduction. But this is not necessary if the dog is put under the influence of chloroform, by which the muscles are rendered incapable of resistance, and the head of the thigh-bone may then be replaced in its socket without much difficulty, if the accident has not occurred more than a day or two. The longer the interval the greater the difficulty, and when adhesions have formed it is almost impossible to effect a reduction. In the dog, the direction of the dislocation is almost always forwards—very rarely backwards.

HÆMORRHAGE.

WHERE THE BLEEDING is very profuse, in consequence of a stake entering the chest, it must be stopped by plugging the wound. It is rarely of long continuance in the dog, unless a large artery is wounded, and generally in such a situation (as, for instance, the space between the points of the shoulders) as to prevent our tying it with a ligature. In the legs, the arteries are too small to require such an operation, as a little pressure with a compress and bandage will always suffice.

RUPTURES.

RUPTURES at the navel are exceedingly common in the greyhound, especially among bitches. They can seldom be detected before the third or fourth week after birth, and when small, may often be cured by directing the kennel-man, after every feeding, to press them up into the belly with his finger. Nothing conduces more to this malformation than the practice of handling puppies— especially after feeding. When the rupture already exists, the puppy ought never to be lifted at all, or, if absolutely necessary, then by the tail only. When the puppy is raised in this way, the tendency is to draw the protruded bowel back again into its place, and consequently no harm is done; but by letting him lean all his weight upon the hand placed under the chest, as is too often done, the strain upon the delicate structures which close the opening at the navel is too great, and they give way, causing the rupture. It would be easy to remedy this defect by operation, but that the tendons here are so thin as to prevent the possibility of gathering them up by a needle without absolutely transfixing them. This is especially the case in the young puppy; and in older dogs, though the textures become thicker, the resistance of the animal also would be greater, and without chloroform would foil all the efforts of the operator. I once operated on a large and powerful dog, which had a rupture from an accident in the side of the belly, and increasing to a great size on any exertion. My intention was to open the sac, replace the bowels, and then sow up the opening after paring the edges in order to effect a union. But no sooner was the sac opened than the struggles of the dog forced almost all the intestines out, and as fast as they were replaced they protruded again. My only course was to bleed him till he fainted, which I did—the action of chloroform not having then been discovered—and then I easily effected my object, and the case ultimately did well; but the dog never recovered his powers, in consequence of the loss of blood, and, though apparently in health, was utterly useless. I have repeatedly tried to cure rupture by the ligature, but have not yet succeeded, in consequence, apparently, of the delicate structure of the tendons around the opening. These are not thick enough to allow of a thread being passed in and out, as in the case above mentioned, and if the opposite edges only are pierced and tied together, an adhesion may be effected, but, like the tinker, in mending one hole another is made. It is possible that if a pointed compress could be confined on the outside of the rupture, it would, as in the human subject, effect a cure; but as long as the puppy is with its mother no such application would be allowed by her to remain, and after it is weaned its own teeth would soon remove it. I am afraid, therefore, that there is no hope of curing ruptures in the greyhound; but fortunately it happens that they are seldom injurious, either to the health or running powers of the greyhound. Indeed, it is only when very large that they are of the slightest inconvenience.

CHAPTER VIII.

WORMS AND OTHER PARASITES INFESTING THE DOG.

Natural History of Intestinal Worms—Prevention—Curative Agents—Other Internal Parasites—External Parasites—Fleas, Ticks, Lice—Mange Insect.

NATURAL HISTORY OF INTESTINAL WORMS.

SINCE the first edition of 'The Greyhound' was published, the natural history of intestinal worms has been deeply investigated, and the labours of Von Siebold and Küchenmeister have brought to light much that was previously unknown. There still, however, remains a vast field for the observer; and although the old theory of spontaneous generation is exploded, its place is not supplied so as to account for the presence of worms in the newly-born whelp. Yet such cases are recorded on the high authority of Blumenbach, and other equally careful observers, in reference to the tape-worm, while I can myself speak to the existence of the nearly adult round-worm (*Ascaris marginata*) in the puppy while still blind. No rational explanation has yet been given, as far as I know, of this development of worms *in utero*; and certainly the present theory of their generation will not suffice. Still there seems to be little doubt of the truth of their natural history under other circumstances, as described by Küchenmeister and Von Siebold; and its importance cannot be overrated when we consider that upon it depends the power of preventing the development of intestinal worms altogether. Every experienced courser knows the difficulty of expelling them without injuring the health of the dog, and would appreciate any means likely to lead to their prevention in preference to their cure. I shall therefore endeavour to put my readers in possession of the present state of our knowledge on this abstruse subject.

Though the highest authorities on the generation of parasitic worms are not quite agreed on minute points, yet they all come to nearly the same general conclusions as to their progress from the ova to the fully-developed worms, the most remarkable feature in which is the fact that a great part of it goes on independently of the intestine of the dog. In the *Tænia serrata*, and very probably in the *Ascaris marginata*, if we could isolate the dog from the sources whence these animals are derived, we should altogether prevent their existence in his alimentary canal, but in order to do this it is necessary to ascertain what those sources are, and, as far as I know, that of the *Tænia cucumerina* has yet to be ascertained. It appears pretty clear that the heat of boiling water or of the oven will destroy the ova of the parasitic animal in any stage of development, and thus it is easy to prevent their entrance with the food; but as worms are often developed in kennels where no uncooked food is ever given, there must be other sources from which they are derived, and these are the points of special interest to the courser.

The DEVELOPMENT of the tape and round-worms is altogether different, and each must be studied by itself to enable us to take proper precautions against their invasion of the intestines of our dogs. With regard to the maw-worm, although I can find no special description, either of the worm itself or of its development, in Von Siebold or Küchenmeister, nor do I find it mentioned among the parasites infesting the dog enumerated by the latest French authority (M. C. Davaine), yet there is no doubt that it is a thread-worm (*Oxyuris* of Küchenmeister and Davaine), and its natural history similar to that given by these writers in treating of this worm in man, the horse, and other animals. This is a curious omission, as the thread-worm is found in the dog much more commonly than any other species of worm, and also more frequently in him than in any other animal, as far as I know. From its pure white colour it is often confounded with the tape-worm by careless observers, but this could scarcely have happened to the German writers I have quoted, nor, indeed, to any scientific enquirer. The omission is a remarkable one, and I am entirely at a loss to account for it.

The TAPE-WORMS ordinarily infesting the dog are the *Tænia serrata*, which so closely resembles the *Tænia solium* of man that Siebold declares the two to be identical, and the *Tænia cucumerina*, which can readily be distinguished. Besides these two, admitted by all authorities, Siebold describes a species of *Bothriocephalus* as having been found in a Pomeranian dog, and both that author and Küchenmeister succeeded in developing a species of *Tænia* in the dog from the *Cænurus cerebralis* of sheep, which the latter distinguishes by the name of *Tænia cænurus*. For all common purposes, however, the tape-worm in the dog

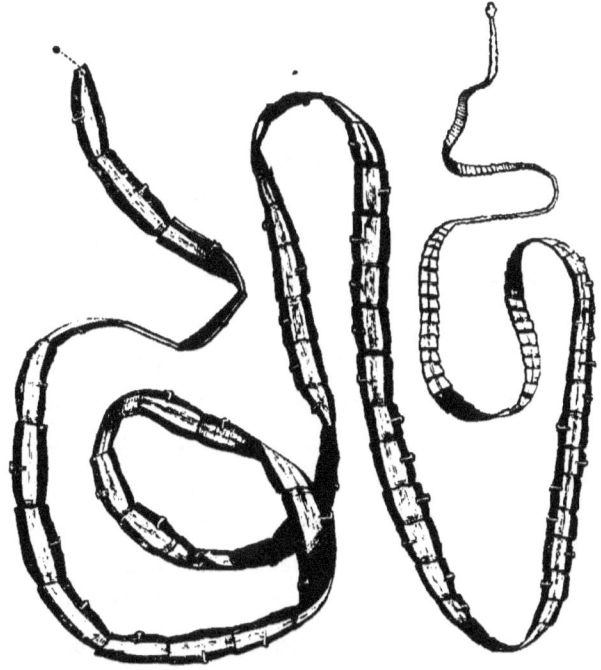

Tænia serrata.

may be described as consisting of two species only, *T. serrata* and *T. cucumerina*. *Tænia serrata*, as met with in its fully developed state, consists of a head (*scolex*) surmounting a series of whitish joints (*strobila*). Each of these joints (*proglottis*), when fully developed, is capable of separating itself, and progressing by its own vermicular motion for any reasonable distance, containing within itself a mass of eggs, which are only hatched in the stomach of the rabbit, sheep, or other herbivorous animal after the integument is digested and they are thereby set free. This tape-worm often attains a length of many feet, and may readily be distinguished by the square form of its joints from the *T. cucumerina*, whose joints are oval, and exactly resemble the seeds of the cucumber, from which it derives its specific name. It appears to be clearly ascertained from careful observation, that when this tape-worm is mature, segments (*proglottides*) are continually given off, which may be considered as distinct animals, or perhaps it would be more correct to describe them as being ovarian bags, provided with muscles for locomotion. By this means they are able to leave the mass of *fæces* with which they have been passed out of the rectum of the dog, and creep away to the nearest grass, where they either die from being dried up, or they are swallowed, in contact with its food, by some rabbit, hare, sheep, or other ruminant. In the stomach of either of these animals the envelope is digested, and the eggs are set free, each of which is soon hatched, and by its boring powers reaches the blood-vessels, through which it is transmitted to its proper seat. It is most probable, though this fact is not yet demonstrated, that these ova in the hare and rabbit are developed into the cestoid-worm, known as *Cysticercus pisiformis*, which is found very commonly attached to the viscera of the rabbit and hare in the form of small globular vesicles or cysts. Again, when they are developed in the sheep or cow, they either reach the brain in the same way, and become the *Cœnurus cerebralis*, which has been actually demonstrated by Professor Haubner at the Veterinary School of Dresden, though on this point the opinions of Siebold and Küchenmeister are directly opposed; or, should the ovum take another direction, it becomes the *Cysticercus tenuicollis*, being attached to the serous membrane of the abdomen or thorax, but chiefly in close proximity with the liver. Lastly, when it is swallowed by the pig, it reaches the muscular substance of that animal, and becomes the *Cysticercus cellulosæ*, which gives the appearance known as measly pork. Siebold is again at variance with Küchenmeister on this point, the former maintaining the possibility of producing the *Tænia serrata* from *Cysticercus cellulosæ*, while the latter disputes it altogether. An affirmative experiment is, however, always stronger than a negative one, and I am inclined to place great reliance on the observations of Von Siebold, so that I do not hesitate to accept his experiments on this subject. I am led to this conclusion from knowing that these two authors disagree on the identity of *Tænia solium* and *T. serrata*; but as I confess that I can see no difference between the two worms, either with the naked eye or under the microscope, I am led to believe Von Siebold, with whom my own observations agree.

THE FOUR FOLLOWING CESTOIDEA may therefore be considered as the origin of *Tænia serrata* in the dog, viz.: 1. *Cysticercus pisiformis*, found in the rabbit and hare; 2. *Cœnurus cerebralis*, infesting the brain of the sheep, calf, &c. producing 'gid;'

and, 3. *Cysticercus tenuicollis*, whose *habitat* is the serous membrane of ruminating animals, and also occasionally of the pig. 4. *Cysticercus cellulosæ*, found in the muscles of the pig, and known as producing measly pork.

The following illustrations, copied from Siebold, show the *Tænia* in its several stages of development from *Cænurus cerebralis*. The experiments are related with great minuteness, and I see no reason to doubt their correctness, for positive evidence is not necessarily upset by experiments attended with a negative result.

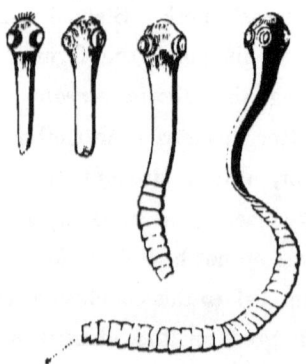

It may readily be imagined that some one or more of these cysts may be swallowed by the butcher's dog, or by others fed like them with offal, and also by the greyhound and other hare-killing dogs when they meet with a liver of that animal, or of the rabbit, containing the *Cysticercus pisiformis*. On reaching the stomach the cyst is soon transformed into *Tænia serrata*, as has been clearly demonstrated by numerous experiments performed by Küchenmeister and

Siebold, as well as by other observers at the request of the former of these authorities. This *Tænia* has been actually developed in the dog from *Cysticercus pisiformis* by Küchenmeister, Van Benedin, Siebold, and Baillet; from *C. tenuicollis* and *C. cellulosæ* by Siebold, and from *Cœnurus cerebralis* by Von Siebold and Van Benedin. It is possible that there may be some inaccuracy in the details of their experiments, but from this concurrent strong

Tænia cucumerina.

testimony there can be no doubt that *Tænia serrata* in the dog is developed from some one or more cystic worms infesting an herbivorous animal, which in its turn has received the ovum producing it from the intestine of the dog.

The *Tænia cucumerina*, as already observed, differs from *T. serrata* in being shorter in its entire length, seldom reaching to more than one quarter of that to which the longer worm extends, which varies from two to three yards. It gives off its segments like *Tænia serrata,* containing ova. These segments are oval instead of square, as in *Tænia serrata,* and have two marginal sexual apertures, while the latter has only one. The colour varies also, being milk-white in *T. serrata,* and pinkish-white in *T. cucumerina.* Of the development of this tape-worm nothing has yet been discovered, but there is little doubt that it is very similar to that which has already been described. Of course, this being the case, the exact cystic worm with which it is identical cannot be defined.

The *Tænia echinococcus* of Siebold is very small, being composed of a head and only two or three segments, and is developed from the *Echinococcus veterinorum* infesting the liver and lungs of the ruminants as well as the pig. This tape-worm is very rare in comparison with the other two to which I have already alluded, and practically its natural history is of no importance to the courser.

Besides the *Tænia,* two intestinal worms are frequently found in the dog, both belonging, in common with several other rare parasites, to the nematoid order of *entozoa,* according to Rudolphi's classification. These are usually known as the round-worm (*Ascaris marginata*), and the maw-worm, which I cannot find described by any of the foreign writers on the *entozoa,* but which is evidently a thread-worm, and would then fall under the genus *Oxyuris,* or sharp tail. Unlike the *Tæniæ,* which are androgynous, the *nematoidea* require the contact of the male to fertilize the ova in the female ovary. As soon as these are matured they are passed into the intestine of the dog, and mixing with his *fæces* get into some sewer or cesspool, where they remain till they are conveyed to the fields in the shape of manure. From this point it is difficult to trace their course with certainty, but it is believed that they have the power of supporting their vitality till they reach some collection of water by the agency of rain and the ordinary drains of our fields. In 1853, Verloren placed a fragment of a mature female *Ascaris marginata* from the dog in water, examining the eggs from time to time. The development of the young immediately commenced, and in about fourteen days was completed, perfectly developed young worms making their appearance within the egg-shells, but *not breaking them, although kept in different temperatures for more than a year.* This fact is very remarkable, being in direct opposition to the ordinary course of nature, which usually provides for the preservation of *ova* under many vicissitudes of heat and moisture, but when once the animal begins to be developed, its progress must be steady or it dies. Here, however, the developed embryo is arrested in its shell, and becomes, as it were, torpid, till it reaches its proper *habitat*, the intestine of the dog who has swallowed the water in which it has been suspended.

Such is a brief summary of our knowledge (much of which is hypothetical) of the generation of these worms, and it will be apparent by comparison with the natural history of the *Tæniæ*, that less is known of the round-worm than of the tape-worm. Still I think it may be accepted as true in the main, or sufficiently so to put us on our guard against the chief means by which these worms enter and infest the inmates of our kennels. How the ova find their way into the intestines of the unborn whelp is beyond my knowledge, as it is not supposed that in any stage either the *Ascaris* or the *Oxyuris* have any boring apparatus, like the embryo of the *Tænia*. It is true, as we shall presently see, that the latter often wanders in its mature state from the rectum of the animal which bred it, and it is very possible that it might in this way reach that of any other dog, supposing the latter has left the uterus and been born. But as we know that the fœtal animal is invested by a membranous covering while in the uterus, this would not explain the appearance of the maw-worm if found in it; and, moreover, the only worms I have ever known or heard of being found in the newly-born puppy, are the *Tænia cucumerina* and the *Ascaris marginata*. We know, however, that embryo entozoa are in some way transferred from the internal surface of the stomach to the interior of the blood-vessels, and through them conveyed to their proper nidus. It is, therefore, equally possible that the nematoid worms may in this way reach the circulation of the mother, and thence pass to that of the fœtus, but even then they would have again to be transferred to the intestine of the latter. The subject is one very difficult of comprehension, and in our present state of ignorance we can only say that we know nothing about it except on the most vague hypothesis.

I shall now proceed to describe the appearance and habits of the two round-worms which infest the dog so commonly as to make their presence almost the rule rather than the exception. M. Davaine enumerates three others, namely, *Holostomum alatum*, *Trichocephalus depressiusculus*, and *Dochmius trigonocephalus*;

but they are so exceedingly rare as to be only interesting to the naturalist, and are therefore of no practical importance.

The ROUND-WORM (*Ascaris marginata*), which a good deal resembles the common garden-worm, varies from four to seven inches in length, the male being much smaller than the female. It is, as may be gathered from its prefix, *round*, firm, and of a pale pink colour, its two extremities, which are alike, being pointed, but slightly flattened. It is found either alone, see (*a*), or in a group, as shown in the engraving (*b*), which was drawn from a knot of

Round Worms.

worms as actually expelled from the dog. I have already alluded to one peculiarity attaching to its generation, but there are several other points of great interest to the physiologist connected with the development of its ova. They have caused a great deal of controversy, but as they are not yet settled it is scarcely worth while to encumber my pages with them. It has been ascertained, without doubt, that the worm deposits an immense number of eggs, which under the microscope have somewhat the appearance of rough limpet-shells, and may be also recognised by the naked eye in the fæces. There appears to be little doubt that these ova are not hatched in the intestines of the dog, but pass out with the fæces, and remain for months in a torpid state, as I have already described. The accuracy of these statements is of the greatest importance, as upon them depends a good deal in the treatment by prevention, and expulsion of these worms; but though I see no reason to doubt the facts and theories of the German writers on this subject, I do not think they are sufficiently made out to be fully depended on.

The MAW-WORM, whose scientific name I am unable to give, for the reasons stated at page 154, is a white worm about an inch to an inch and a quarter in length, with one extremity truncated, and the other pointed (see engraving). These worms often exist

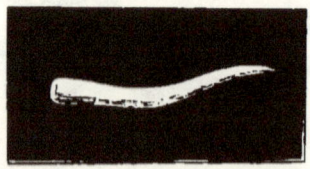

Maw Worm.

in large numbers, chiefly in the rectum and colon, but sometimes extending to the small intestines. Of their generation and development I know nothing, except from analogy with the nematoid worms in general, to which order they belong, and whose development I have described at pages 160, 161.

PREVENTION OF INTESTINAL WORMS.

I have already shown from the experiments of foreign observers, that all the intestinal worms in the dog are incapable of being propagated within his body, with the exception of the maw-worm, of whose development I have not been able to obtain an account. The tape-worms can only procure an entrance with his uncooked food, *or from this being placed in vessels which have not been properly cleansed since they contained it when in a raw state*. This I am led to believe is one means by which the tape-worm is introduced into the intestines of the dog, for there are now few coursers who feed their greyhounds upon raw food; and there can be no doubt that the heat of boiling, frying, or baking destroys animal life in any stage, whether ovum, embryo, or mature worm. Kennel-men should therefore be as particular as dairy-women in scalding out the vessels from which greyhounds are fed, and also those in which the food is stored after it is cooked. It is a common practice to deposit trotters, paunch, or other kind of food, after it is cleaned and before it is cooked, in the same vessel which is afterwards used for storing it; and when this is done it may readily be supposed that a *Cysticercus* or *Cænurus* has been left behind, and when the cooked food is replaced, mixes with it, and is thus admitted into the stomach of the dog. In this way only can I explain the occurrence of tape-worm in kennelled dogs carefully fed on cooked food, and well looked after when at exercise; though, of course, with every precaution it will happen sometimes that dogs get to offal or some kind of raw food out of doors, and in that way upset all pre-cautions at home. But the most fertile source of tape-worm is no doubt the intestines and liver of the hare, which are so commonly given to the young greyhound to encourage him to kill savagely, or which he himself will often tear out when he has been allowed to do so. As these contain the *Cysticercus pisiformis*, which becomes developed into *Tænia serrata*, it needs no other explanation of one mode of introduction of tape-worm. As the origin of the *Tænia cucumerina* has not been ascertained, precautions cannot be taken against its special source, but by avoiding all kinds of raw food no doubt it may be altogether prevented.

There is more difficulty in preventing the development of round-worms, because, though it is easy enough to boil all the water which is used in the kennel, it is almost impossible to keep dogs from drinking when out at exercise, and it is in ponds and stagnant water that the eggs of the round-worm, and most probably of the maw-worm, are stored up, ready for bursting their shells when they are swallowed by the dog. Clearly, however, the water used in kennel should always be boiled, and greyhounds should not be allowed to drink at pools, or, indeed, anywhere out of doors when it can be avoided. A muzzle will not prevent the dog from lapping water if he is very thirsty, otherwise a light wire one might be always worn, and no doubt its use is advantageous, both in tending to prevent to some extent the lapping of water, and also in effectually keeping the dog from getting at garbage.

My advice, therefore, to all coursers would be to take every precaution against the development of worms: 1st, by boiling, frying, or baking every article of food, and by taking care that the kennel-man does not use the same vessel for storing it after it is cooked as he had previously employed; 2nd, to boil every drop of water used in kennel; and, 3rd, to make the dog habitually wear a light wire muzzle when at exercise. The importance of superseding worm medicines can hardly be overrated, and if by these precautions the invasion of worms can be entirely prevented, the little extra trouble incurred by them will be amply repaid.

SYMPTOMS OF WORMS.

When the dog looks ragged and 'unkind' in his coat, being lower in flesh than he ought to be in proportion to the food he takes, and when he is constantly passing small quantities of fæces at exercise, the presence of worms may be suspected. Still it should be known that frequently large numbers of the maw-worm, and even sometimes the round-worm, or tape-worm, may be present without these signs making their appearance. One of the most certain symptoms is, however, the passage of small lumps of solid fæces, enveloped by a mucous secretion of a frothy appearance, and in addition to this it will usually be found that the dog is dull and heavy, his coat seldom looks blooming, but stares, and is rough, and the skin feels hard and unyielding; the nose also is generally dry, and the breath hot, the appetite voracious, and, when fully gratified, not producing the degree of fatness which might be expected; in fact, the dog infested with worms can seldom be got into good condition, either for rearing purposes or, when adult, for running.

REMEDIES FOR WORMS.

The proper plan to be adopted for removing worms will depend upon the kind infesting the dog. Where, therefore, they are supposed to exist, his droppings should be carefully watched, in order to ascertain the species which infests him, and when this is ascertained proceed as follows:—

For MAW-WORMS the most certain remedy is the Indian pink (*Spigelia Marilandica*), of which half an ounce is to be infused in a pint of boiling water for two hours, then strain the infusion, and by mixing one or two tablespoonfuls with some good thickened broth, the dog (after twenty-four hours' starvation, which is essential to the cure) will readily swallow it without forcing him. This should be given him at night, so that it may gradually pass through the bowels, and thus allow time for the worms to be submitted to the action of the remedy, which is a poison to them. The next morning a dose of castor oil should be given, and in a few days the dose of Indian pink should be repeated, and, to make assurance doubly sure, a third time, with a similar interval. If the worms are very numerous and strong, the infusion should be given as a drench, without broth; but though I have given Indian pink in a great many cases with perfect impunity, yet I have known it produce severe inflammation of the bowels, and in one instance prove fatal. Coursers should therefore be aware that they run some risk in using it. Many give a small tea-spoonful of pounded glass mixed up with butter or cocoa-nut oil, but I have found it fail so often that I place no dependence upon it. The stinking hellebore I have also tried in half-drachm doses of the dried powder, and prefer it to the powdered glass, but both are I think inferior to the Indian pink; the only advantage of the glass is that it may be given even during training, without much injury to the dog; but as I know of no harm which a little delay would occasion, I should prefer waiting till a week could be spared for the exhibition of the Indian pink. Worm seed (*Santonicum*) is a very efficacious remedy for round worms, and does not disorder the stomach so much as Indian pink. It should be given as a pill, made up with a few grains of the Compound Rhubarb Pill, and the dose should be one grain of the powdered seed for every month the puppy is old, up to six months, six grains being the full dose for the dog. This should be given two or three times a week, till the dog seems clear of worms. By far the safest of all worm medicines is the areca-nut (*Nux areca*), introduced into this country by Major Besant about the year 1851. The dose for the full-grown dog is about two drachms of the freshly grated nut, which should be mixed with some strong broth, just before it is wanted, as it speedily imparts a bitter taste if allowed to stand. In any case of giving worm medicine the dog should be fasted for twenty-four hours, that the efficacy of the medicine may not be lost by mixture with the food. This has also the good effect of making the animal, from hunger, ready to eat anything, and broth, even if a little bitter, will be readily swallowed. Six hours after giving the areca-nut, a mild dose of castor oil should follow; and by repeating this treatment every five or six days, any kind of worms may be exterminated. Like the Indian pink, however, the effects are sometimes, though very rarely, severely felt by delicate dogs.

ROUND-WORMS may be removed by the same remedies as mawworms, but they are more difficult to destroy, and require the drug to be administered more frequently. The areca-nut, if given every four or five days (carefully fasting the dog), will generally suffice, and this is certainly the safest plan; but where it fails, Indian pink will almost invariably succeed. I should therefore advise a fair trial of the former, failing which, the latter may be given, with full confidence in a cure, if it does not kill, which in obstinate cases it is well to know.

TAPE-WORMS are, however, the chief pests of the kennel, and

many is the dog whose constitution is destroyed in attempting their removal. Until lately, turpentine was considered to be the only effectual remedy for this worm, for the root of the male fern, though really efficacious, had somehow or other been forgotten. Some remedies which are sufficient to destroy the round worms are totally inert against tape-worm, and because turpentine was found to succeed in the human *Tænia* without injury to the patient, it was exhibited in all cases to the dog, though often to the great injury of his constitution. . It is customary to give this powerful remedy to the dog tied up in a piece of bladder or intestine, in order that it may not be rejected by vomiting, which is always the case if given in an emulsion as a drench; the bladder soon becomes digested, but not until it has passed into the small intestines, and the consequence is that the acrid spirit of turpentine in all its strength is applied to the delicate mucous membrane of the bowel, and produces such a degree of inflammation as will take many weeks, or even months, to recover from. The human stomach, on the contrary, will bear the presence of the turpentine; and it is there mixed with food and mucus and other diluting matters before it is passed on into the delicate small intestines, and the injury done is consequently small. But, within the last few years, a remedy has been introduced into this country from Abyssinia, which destroys the tape-worm without any appreciable injury to the constitution, and acts equally well upon man and dogs. This remedy is the Kousso, of which four drachms to one ounce, according to the age and size of the dog, should be infused in half a pint of boiling water; the whole, when cold, should be mixed with a table-spoonful of lemon-juice, and given at night to a dog previously starved for twenty-four hours, and a dose of oil administered in the morning. The remedy should be repeated at the end of a week, and again in a month or two. It is, perhaps, as well, in order to make sure that the whole animal is expelled, to examine the worms passed for the head, which is about as large as a very small horse bean, with a long narrow neck. Like Indian pink, and, indeed, all other worm medicines, Kousso has sometimes produced mischief, and it cannot certainly be regarded as *perfectly* safe. As a general rule, however, it is an innocent remedy, and no doubt it is a very effective one. The areca-nut, if administered according to the directions given at page 170, will generally clear the dog of tape-worm; but it sometimes fails, and I have repeatedly known Kousso succeed afterwards. The leaves and oil of the root of the male fern are strong in their power of destroying tape-worm. The plant should be dug up in the summer, and the top powdered, and carefully preserved in a stoppered bottle. The dose is from one to two drachms made into a bolus, and followed by a dose of oil in a few hours. Of the oil which is sold in the shops eight to ten drops form the dose administered in a bolus, and repeated the next morning.

The following are the doses of each vermifuge, which must be varied according to the age and strength of the patient:—

Areca-nut (*Nux areca*). Two grains to every pound the dog weighs.
Stinking Hellebore (*Helleborus fœtidus*). One grain to every six pounds the dog weighs, mixed with double its weight of jalap.
Indian pink (*Spigelia Marilandica*). Half an ounce to be infused in a pint of boiling water. Then give a full-grown dog from one to two table-

spoonfuls, and to the puppy from half a tea-spoonful to a dessert-spoonful, according to age.

Spirit of Turpentine (*Spiritus terebinthinæ*). To young puppies give two or three drops mixed in a tea-spoonful of olive oil or a little suet or lard. Old dogs require half an ounce for a dose, which should be mixed with an equal quantity of oil and tied up loosely in a piece of bladder, so as to offer no impediment to being swallowed.

Kousso (*Brayera anthelmintica*). Half an ounce is the full dose of this drug, which should be infused in half a pint of boiling water, and when cool, the juice of half a lemon should be added. The dog must be drenched with the whole mixture. Half a drachm is an ample dose for a young puppy, and for intermediate ages in proportion.

Wormwood (*Artemisia absinthium*). From five to thirty grains in syrup or honey.

Santonine (*Artemisia contra*, active principle of). The brown variety is the best, the dose being from quarter of a grain to three grains, mixed with eight to fifteen grains of jalap.

Pomegranate bark (*Punica granatum*). Dose, from one drachm to one ounce of the bark, which is to be infused in cold water for twenty-four hours, and then boiled down to one-half its bulk and filtered. One-third of this quantity is to be given at intervals of half an hour till the whole is taken.

The leaves and oil of male fern (*Filix mas*). Dose of the former from ten grains to two drachms; of the oil, from two to ten drops, mixed up with linseed meal.

OTHER INTERNAL PARASITES.

The dog is liable to the invasion of *Cysticercus cellulosæ* into his muscles, but such cases are extremely rare. I am not aware that any variety of *Filaria* has been found in the pulmonary mucous passages of the dog; but in the nose Rudolphi met with three cases of the existence of a worm which he classed as *Pentastoma tenioides*. The kidney-worm (*Strongylus gigas*) has, however, been several times found in the kidney of the dog, and is perhaps more frequently the cause of the disease of that organ than is usually supposed. Still its occurrence is rare, and it will seldom be of importance to the courser to ascertain its existence. In appearance it resembles in general form the round worm, and if a worm of somewhat the size and shape of the latter is met with on opening a dog's kidney after death, it may be considered without doubt the *Strongylus gigas*. But as its existence cannot be diagnosed during life, nor could it be removed if ascertained, no description of treatment would be of any avail.

EXTERNAL PARASITES.

The parasites infesting the skin of the dog include the flea, tick, louse, and mange insect; to which may be added several vegetable parasites not accurately made out, and causing diseases of the hair.

The FLEA is too well known to need description. Its occurrence in large numbers may best be prevented by the use of shavings of red deal, or by sprinkling turpentine upon the litter some little time before it is introduced. To remove fleas when they abound, soft soap and carbonate of soda should be mixed into a paste, and rubbed into the skin, on which the mixture should be allowed to remain for half an hour, then put the dog in warm water for ten minutes, so as to allow the fleas to be soaked in the solution, taking care to immerse the head up to the eyes and nose. After this wash all completely out, and dry the dog either by the fire with towels, or by letting him run in the open air. In warm weather neat's-foot oil rubbed into the skin of the whole body will destroy every flea, but it can only safely be employed when the weather is perfectly sultry, as it chills the dog almost as much as water, and not drying, the chill is permanent for two or three days. Great care, therefore, is necessary in the use of oil. The various insect powders sold by Keating and others, also destroy fleas, if the expense is not objected to.

LICE also are easily recognised, and may be destroyed in the same way as fleas, but a more easy plan is to rub some powdered white precipitate into the roots of the hair over the whole body. Put on a muzzle, and leave the dog with the powder on him for six hours, or longer if the parasites are very numerous. Then brush all out, and the lice will be found dead. The remedy must, however, be reapplied in a few days, to make sure of success. The dog should be kept dry, or the powder may be absorbed through the skin.

The TICK (*Ixodes ricinus*) is small, spider-like, and tough, as represented in the annexed engraving. In colour it is a bluish-red, and it may readily be known by its adhering strongly to the skin. In size it varies from the magnitude of a small pin's head, to nearly half an inch in length, when it has long been allowed to infest the dog. To destroy ticks, the best remedy is the white precipitate, used in the same way as for lice; but mercurial ointment

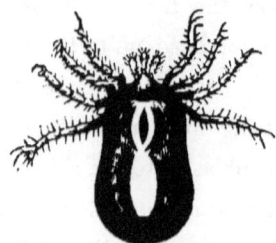

The Tick, magnified.

will do equally well, the objection to the latter being that it makes the dog greasy, and in cold weather chills him considerably.

The MANGE-INSECT (*Sarcoptes canis*) is slightly smaller than that of the horse, which it closely resembles in other respects. It burrows into the skin, leaving a protuberance at its entrance, from

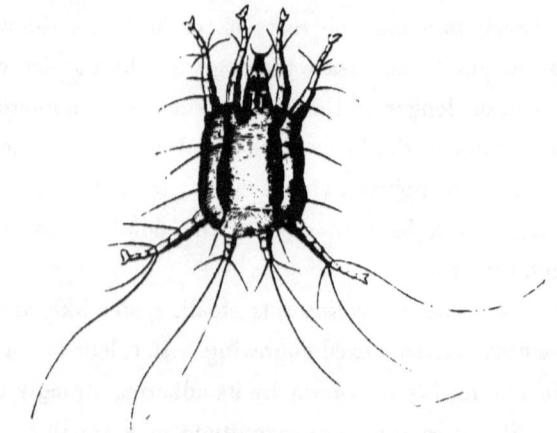

Male Mange insect, magnified.

EXTERNAL PARASITES. 177

which it works its way gradually along a little gallery, at the end of which it sits and with care may be found, presenting with a good glass the appearance shown in our engravings of the male and female. The colour varies with that of the dog, but the insect is always more or less tinged with the blood it has

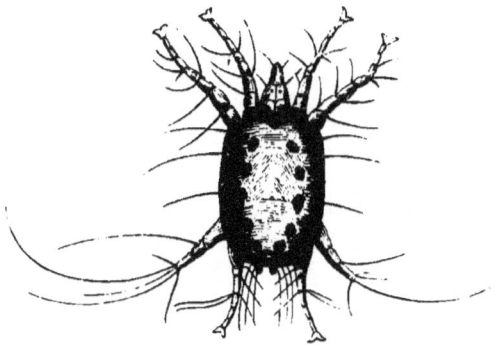

The Female Mange insect magnified.

devoured. Its eggs are very large, and coated with a sticky substance, by which they adhere to the legs of the female till they are deposited in the gallery made by her. When first hatched the young are small, but quickly grow, and each making a separate gallery or passage, the irritation in the skin rapidly increases, and the true scabby mange described at page 141 is produced. It is unnecessary to repeat the treatment which is alluded to at that page.

'CERITO.' *

CHAPTER VIII.*

Innocence of Public Coursing compared with Racing—Its Suitability to the man of limited means—Advice to Young Coursers on the best means of obtaining a Stud of good Dogs—Selection of Brood Bitches—Examples of good and bad ones.

BEST MODE OF OBTAINING A STUD.

In the first three chapters of this treatise, I endeavoured to describe the most desirable form and blood for the public grey-

* For pedigree &c. of Mr. Cooke's 'Cerito,' as well as the other bitches alluded to in this Chapter, see Appendix.

hound; in the subsequent chapters, the mode of keeping him in health has been considered, and now I shall proceed to examine into a still more difficult subject, namely, the best mode of obtaining a stud of these animals. This object may be effected either by purchase, or by the selection of a sire and dam, as perfect as possible in blood, form, and health, and then proceeding to breed from them.

One chief reason for my undertaking to give publicity to my opinions is, that I believe coursing to be the most innocent public amusement, connected with the indulgence of the hunting propensity so natural to every man, and more especially to every Briton. For I think it may be shown that, *properly conducted*, the pursuit of the hare by the greyhound at public meetings may be carried on with perfect innocence, as regards the morals, both of the parties actually engaged and also of the spectators. Now this can be said of scarcely any other amusement of the kind. In horse-racing there is much which is reprehensible, and though its encouragement is necessary to keep up the breed of horses, yet I much doubt whether its disadvantages do not counterbalance its advantages. Fox-hunting can only be enjoyed by the wealthy, and even by them is only attainable in certain favoured districts. Shooting, also, is confined to those who possess landed estates or the right to shoot over them, and is now out of the reach of most men of moderate means, except as a rare treat; but there are few who may not find the means to keep one or two greyhounds, and this number will engage the attention, and delight the eye, of the man of limited means quite as much as the extensive studs of our large public coursers. I propose, therefore, to show all who may be desirous of obtaining the information, how they may best enter upon this sport, with the least expense to themselves, and with the greatest prospect of success; remembering always, that money as a prize should not be the *desideratum per se*, but solely, as was observed by the late Lord George Bentinck, as a proof of success. Everyone who knew him was aware how little value he set upon gold, but no one would strive more ardently than he to succeed in obtaining it, when held out as the test of success, in a sport to which he devoted his whole mental and bodily energies, till called by what he considered his duty into another sphere of action. Although much has been written on this subject, and sometimes the information is of great value, yet it has been universally admitted that the information thus offered is so diffuse, and given in a form so unintelligible to the beginner, that it is almost wholly useless to him. Mr. Thacker's two volumes contain a vast amount of useful and interesting matter, but with the good corn there is much chaff, and it is only to the practised courser that they are really valuable. As a Coursing Judge he certainly astonishes the reader of his notes, by the extent of his knowledge of the merits of the greyhound, but as a greyhound manager, from a want of experience, he was obliged to obtain his information from others and is not in this department so much to be depended upon. Since his time nothing of any value has appeared, and I believe that no one would have much prospect of success in public, if depending solely upon what he may find in print. At all events, until he has submitted to such a series of losses as, in all probability, to disgust him with the sport, he has no chance of finding out the right way from the wrong. In training, for instance, nothing but experience can direct the exact amount of work which each particular dog will bear; but it is easy to direct the average quantity, to be regulated according to the age and constitution of the individual. The same holds good with respect to food and the number of courses which puppies should have before they appear in public. In this last point so much depends upon the breed and rearing, that an experienced person alone can say when a puppy is fit to meet the Judge's eye. But the whole subject is now so enveloped in mystery, so much is thought to be done by the trainer which no man can do, that the novice is frightened from attempting the task, and, if determined to commence as a public courser, he trusts entirely to some dog-man, who probably knows as little of the proper management of the greyhound as the horsekeeper of a wayside public-house does of the management of a race-horse. Hence the miserable failures which are so often made. Greyhounds are brought to the slips as fat as bullocks, or else like living skeletons, or, perhaps, in condition fit to run for a man's life, but having had no experience, they either lose their course by running wide, or do not kill their hare when they have the power to do so. It is my object, therefore, to enable any man who understands the management of dogs generally, or even his own species (since the points of similarity in constitution between man and his companion, the dog, are so great as to make it easy to do the one if the other has been mastered), to undertake the control of a stud of greyhounds, without the assistance of a *special trainer*; or, if he prefers to entrust them to some person learned in the mysterious art, still to enable him to check his servant in his absurdities, and to know whether he is really going on in the right road without doing too much or too little. I have known a master charged three shillings a day for each dog for rabbits and eggs!!! without, as may be expected, seeing any superiority of condition manifested by the stud. I have seen naturally good dogs fed at first-rate meetings, upon fat necks of mutton, with at least four times as much fat as lean—and with the inevitable result of losing their courses from want of condition, the master all the while ignorant that his chance was being thrown away by the incapacity of his servant. Indeed, it is truly astonishing how some dogs run at all, when we see how they are mismanaged—what with improper food, sherry and eggs, and other stimulating articles, to which the dog's stomach is not easily accustomed. There is no animal which will digest bones more quickly than the dog, which has led people to suppose that his stomach can digest anything; but there is scarcely any domestic animal whose stomach is so readily upset by unaccustomed and improper food.

The first advice I would give to an inexperienced courser would be, to get a few greyhounds at the lowest possible price, without any hope of running in public, but in order to gain experience in their management. Of course it is desirable to get as good dogs as possible; but it is useless for the tyro to hope to procure greyhounds, by purchase, of such a character as to win a stake in public; for, except under particular circumstances, no one will part with them. Even in the sale of an entire kennel, there are always some few in the secret who buy up the valuable lots, and the inexperienced eye has little chance in competition

'MOCKING BIRD.'

with the man who is in the secret, and has made it also the business of his life.

It may be said, and it is quite true, that 'Mocking Bird' was bought for a small sum by auction, but it was by a good judge, who was also in the secret as to her capabilities. 'Movement' likewise was sold in the same way, and some few other winners might be enumerated, but they are only exceptions to the above rule, such as 'Cerito' for instance, which bitch was bought at an enormous price after her first successful performance, and afterwards won the Waterloo Cup three times.

Mr. Spinks has also been more successful in purchasing than in breeding, having obtained 'Seacombe,' 'Sea Rock,' 'Sea Pink' and 'Sea Foam' by the former plan, which have been far more useful to him than his numberless puppies. On the other hand Mr. Randell has never bought a first-rate dog at full age, with the exception of 'Rival' purchased of Sir St. George Gore, 'Riot' and 'Ranter' having been obtained from Mr. Pridmore when whelps.

Besides, a young hand would be more likely to select a good-looking dog which has had all his work taken out of him than one which would be really useful to him. It is better, therefore, to devote all your energies and money to the procuring a good brood bitch or two, and while her progeny are growing up, to try the ''prentice hand' upon what you can easily buy at four or five pounds a piece, confining your trials to a friendly competition with your neighbour's dogs. In this way you will gain the experience at little cost which would otherwise empty a long purse to obtain. Many a man has spent five or six hundred pounds in the purchase of a lot of useless animals, and has lost as much more in the first season in stakes and expenses. It is not even safe to buy a winner, for a dog may be of such a constitution as to be only in condition once or twice a year, especially with the physicking system which so much prevails; and of course on such a dog the severe trials run in winning his stake will tell with double effect. With the exercise of patience in this way, a small kennel may be collected

'MISS HANNAH.'

at very little expense, and a small kennel well managed will be more likely to produce winners than the large and consequently unhealthy lots of many of our public coursers.

In this way, whilst gaining the necessary experience in the

management of the adult, the young courser may hope also to obtain some little practical insight into the *arcana* of the breeding stud. I have already said that he has little chance of purchasing a first-rate animal, and the only resource is to set to work and breed one. But to do this requires great care in the selection of the brood bitch, equal or greater care and knowledge in the choice of a good cross for her, and some considerable time, trouble, and expense in rearing their progeny. Much depends upon the nature of the ground where you intend to enter your dogs; but, as I have already said, I believe there are some breeds which are calculated to run well in all countries, though certainly better in some than in others. Thus 'Mocking-Bird' ran well at Newmarket, at Amesbury, at Barton-on-Humber, and at Altcar; 'Miss Hannah' also won the Great Western Cup, in Wiltshire, as well as The Purse at Altcar, and by some is considered to have run even better at the latter than the former place; and 'Riot,' though unfortunately never able to take part in the Waterloo Cup contests, was equally good at Newmarket, Amesbury, and Altcar. The same may be said of 'David,' and latterly the members of the Altcar Club, including more especially the Earl of Sefton, have been quite as successful in the south as in the north. Curiously enough, however, his Lordship's most successful greyhound in the south ('Sapphire') is descended through her dam from 'King Cob' and 'Foremost;' indeed, the 'King Cob' and 'Foremost' blood seems to acquire fresh laurels in new districts every year. Whether we examine the returns from Scotland or from Altcar, from Wiltshire or Newmarket, an overwhelming proportion of the winners will be found to consist of their descendants. In the list of great winners which I compiled for another purpose, from 1843 to 1853, and comprising 123 dogs, 41 of them were descended from one or other of the above-named celebrated stallions. Of these, fourteen are by 'King Cob' himself, six by 'Figaro,' two by 'Miles,' one by 'Kotzebue' (all sons), two by 'Sam' (grandson), out of 'Tollwife' (a daughter), and one out of 'Queen of the May' (another daughter), whilst the remainder consists of twelve by 'Foremost' himself, two by 'Czar,' and one by 'Rocket' (his sons). Since that time the proportion of winners descended from 'King Cob' has been largely increased, and his grandson, 'Bedlamite' has been undoubtedly the most successful stallion of modern times, while 'David,' who has two lines of 'King Cob' blood, is of nearly equal celebrity. 'Effort' and 'The Brewer,' 'Jacobite,' 'Selby,' 'Baron,' and many other successful sires may also be adduced in support of his fame, while the 'Foremost' blood has almost disappeared, being chiefly preserved in the kennels of the Earl of Sefton and Mr. Loder.

SELECTION OF BROOD BITCH.

Leaving the consideration of particular breeds, let us now consider the essentials of a brood bitch for all countries. First and foremost I should place stoutness; secondly, speed; thirdly, honesty; and fourthly, working powers. Now stoutness I have already supposed to reside in the whole nervous system; it is, in fact, a constitutional peculiarity, giving the power of endurance under long-continued exertion, and depending upon the degree of perfection of the nervous system, as well as the lungs, heart, and general muscular system. It is also in great measure due to the

'RUBY.'

state of the health of the individual, and this ought to be carefully attended to in the brood bitch, for no animal, however naturally stout, can either continue so herself or transmit the quality to her progeny, unless she is in high health and condition; care should

SELECTION OF BROOD BITCH.

therefore be taken that the brood bitch has not yet been injured by training or subsequent neglect. In all these requisites it is desirable that the brood bitch should herself partake, but in speed it is not so necessary that she should in her own person shine; but she should certainly be of a speedy family, if it is expected that her produce should inherit that quality. It often happens that one bitch out of a litter of fast greyhounds is too small, and perhaps too thickset, to attain high speed, and she, though useless as a public performer, is the very animal to breed from, if stout and honest, with enough destructiveness to render her anxious to do her best towards killing her game. In fact, I should as soon select such a bitch, which has been thrown aside as useless by the public courser, as his more successful but worn-out favourite, even though the winner of as many stakes as 'Mocking Bird,' 'Cerito,' or 'Birdlime.' I repeat, then, let the family to which the bitch belongs be your guide rather than the individual herself, except in the two points of stoutness and honesty, which should certainly be possessed by every brood bitch. In every other particular it is more likely that the produce will possess the general characteristics of that family than the peculiar properties of the individual bitch. Thus, a large roomy bitch, if got by a little dog out of a similar bitch to him, but accidently forced into her increased size, will most probably 'throw' a lot of under-sized greyhounds; and the reverse holds good with a small animal belonging to a family of good-sized greyhounds. If, therefore, you can get a small muscular bitch of from 45 lbs. to 50 lbs. weight, belonging to a winning family whose general properties you admire, and who are most of them of a proper size, by all means select her in preference to a larger animal, for the following reasons: 1st. The small bitch is more easily obtained, because she was very probably not large enough to win, and has also been less used in consequence; 2ndly. The large bitch, if not good enough to win, must be defective in some other point than want of size, and if a winner, is injured, to a certain extent, by the work she has done; 3rdly. The small bitch is generally a better nurse, and more hardy in every respect. I have made the remark that it is not important that the brood bitch should have been a public winner, but I should go still further, and maintain that she is rendered less valuable for breeding purposes by her successes. When we consider the care that is generally taken in putting celebrated bitches to first-class dogs, it is wonderful how few have produced a fair proportion of winners. I may adduce as an instance the celebrated 'Dressmaker,' which, though a wonderful performer, has, out of four or five litters, only produced one first-rate greyhound, and in fact only three winners altogether, viz. 'Staymaker,' 'Cinderella,' and 'Perseverance,' whilst her brother, 'Pleader,' has got more than a dozen out of a very limited number of bitches, though in himself very inferior to her. Besides 'Dressmaker,' the following noted bitches may be enumerated, viz. 'Breeze,' the no less celebrated 'Harriet' and Birdlime,' 'Regina Victoria,' 'Lady Harkaway,' 'Highland Lassie,' 'Kizzie,' and last, though not least in public estimation, Mr. Fyson's 'Fairy.' This bitch, when compared with his 'Frederica,' is a good illustration of my argument, for though she was

SELECTION OF BROOD BITCH.

greatly superior to her as a runner, she has been totally useless as a brood bitch, whilst 'Frederica' has produced a long list of successful greyhounds. On the other hand, certainly, some brilliant exceptions may be adduced, as, for instance, Lord Strad-

'DRESSMAKER.'

broke's 'Minerva,' and her daughter, 'Queen of the May.' 'Titania' also has produced a lot of good second-class greyhounds.

But since the first edition of this book was published several striking examples of success in breeding from good winners have occurred. 'Mocking Bird' and 'Riot,' which I have adduced at page 16, among the examples of greyhounds running well in all countries, have each bred several successful litters, the former being the dam of 'Mœris,' 'Mimosa,' 'Mansoor,' 'Mechanic,' and

'TITANIA.'

Marqueterie,' and grand dam of 'Clive,' while the latter can boast of 'Regan,' 'Rebel,' 'Referree,' 'Rienzi,' and 'Rosy Morn,' among a numerous lot of less successful puppies. Neither, however, has bred a greyhound equal to herself, and it is to Mr. Campbell's

'Scotland Yet' that we must look for the best instance of a successful runner and brood bitch combined in one. She was in every respect but pace a first-class greyhound, and is the dam of 'Canaradzo,' 'Coorooran,' 'Canopy,' 'Cazzarina,' 'Sea Foam,' 'Sea Pink,' and 'Ciologa,' besides several other good second-class greyhounds. These bitches, however, were all, I believe, uninjured by their work, either in honesty or bodily health; and in this fact will, I believe, be found the secret of their success as brood bitches.

Almost all great winners have, in the severe work necessary to the completion of their tasks, learnt a trick or two. Now, we know that the mental as well as the bodily powers are transmitted from parent to offspring, as, for instance, in the pointer and setter, in which breeds it is well known that it is exceedingly difficult to break the puppy-bred from badly-broken sires and dams, especially in the acquired and unnatural accomplishment of 'backing;' whilst, on the other hand, the well-bred young pointer stands and backs the first time he goes into the field. So, in the greyhound, we have frequently the grievous disappointment of seeing the sapling 'wait,' and, in fact, show the same signs of foul running as his experienced sire; but this early display of cunning is seldom seen except in breeds which have been famous for speed, because the fast greyhound finds out by experience that he can safely allow his assistant to knock the hare about for a time, and then he can 'go in and win' when he likes. The slower animal, however, can take no such liberties, and his offspring, therefore, seldom show the tendency so early, if at all. The fact is, that they have no inheritance of vice, and, however slack in running they become, they do not generally reserve their powers to the end of the course, but whatever they do, they do the same or nearly so, from beginning to end. I would therefore caution breeders against selecting a brood bitch which is no longer honest, and also against using their brood bitches 'for pot-hunting' purposes, as is so often the case. The same will apply to the stallion dog, though perhaps not in the same degree, since it is generally believed that the mental faculties of the offspring are more dependent upon those of the female than the male. But it is not only from dishonesty that the great winner is unfitted for breeding purposes, but also because in all probability she has been kept in an unnatural state of virginity for several seasons. This deprivation alone interferes with the due performance of the natural functions, both prior to, and after, devoting her to breeding purposes, and I believe almost all the above successful brood bitches were put to the dog at their first or second heat. 'Titania,' I know, won the Waterloo Cup only four months after breeding a litter of whelps; 'Flirt' ran second for the same cup with 'War Eagle' in her belly; and 'Riot' never ran better than when she won the Altcar Cup in October 1857, some few months after she bred her first litter of puppies. 'Bessy Bedlam' did not breed 'Bedlamite', till she was five years old, but then she had never previously been 'in season,' so that her case tells for nothing except that being herself a good runner she was the dam of a wonderful litter of greyhounds, perhaps altogether as good as ever was whelped. Neither does the act of training improve the constitution, so that, in every way, of two equal bitches, one put to the dog at two years old, and the other trained and run till five, I should expect the produce of the former to be very superior to that of the latter. The reason of this probably is, that in training,

'TENDRESSE.'

the organs of generation are kept as much as possible in abeyance, whilst the muscular and respiratory systems are developed to the highest extent of which they are capable. As instances of successful brood bitches, which were themselves inferior runners,

I may adduce Mr. Bagge's 'Madré' (sister to his 'Traveller,' and dam of 'Twilight,' 'Turquoise,' 'Tendresse'), &c.; Sir James Boswell's 'Rosebud' (sister to 'Mildew' and 'Evergreen,' and dam of 'Auchinlech,' 'Vraye Foye,' and the 'Curler'); Mr. Gregson's 'Grace' (sister to 'Burdon,' 'Tunstall,' &c., and dam of 'Neville' and 'St. Godric'); Mr. Cooke's 'Catch 'em,' dam of the 'Czar,' 'Forward,' and 'Cannon Ball;' also his 'Tippitywitchet' (sister to 'Kotzebue, and dam of 'Sam' and 'Sable'); besides which is to be found 'Faith' (sister to Scott's 'Marquis,' and dam of 'Cinneraria' and 'Rocket'). Going still further back, we find plenty of examples, but they are not so remarkable, because public competition was not so general as at present; but still we find Mr. Blake's 'Blacklock' and 'Birdlime,' out of sister to 'Priam,' and Mr. Slater's 'Sandy,' out of sister to 'Solomon,' as well as many other examples of the same kind—for it is remarkable, in looking through the pedigree-lists of Messrs. Thacker and Welch, how many winners are out of the sisters of celebrated dogs, they themselves having been so unknown to fame as to be without a distinguishing name. Of late years almost every greyhound has had a name, so that these remarks cannot be carried on through the *Coursing Calendar*, but numberless examples of good greyhounds from moderate dams might be enumerated, including ' Romping Girl ' out of ' Redwing,' who is also the dam of ' Skedaddler,' and two or three other fair second-raters. On the whole, however, I think that the preponderance of evidence is in favour of breeding from winners, provided that they are not worn out by training and hard running, and especially

SELECTION OF BROOD BITCH.

if such an animal as 'Riot,' 'Mocking Bird,' or 'Scotland Yet' can be obtained, which is not an every-day occurrence.

I have thus endeavoured to show that the tyro need not have

'RIOT.'

any difficulty in procuring a draft bitch from some celebrated stock, which will be likely to produce him a successful litter of greyhounds, and that a little discarded bitch, if possessing the qualities I have enumerated, will most probably answer his purpose as well as her more valued sister, although the latter may be of more imposing appearance, and have a long list of victories to boast of. The reasons for this I have endeavoured to make clear, and I have also attempted to prove the truth of my assertion, by adducing a list of examples in illustration of it. That familiar aphorism of the breeder, 'like begets like,' is true enough in the main, but is not to be interpreted too strictly. It should be rendered thus,—every animal has a tendency to reproduce the likeness of itself, *or of its family*, and if the individual in question is an exception to the general form of the family, then the produce will be more likely to follow the rule than the exception. Bearing in mind, then, this amended aphorism, which I believe to be the true interpretation, let the breeder only decide on the best blood from which to make his selection, and then let him without fear obtain such a draft as I have described, which he can do at a much less cost than if purchasing a successful favourite.

It will be said by the young courser, that I have given directions for selecting the brood bitch in every particular but the one most essential, namely, her 'breed' or 'pedigree,' and this is quite true, though I have indicated one strain which experience has shown is good in all countries, viz. the stock of 'King Cob,' and especially as handed down to us through 'Bedlamite' or 'David.' Other sires have occasionally bred greyhounds which have carried off good prizes both in the south and north; but taking public running as our only sure guide, these two sires have been the most successful of late years in all countries, and I should

SELECTION OF BROOD BITCH.

myself select a brood bitch possessing one or other of these fashionable names in their pedigrees, but taking especial care that the other names coupled with them should belong to animals of stout, honest, and good-working blood.

If the produce are intended for Altcar and Lytham alone, or indeed for any north country coursing, there are several strains which will perhaps succeed even better than the descendants of 'King Cob.' Among these I may mention 'Judge,' 'Skyrocket,' (the latter being almost as well suited to the south as the descendants of 'King Cob,') 'Canaradzo' (combining Mr. Borron's 'Blue Bugle' blood with the extreme cleverness of 'Wigan's' stock); 'Beacon' and 'Black Cloud' (two brothers bred by Mr. Borron and almost equally successful at the stud, though the former has certainly the advantage in having got two Waterloo Cup winners, in 'Canaradzo' and 'Roaring Meg,' besides another through Canaradzo, in 'King Death'), the descendants of 'Jason,' through 'Vraye Foy,' 'Egypt,' and 'Lopez,' and of 'Larriston' through 'Effort.' 'The Brewer' and 'Woodman' have also done well in the south, and the young courser who can obtain a brood bitch by any one of the above dogs, combined with other strains equally good, may consider himself extremely lucky. In the north, 'Jacobite,' combining the blood of 'Judge' and 'Bedlamite,' has been justly successful, but though his sons 'Cardinal York' and 'Picton' have got some greyhounds above the average, I have as yet seen nothing very striking by them. Since the 'Beacon' and 'Black Cloud' litter, no greyhound much above the average has appeared from the Ardrossan kennel, but such is the luck of the courser, and curiously enough Mr. Randell, who was the only formidable rival to Mr. Borron, when at his zenith, declined about the same time, and has since been equally unfortunate, though neither gentleman has spared any pains or expense to develope his plans. 'Sam' carried all before him for a time in Scotland, his fame being supported mainly by 'Toll Wife,' who was certainly a good wife, producing three good litters to him, and failing as completely when put to Malpas' 'Merrylad.' But his sons, used by Mr. Gibson at the stud, have done nothing, and he has fallen back upon that wonderfully game and honest dog 'Coorooran,' bred by Mr. Campbell.

There are no doubt many valuable local breeds with which I am unacquainted, but I can only speak as far as my knowledge goes, and beyond that depth I should be misleading my readers.

Among the portraits which I have been enabled to give, 'Mocking-Bird' may be adduced as an instance of the form of a most successful runner, and as being the dam and granddam of some excellent greyhounds, though, as I before remarked, not quite coming up to an equally winning progeny; but I confess that I should much prefer the form of Mr. Randell's 'Ruby,' whose portrait is given at page 188, even if I did not know that she had produced such a long list of winners. Her stifles and shoulders show the perfection of shape, and she has transmitted this peculiarity to many of her progeny, one instance of which is shown in the frontispiece to this book. The shape of 'Dressmaker' also is to be desired as a runner; but not as a brood bitch, being too open and racing like. 'Miss Hannah,' on the contrary, is too small in the bone for my liking as a brood

SELECTION OF BROOD BITCH.

bitch, though a beautiful runner; and Captain Wyndham's 'Whiff,' whose portrait is here produced, may be cited as an instance of a successful runner, contrary to all expectation from her shape, and as being from that criterion perhaps unlikely to produce a litter of winners, which she proved herself to be, having only bred

'WHIFF.'

one average greyhound in Sydenham, winner of the Great Western stakes, but soon losing all form.

As a contrast to 'Whiff' may be adduced her aunt, Mr. Long's 'Cactus,' whose portrait I think exaggerates the really extraordinary length of body which she possessed. This bitch was a first-class greyhound in every particular but her feet, and ran well at Newmarket as well as in Wiltshire. Her portrait, as drawn by Mr. H. Hall, is *too long* in the middle, but otherwise she was the model of a brood bitch. She produced two litters, one out of the first of which, called 'Moss Rose,' was successful at Amesbury, and afterwards ran well in Lancashire, while 'Lady,' one of the second lot, has served Mr. Loder well as a brood bitch, being the dam of ' Laban,' ' Leah,' Luke,' and ' Lyra,' a very good average litter.

'CACTUS.'

'KING COB.'*

CHAPTER IX.

General principles of breeding.—Modern theory of Generation.—Remarks on the above.—Instances of successful Stallions, not good Runners.—Reason for this.—Explanation of the nature of what is called 'a Hit.'

AFTER the selection of the brood bitch, the next thing is to determine upon the most suitable dog to 'cross her with.' It is not to

* The pedigrees of this dog and other stallions are given in the Appendix.

be supposed that the breeder has obtained perfection in all respects, and his object therefore must be to rectify her defects, and retain her perfections if any. To do this with advantage, it is necessary to be aware of the principles upon which breeding in general should be conducted, and also to be practically acquainted with the qualities of the various public stallion dogs which are offered to his choice.

THEORY OF GENERATION AND GENERAL PRINCIPLES OF BREEDING.

These are not very fully known, but what little we do know on the theory of generation, and the practice of breeding, is comprised in the following abstract, which for convenience is divided into sentences necessarily in a dogmatic form, because the arguments *pro* and *con* would occupy the whole of that space which must be devoted to other matters. It comprises, however, the most modern and generally received opinions upon those points which interest the breeder of domestic animals, and which may be studied more at length in the physiological works of Todd, Bowman, and Carpenter, and in the more practical one of M. Harard, ' *Des Haras Domestiques*,' also in a highly interesting paper on the breeding of sheep, by M. Malingie, in the last number of the ' Transactions of the Royal Agricultural Society of England.'

1st. In the process of generation the action of the male consists in the emission of the semen into the uterus of the female, where (or near which organ) it reaches and fertilises the *ovum* of the female. The essence or precise nature of the semen is not known, but it is not fruitful unless it contains what are called *spermatozoa*, which are capable of moving themselves, and were formerly supposed to be animalcules. These are now considered to be no more than automatic particles, like those formed in the *pollen* of some species of plants, which often show a great degree of activity after leaving the parent flower; they seem to be intended to convey the essential particles or ' sperm cells ' of the semen to that part of the uterine system of the female where their presence is required.

2nd. The share of the female is greater than that of the male, because she not only furnishes the ' germ-cell,' which is a part of the ovum, analogous to the ' sperm-cell ' of the semen, but she also supplies them both with the materials necessary for their development, till they are able to support a separate existence. The ' germ-cell ' and the *yolk*, together make up the ovum, which is formed by the *ovarium*, and carried off by the *oviduct* just as the semen is secreted by the testes, and carried off by the *vas deferens*.

3rdly. The ' sperm-cell,' being furnished by the male, and the ' germ-cell ' by the female, must be brought into contact before the latter is fertilized, and a perfect embryo formed. As soon as this contact has been established, the ' sperm-cell ' becomes absorbed into the ' germ-cell,' and a tendency to increase in size is set on foot and kept up by means of the nutriment contained in the yolk of the ovum, until it has attached itself to the walls of the uterus by its umbilical system of vessels and placenta.

4thly. The difference between the ovum of mammalia, and that of birds and reptiles, chiefly consists in the larger size of the yolk in the latter, which is necessary, because it has to support the growth of the embryo until able to digest food by means of its stomach; whilst, in the mammalia, the placental attachment affords a supply of nourishment by means of the blood of the mother during the interval between the entrance of the ovum into the uterus and its birth—a period which embraces nearly the whole time between conception and birth, and is called utero-gestation.

5thly. The period of 'heat' is the time when one or more ova are being shed from the ovarium, and are passing on into the uterus; the latter part of this period is, therefore, the best time for the union of the sexes, because the semen then at once arrives at the ovum, in or near the uterus, without either waiting for its descent, or having to go in search of it by means of the automatic power of the *spermatozoa*.

6thly. The semen will continue to retain its fructifying powers for a considerable time, probably, in some cases, for many days when in contact with the lining membrane of the uterus, but soon ceases to be productive if confined in a vessel whose walls are composed of dead matter. A single perfect act of impregnation in the dog is, therefore, more likely to be efficacious than if followed by a second, since the semen is not soon secreted again of an activity equal to the first.

7thly. As the female parent furnishes the greater part of the materials of the egg in all animals, and also supports the young of the *vivipara* during the period of utero-gestation, it might, *à priori*, be assumed, that she would exert a greater influence than the male upon the offspring, but the fact is not clearly proved, and many cases may be adduced in which the character of the offspring partakes even more of the male than the female, though, as a whole, the preponderance of evidence is in favour of the greater influence, in a small degree, of the female.

8thly. The influence of the male is not necessarily confined to the period of conception only, since the semen itself continues to exist for some time, and its 'sperm-cell' is actually absorbed into the 'germ-cell' of the ovum. So that the embryo is really part and parcel of the father, as well as the mother, in whose favour the only balance is the fact of her affording the entire nourishment to the embryo from her own blood.

9thly. The greater influence of one parent, in some cases, seems to depend upon greater strength of constitution, either in the individual, or in the stock, to which he or she, as the case may be, belongs.

10thly. No general law is known as to the transmission by either parent in particular of temperament, health, bodily or mental power, colour, or conformation. In some animals, the colour of each is combined without alteration, as in the piebald and brindle, whilst in others, the shade is uniformly changed to an intermediate stage between the two, as in the various shades of blue and fawn, and in the mulatto of the human species.

11thly. Acquired qualities of mind as well as body may be transmitted by either parent, as in the case of Dr. Brown's 'Heather Jock,' whose prick ears were an acquired variety, and yet have very frequently been transmitted; but the converse is not to be maintained, if only accidental, since the deprivation of a limb or other organ by accident, is not perpetuated. But if a variety, in which an organ is deficient, can be established without violence, such a deficiency will often be propagated, as in the tailless cat, short-tailed pointer, &c.

12thly. The purer or less mixed the breed, the more likely it is to be transmitted in the same form as the parent, and as the blood of the male is generally more carefully attended to than that of the female, it often happens, as a consequence of its greater purity, that his form will predominate in the offspring. But if the male is more crossed than the female, the contrary will generally be the case.

13thly. Bad as well as good qualities may be transmitted, and therefore it is clear that, to improve any stock, a male should be chosen which has not only the requisite good points, but is free from those defects, which are to be got rid of in the female. The breeder must also select a male, in whose family these good points have been long resident, and are not in him accidental occurrences.

14thly. Breeding 'in and in' cannot be shown to be injurious in wild animals, since it is well known that, in gregarious wild animals, the strongest male retains his daughters, grand-daughters, and often great-grand-daughters, as part of his train. Nor is there reason to believe that it is so prejudicial in the domestic animals as in man, with whom the adoption of the practice seems especially to be avoided, and has been forbidden by most of our lawgivers, human and divine.

15thly. Many physiologists believe that the influence of the first impregnation extends to the next and subsequent ones. Haller was the first to remark, that a mare which has bred a mule, begotten by an ass, if put to a horse the next time, will often again breed a mule. Recent experiments have also shown that a mare which had been put to a male quagga for three years, subsequently bred several foals by an Arabian horse, which showed the quagga markings, though each time more and more faintly. Burdach has remarked the same in the sow and bitch, and in the human female the observation has frequently been made, but of course in none is it so strongly marked as in the mule and quagga. If these facts are correctly stated, it is highly important to guard against a brood bitch being warded at any time by a mongrel, or even by a badly-bred greyhound.

It will thus be seen that, though few, there are some brood landmarks which may serve to guide the breeder, and that by studying them he may hope to avoid the grievous errors so often made by those who think breeding in all cases a complete lottery. Indeed, by those who pride themselves most upon their experience and success, it is very commonly supposed that the breeder has nothing to do but to correct any defect in his bitch by fixing upon a stallion which possesses in an eminent degree the quality defective in her. But this will not do in practice. It is necessary to go deeper, and not only to do this, but to detect the cause of the defect, and then to select an animal which possesses, both in himself and family, the peculiar conformation of body and brain which will insure its correction. Thus a slow bitch may be defective, either from her form being *generally* too thick and compact, or, *in particular*, from having clumsy shoulders, or weak hind-quarters, or lastly, from a weak or sluggish nervous organisation. Now each of these deficiencies would require a different stallion to rectify it. As for instance, a slow and clumsy-shouldered bitch would not be likely to produce a fast litter of whelps by putting her to a fast dog, which had nevertheless, as is sometimes seen, equally clumsy shoulders with herself. But if put to a dog with good racing, yet powerful hind-quarters, and shoulders well sloped and light, and belonging to a family of similar form, her produce may possibly even exceed our expectations. Again, it would never answer to put a bitch deficient in courage to a dog of the same worthless class. But with this general principle in view, there is another also to be considered, and that is, not only to endeavour to rectify defects, in which aim you are often likely to fail, but also to retain, and if possible improve, those points which are already well developed in the bitch, by selecting a dog which has them also in a state of perfection, and in the *same form and style.* Now this I take to be one of the great secrets of breeding, and one which is less attended to than it ought to be. To explain my meaning, I shall venture to give an illustration. The celebrated ' Cerito,' as I have elsewhere remarked, though constantly victorious at Altcar, was not so successful in Wiltshire and similar counties, owing probably to her great length of stride. In regard to the reason for her Wiltshire failure, there may be a difference of opinion; but, assuming that it was as I believe, how are we likely to rectify the defect, supposing it is the object to breed Wiltshire greyhounds from her? Now many would have advised her to be put to a good Wiltshire short-running dog, such as 'Fire Office' or Wiltshire 'Marquis,' which are the very opposites to 'Cerito.' But the correct principle, in my opinion, would have been to select a dog such as 'Bedlamite,' who actually succeeded in getting 'Hopmarket,' going *somewhat* in her style, but without her excessive and almost overreaching mode of galloping; or 'David,' who, I think, would have been even more successful: in fact, to avoid the attempt to unite the two extremes in a happy middle point, which I am convinced will generally fail; but, on the contrary, to tone down superabundant action, or raise up deficient powers, by selecting a cross exhibiting a tolerably near approach to the bitch, but either a little above or below her standard, as the case may be, and which, in her instance, I think, might have been found in the stallion at the head of this chapter, if alive. The neglect of this principle is the cause, in my belief, of the many failures in breeding, not only in the first generation, but in all the subsequent ones. Nothing is more common than to see a greyhound with the fore-quarters of a thick lumpy dog, and the hind ones of a racer, or *vice versâ*.

But it is also requisite to pay attention to the twelfth section of the above abstract, which declares that the purer the blood the more likely it is to be represented in the produce. This is well exemplified in the experiments of M. Malingie on the sheep, to which I have already alluded. This gentleman, being anxious to improve the old French breed by crossing it with the English ram, found that it took several generations to effect his purpose, because the French sheep is of a much older and purer stock than the modern and improved English breed. By the time, therefore, that he had obtained the desired form, the produce inherited so much of the English constitution as to be totally unfit for the French farmer. But by breaking down the purity of the blood of the French ewes, by first of all putting them for two or three generations to French rams of as dissimilar breeds as could be found, he arrived at the following satisfactory result. On taking an ewe—the result of this French crossing, but still possessing all the peculiarities of her race, being of small size, of late maturity, and little disposition to fatten—and crossing her with a Leicester ram, the lambs at once showed the size, form, and disposition to fatten of their English sire, and yet retained the constitutional peculiarities of their dam to such an extent as to bear the climate and food of France. This experiment, therefore, goes to prove that the greater the purity (or antiquity, for in our present discussion they are synonymous terms) of the breed, the more likely it is to be represented in the cross. Consequently, a bitch of pure blood—that is to say, one bred for some generations from sires and dams of a particular breed—if put to a cross-bred dog will throw puppies resembling herself in a much greater degree than the sire, and the reverse would happen if the sire were of purer blood than the dam. This theory also explains the reason why a greyhound of mixed blood generally gets stock resembling that branch of his pedigree which is the oldest, unless overwhelmed by an unusual preponderance of other more impure or modern blood. This fact I shall again have to refer to when I come to allude to particular pedigrees. It is sufficient for my present purpose to notice the fact, and hereafter to return to the subject in considering the value of individual stallions.

No single fact in breeding is so well established as this, and yet it seems to have been totally neglected in the breeding of the greyhound, as far as I know: indeed, the ignorance of the true principles of conducting the entire management of the greyhound kennel is very remarkable, considering that the animal has been so long the pride and glory of a large body of educated men, numbering among them kings, dukes, earls, and judges of the land, and even bishops, to say nothing of inferior members of the three learned professions.

But it must be remembered, that, in searching for a particular quality in the stallion, you will often succeed if you select one who, from the very excess of that quality, was in public a very middling or inferior performer. Thus, a dog may be so fast as to overrun himself, or so venomous as to be constantly overtaxing his energies in his desire to kill; and yet such a dog will get good stock, because his progeny will seldom come up to him in these

214   GENERAL PRINCIPLES OF BREEDING.

valuable qualities, but will have exactly the proper proportion. 'King Cob'* and 'Foremost'* were both beaten as often as they were victorious, and it is notorious that they were not either of

'FIGARO.'*

them by any means good running greyhounds. 'Figaro,'* also, was what is often called an unlucky dog, and 'Jason'† was not

* See Appendix ('King Cob,' 'Czar,' and 'Figaro').
† See Appendix (Pedigree of 'Vraye Foy').

often successful. 'Jacobite,' likewise, though winning the Altcar produce stake in good style, was like 'Figaro,' an extremely wide worker, yet many of his stock have been remarkable for the opposite quality. On the other hand, 'Tyrant,' 'Senate,'* 'Sefton,' and 'Oliver Twist'* had just tact enough as runners, in which capacity they were very superior to 'Foremost' or 'King Cob,' but unfortunately they have transmitted rather too much of it to many of their descendants.

But something more yet is required than attention to the form of the individuals implicated. Every greyhound, whether dog or bitch, must be considered as a compound animal, made up of a sire and dam, also of two grandsires and granddams; and sometimes even the four great-grandsires and great-granddams must be taken into account. This is only necessary when there has been much cross-breeding, for in those cases where the same blood has been bred 'in and in' this principle does not apply. But in all dogs bred from different strains, if those strains are remarkable for opposite qualities, you are as likely to get the one extreme as the other. For instance, suppose you put a bitch to a dog got by a racing sire out of a little short-working dam, then, granting that the sire and dam were types of their families, and not exceptional cases, you are just as likely to breed a litter like the granddam as the grandsire, or perhaps more so, since I am inclined to believe that the dams and granddams have more influence on the produce than the sires and grandsires. But much would depend upon the form and blood of the bitch, since she would be most likely to

* For Pedigree, see Appendix ('Sefton'), and Thacker, vol. vii.

appropriate to herself, as it were, those particles which are most like herself and her progenitors in the compound or crossed stallion put to her. Suppose, for instance, a bitch to be composed of the blood of four different strains, which we will call A, B, C, and D: then, if put to a dog composed also of blood from four different strains, one of which was B itself, or a strain like B, but united with three others, E, F, and G, then the result would be that the produce would be more likely to inherit the characteristics of the B strain than of either A, C, D, E, F, or G. If these characteristics are desirable, the result is called 'a hit;' and it is very extraordinary how far back these 'hits' will sometimes go; the dog and bitch may not be related for six or seven generations, at which point in their pedigrees they may each own a particular dog as their progenitor, and yet their produce will appear to go back to that particular dog in preference to all the others. This fact has been very evident in crossing between rough and smooth greyhounds, in which the nature of the coat of the puppies is apparently very capricious, but really founded upon the above principle. But it is also seen in form and colour; a bitch descended from a celebrated dog will sometimes breed two or three different litters without producing one at all like him in form or other characteristics; but if put to a dog also descended from him, and perhaps totally unlike him, a litter will result resembling in form, colour, and style of going, their famous great-grandsire, or still more remote ancestor.

This I take to be the reason why 'in and in' breeding has often been so successful. Certain dogs have been conspicuous in the field for particular qualities, and have been put to the stud, and perhaps to bitches totally unlike themselves. But their sons and daughters have still, though only half of their blood, been expected to carry on the whole of their characteristics, and have consequently failed in pleasing their owner, who perhaps was wedded to the peculiarities of their sire. In order to recover those peculiarities, he has had recourse to the old stock, or a son perhaps by another bitch, and with the happiest effect; because if the sire and dam were half brother and sister, the produce would be composed as follows, viz. one-half of the grandsire whose blood is prized, and the other half made up of equal proportions of the blood of the two granddams; and the consequence would be that the half would preponderate over each of the quarters, in the proportion of two to one. This is still more clear the further the remove, since sometimes, without any *very* near breeding 'in and in,' you may succeed in obtaining two or three quarters of a particular blood, and not more than one-sixteenth or one-twenty-fourth of any other distinct and separate strain. As an illustration of this principle, though not in a very high degree, the pedigree of 'Blacklock'[*] may be taken. This celebrated flyer was composed of five-sixteenths 'Streamer' blood, four-sixteenths 'Emperor' blood, and the remainder of smaller proportions belonging to various bitches; the consequence has been that his stock have all inherited the peculiarities of 'Streamer,' and none that I ever heard of have followed those of 'Emperor,' though the balance was only as five to four. Another illustration may be afforded in the produce of

* For pedigrees, &c., of the dogs alluded to, see Appendix.

'Perseverance' (by 'Worcester Marquis' out of 'Dressmaker'). This bitch has been thrice put to 'War Eagle,' which is composed, one half of 'Foremost,' one quarter 'Marquis,' and one quarter 'Coquette.' The produce, as might have been expected, have all been, more or less, 'Marquises,' in style of going and general appearance, though with some peculiarities of form, which have almost invariably adhered to the descendants of 'Coquette,' as, for instance, the cat-like foot. Not one has resembled 'War Eagle' himself, or the 'Foremost,' or 'Bugle' blood, because they are composed of three-eighths of the 'Marquis' blood, two-eighths 'Foremost,' two-eighths 'Dressmaker,' and one-eighth 'Coquette;' and as three to two is an overwhelming preponderance, the result has been as already stated.

'CZAR.'

CHAPTER X.

PECULIAR CHARACTERISTICS OF VARIOUS STALLIONS.

Greyhounds divided into Newmarket — Wiltshire — Lancashire, Scotch, and Yorkshire Varieties. — Descriptions and examples of each.

BUT, in addition to an acquaintance with the *general* principles upon which to conduct the management of a breeding stud, it is highly desirable to be conversant with the *peculiar* characteristics of the various public stallions from which the breeder is to pick the sire of his future young hopefuls. To insure success it is necessary to study the public performance of the various breeds, and to balance the successes and failures of the animals themselves, their own immediate families, and their descendants, if any. In accordance with general custom, more than with any real division at present existing, I shall consider the greyhound as consisting of five leading varieties; though they have been so much intermixed for many years past, that scarcely any pedigree can be considered as strictly local. These four classes are—

1. The NEWMARKET, including the greyhounds used in Norfolk, Suffolk, Cambridgeshire, Essex, Bedfordshire, Huntingdonshire, and part of Lincolnshire.

2. The WILTSHIRE dog, confined chiefly to Wiltshire, Berkshire, Dorsetshire, and the Cotswold Hills.

3. The LANCASHIRE, extending over the whole of the Midland counties of England; and

4. The SCOTCH greyhound, which is sufficiently described by his name.

5. The YORKSHIRE, also defined in the same way.

The NEWMARKET GREYHOUND, of which the portrait of the ' Czar ' may be taken as a good example, though only half of Newmarket blood, is characterised by great size, immense speed, a tolerable degree of stoutness, considering their general deficiency in the back and sides, and good working powers, in proportion to their size and speed. Nothing can be finer than the galop of these dogs;

but it must be evident to every one that a racing greyhound, *cæteris paribus*, cannot work so closely as a slower animal. If, therefore, the tyro expects to find a flyer which shall be able to compete with a little, slow, close-working dog (or more especially a bitch), in running a bad hare he will find himself disappointed; that is to say, if the hare is only able to live for a few turns without having strength or heart enough to break away, and thus show to advantage the superior speed of the fast greyhound.

The greater number of the modern fashionable Newmarket greyhounds are flatsided, but the depth of chest is such as to give plenty of bellows room, and they are, therefore, not deficient in wind; but they are also narrow in the hips, so that there is usually not sufficient width of bone either in the ribs or hip to give attachment to muscles sufficient to form the 'back like a beam.' This point is of vast importance, since upon its full development depends the power of springing away again after each turn, which is so essential to success in public running; for it often happens that a dog which is very fast to his game is unable to get away from his turns, and is, therefore, easily beaten by a dog much slower when both are in full swing. The same quality is seen in the steeple-chase, in which the horse, which has such strength of back as to get away quickly from his fences, has often a vast superiority over another which may be able to beat him as easily over the flat. The head of the Newmarket dog is long and narrow, showing little intelligence, and the ears short, fine, and falling over with an elegant droop; the neck beautifully long and thin, being really 'like the neck of a drake;' shoulders often rather too upright, without the power of stooping being sufficiently marked. There is a general air of high breeding and more delicacy of constitution than is always pleasant. These dogs are magnificent in going up to their hare, and have a peculiar style of coming round when she turns, seldom attempting to stop themselves after a rush, which is often wilder than suits their owner's taste, but running as small a circle as they can contrive to turn in, and thus preserving their impetus for the next rush. By this style of running they appear to run out in their turns, but they are able to make magnificent go-byes, and thus often win their courses by a first turn, one or two go-byes and a kill, to equalise which their competitor must make ten or a dozen wrenches and turns. This style of running, however, requires the highest condition, since it is tremendously fatiguing to the dog, and this perhaps induces him sometimes to let his antagonist do a little too much in the middle of the course, by which he cuts his own throat; but when in prime order, a first-rater of this breed just out of the slips is indeed a noble sight to look upon.

Until the year 1842, there has been great difficulty in procuring the best Newmarket blood, which was carefully kept to the kennels of Lord Stradbrooke, Mr. Fyson, Captain Daintree, and a select few; but since the time of 'King Cob' and 'Fantail,' which were then thrown open to the world by Captain Daintree, we have had the following stallions at command, of pure Newmarket blood, viz. 'Foremost,' 'Figaro,' 'David Deans,' 'Mawworm,' 'Maxse,' 'Sherwood,' 'Brutus,' 'Kentish Fire,' 'Kotzebue,' 'Locomotive,' 'Sam,' 'Field Marshal,' 'Esquire' and 'Exchequer,' 'Miles,' 'Mercury,' 'Damson,' and 'Bourdeaux.' I

have not included among these the sons of 'King Cob' and
'Foremost,' which have been crossed with Wiltshire, Lancashire,
and Scotch blood, but shall mention them *seriatim*, after treating
of each of these varieties.

In the above list, 'King Cob' stands out prominently as the
sire of more *large* winners than any dog which ever ran; for though
'Foremost' produced in his best three years 113 winners to
'King Cob's' 111, yet the sons and daughters of the latter won a
much greater proportion of *large* stakes. Thus, taking the best
six years of the running of each of their immediate produce, in
the five principal thirty-two dog stakes, 'King Cob,' from 1843
to 1848, produced the winners of six, and divided two; whilst
from 1847 to 1853, 'Foremost' only produced the winner of the
Newmarket Puppy Stake twice, and the winner of the All Aged
Stake at the same place once, the performance of 'Triste' being
neutralised, as she divided the Puppy Stake with 'Trotzig,' by a son
of 'King Cob.' But, contrasting the value of the stakes won, the
difference is very great, for in opposition to these three Newmarket
performances of 'Cinneraria' and 'Tendresse,' two of which were
puppy stakes, may be adduced, 'Kizzie,' who won the Newmarket
All Aged Stake twice (the first time when a puppy)—'Probity,' who
in the following year divided the All Aged Stake with 'Dewdrop;'
'Miles' the next year dividing the same stake, and 'Amina' winning
it in 1848; and lastly, 'Magician,' who won the Waterloo Cup in the
same season. The account thus stands as follows: —'King Cob's'
stock won four of the principal thirty-two dog All Aged Stakes,
and divided two, besides winning two puppy thirty-two dog stakes
whilst 'Foremost's' stock have only won one thirty-two dog All

Aged Stake, and two thirty-two dog Puppy Stakes: in both cases, the comparison being confined to the Newmarket, Wiltshire, and Waterloo Cups. But it may be said that the performances of the second dogs in these stakes are really as good as the first, luck being taken into account; and certainly, in this view, the difference is not quite so great, though still very remarkable, since the produce of 'Foremost' have run up for these stakes five times to to 'King Cob's' twice, besides winning the Waterloo Purse twice.

But though in the first generation the stock of 'King Cob' and 'Foremost' were very nearly on an equality, since that time the former have completely eclipsed the latter. The sons and daughters of 'Figaro' alone have by far eclipsed all the stock of 'Czar,' 'War Eagle,' 'Wrestler,' and 'Staymaker' combined; while, as we come still nearer to the present time, we find 'Bedlamite,' 'Motley,' 'Field Marshal,' 'Baron,' 'David,' 'Effort,' 'The Brewer,' 'Boisterous,' 'British Tar,' 'Seagull,' 'Sam,' 'Regan,' 'Rebel,' 'Jacobite,' 'Selby,' 'Ranter,' 'The Wizard,' 'Black Adder' and 'Black Eagle,' 'Cardinal York,' 'Picton,' 'Mansoor,' 'Mechanic,' 'Windermere,' 'Railroad,' 'Paramount,' 'Kingwater,' 'Gabriel,' Colchicum,' 'Little Wonder,' 'Lapidist,' 'Ingomar,' &c. &c., all containing more or less of the blood of Captain Daintree's celebrated dog, while the male descendants of 'Foremost' which have been at all used at the stud are confined to 'The Czar,' 'War Eagle,' 'Wrestler,' 'Foremost Junior,' 'Sackcloth,' 'Staymaker,' 'Baron Garnock,' 'Lysander,' and one or two others of still less note.

The chief competitor of 'Figaro' among the stallions of

THE NEWMARKET GREYHOUND.

Newmarket blood was Mr. Gibson's 'Sam,' bred by Dr. Scott, and partaking largely of the Yorkshire strains of Mr. Grayson and Mr. Franker. He was not himself so large a dog as 'Figaro,' but

'SAM.'*

many of his stock have been of great size, and possessed more than average speed, combined with great working powers, a notable example being Mr. Gibson's 'Caledonian.' When put to bitches

* For pedigree, see Appendix.

of King Cob's blood, the cross has done well, and from him are descended in this way 'Motley,' 'Miss Hannah,' and their numberless sons and daughters, including those two first-class dogs (father and son) 'David' and 'Patent.' His portrait which accompanies these remarks is a very good one, and shows the exact shape and general character of 'Sam' remarkably well.

In the following generation 'Bedlamite' was unapproachable, eclipsing every Newmarket competitor in the successes of his stock, and indeed being the fashionable stallion of his day, which lasted longer than usual, as he lived to be eleven years old, and got stock to the last. Oddly enough, he had two grandsires of the name of 'King Cob,' one being the celebrated Newmarket dog, and the other a Nottinghamshire-bred one. The litter to which he belonged consisted of himself and five sisters, all first-rate runners and great winners. 'Bedlamite' ran only at Hornby, Ashdown and Amesbury, running his first and last courses at the first place, where he commenced by winning the Brough Cup (thirty-two dogs) in December 1851, his sister 'Bedlam Bess' being drawn in his favour. He next won the Craven Stakes at Ashdown, after which he was reserved for the Druid Cup in October 1852, where he beat a lot of first-class dogs, including 'Motley,' 'Raven,' 'Lady Dalton,' 'World's Fair,' and 'Merlin.' In the following month, however, he was for the first and only time doomed to defeat, but by no nameless hero, that first-class greyhound, 'Larriston,' having the honour of this victory. 'Bedlamite,' had not perhaps quite the flying speed of 'Figaro,' having been led by 'Merlin' at Amesbury, and by 'Larriston' at Hornby Park; but there were few dogs which could work with him, and his staying powers were undeniable. Fortunately he was never injured by running, and the coursing world are indebted to Mr. Brown for

'BEDLAMITE.' *

so soon reserving him for the stud, for which self-denial, in point of glory, however, he was soon repaid by the annuity which he received for eight or nine years from the services of 'Bedlamite.'

* For pedigree, see Appendix.

His portrait indicates particularly well the characteristic points in his conformation, which have been handed down to many of his best sons and daughters. These consist in the bent and otherwise well-developed stifles which are set on unusually widely, and in the drooping hind-quarters and somewhat arched loin. He was a grand dog in appearance, but to those who stood out for a level back his quarters were always an objection.

WILTSHIRE.*—Next on our list comes the Wiltshire greyhound, which is the very opposite of the Newmarket dog, being a small, muscular, compact animal, more like a terrier than one of Lord Stradbroke's or Mr. Fyson's kennel, but showing more speed than would be expected from his appearance, with untiring energy and great working powers, which are of a totally different style to those of the open, speedy, racing animal I have already described. From his width of chest and back, he is able to stop himself easily, and come round at any angle; and he then shoots out again like the pellet from a boy's pop-gun. By this peculiarity of form, with a short-running yet strong hare, such as are so often found in Wiltshire, he is capable of showing to great advantage; but in going through a stake, he is apt to meet with a straight-backed puss, and then he is almost sure to be put *hors de combat* by a speedier antagonist. Many of these little greyhounds, not weighing more than from 30 lbs. to 35 lbs., have won large stakes in

* The portrait of 'Cactus,' at page 202, gives a good idea of the old Wiltshire greyhound, though longer in the back than the animal herself, and though her pedigree is only composed of one-half of Wiltshire blood. I have not—I am sorry to say—been able to procure any good portrait of the pure old Wiltshire greyhound.

former days. Mr. Hole's 'Alacrity,' I believe, was not more than 28 lbs.; and 'Little Vic' and 'Magic' were not much more. The Wiltshire coursers have, however, found out that a good big dog will always and in all countries beat a good little one; but as there is much difficulty in getting a really stout dog of great size, the little one will oftener win in Wiltshire than in other countries. But it must be remembered that the Wiltshire country and the Wiltshire hares are both materially affected by the recent changes in the agricultural management of the downs. These are now much broken up, and the course is necessarily often over arable land, or even in turnips. Besides this, I am inclined to think that the superior food afforded by seeds and other green crops has enlarged the size of the hares now found on the downs, and consequently they are really faster than the old hare of the district, which was often only 5 lbs. in weight, whereas a full-grown hare of that size is now a rarity, and I have seen many, even jack hares, of 7 lbs. or 8 lbs. each. All of the Wiltshire dogs are, therefore, now crossed with the Newmarket, Lancashire, or Scotch breeds, and no stallion dog is now offered to the public of pure Wiltshire blood, nor indeed do I now know any kennel where this breed is maintained in any approach to purity.

One of the best bitches which ever ran in Wiltshire was Mr. Randell's 'Brilliant,' by 'Chieftain' out of 'Ruby,' and in her there was no old Wiltshire cross, being, on the dam's side, a niece of 'Waterloo;' but she was capable of running the Wiltshire hares in a style superior to most of the indigenous greyhounds of the day. Her form, like her dam's, was the model of symmetry and efficiency, and I have placed it in the frontispiece as the perfection of the greyhound form in the bitch. Another equally good Wiltshire bitch was of nearly double her size, and also of blood extraneous to Wiltshire itself, though belonging to the same district: I allude to Mr. Long's 'Lizzie,' by 'Billy go by 'em,' a bitch whose running on the downs was equal, if not superior, to her old antagonist 'Mocking Bird,' with whom she stands on an equality in their individual contests, each having once defeated the other.

LANCASHIRE.*—Intended for a totally different country to that of Newmarket or Wiltshire, the Lancashire greyhound has been bred exclusively for the plains of Altcar and Lytham, and those of Lincolnshire and Cheshire. Here it is only necessary that the dog shall be fast to his game; but he must also be high enough on his legs to see it while running at one hundred yards' distance, and up to his elbows in high stubble, as is often the case at Lytham. Much has, therefore, been sacrificed to size and speed, even more than at Newmarket; and, as the judge is generally unable to follow the course on horseback, the first part is often all that is seen by him, and then when it lasts for more than a mile, as it often does at Lytham and Altcar, the exhibition of stoutness is thrown away. Still I am bound to confess that many Lancashire greyhounds have shown a fair amount of stoutness of late years; but I cannot help thinking that this quality has been more attended to, since the improvement in drainage has made the

* The portrait of 'Blacklock' will be found at page 1, and those of 'Cerito,' 'Dressmaker,' and 'Titania,' at pages 178, 191, and 192, of pure Lancashire blood; while that of 'Riot,' at page 197, is Lancashire combined with Newmarket blood.

hares of this district more sound, than it was formerly, when a run up a wrench or two, and a kill, formed the average Lancashire course, and when a tremendously long slip was essential to produce a tolerable trial. In any case it cannot be denied that the Lancashire dog has been generally triumphant on his own peculiar ground, and the success of 'Cerito' alone, in having thrice won the Waterloo Cup, must stamp this strain as well fitted for the plains of Altcar. Since the year 1842, when public stallions were first advertised,* the most successful Lancashire coursers have abandoned the pure blood of 'Streamer,' 'Sandy,' and 'Senate,' and have had recourse to extraneous sources to supply their places, as in 'Staymaker,' 'Cinderella,' 'Britomart,' 'War Eagle,' 'Movement,' and 'Raven,' in which the Lancashire greyhound has been crossed with that of 'Foremost;' in 'Neville' and 'St. Godric,' in which it has been united with Mr. Goodlake's 'Gracchus;' and in 'British Lion' and 'Capacity,' &c., with 'Kentish Fire.' The Wiltshire and Newmarket blood, as united in 'Czar' and 'Forward,' also produced, with the Lancashire, some first-rate stock, as in 'Celeste' and 'Saucy One.' But it is to the judicious crossing practised by Mr. Borron and Mr. Campbell that we must look for the breeding of the best dogs in Lancashire within the last ten years. Mr. Jefferson's 'Judge,' and Lord Sefton's 'Skyrocket,' are, I think, the only successful stallions of pure Lancashire blood which have been used between 1850 and 1860. The former certainly has done excellent services, being with his brother in blood

* In the 25th volume of the 'Racing Calendar' there is an advertisement of the stallion greyhound 'Rex.' This was in the year 1826, and is, I believe, the first on record.

'Sunbeam,' perhaps the two best running *dogs* on this ground of their day, and Mr. Jefferson's not only getting good stock out of Lancashire bitches, but also combining well with the Newmarket strains, as in 'Jacobite' and his descendants, and also in

'CHLOE.' *

'Clive,' joint winner of the Waterloo Cup, 'Lady Java,' and 'Impératrice.' His daughter 'Chloe,' who combines her Lanca-

* For pedigree of this bitch, &c., see Appendix.

shire blood with the Scotch, Newmarket, and Wiltshire strains, seen in the pedigree of his dam, has been the most successful bitch over Altcar since the time of 'Cerito,' having won the Waterloo Cup in 1863, and the Altcar Club Cup twice.

'Skyrocket,' though not coming up to 'Judge' in getting winners, has been very useful, and his daughter 'Sampler,' albeit less lucky than 'Chloe' in winning the Waterloo Cup, has twice narrowly missed that much-coveted prize, and would by many good judges be considered the superior animal of the two. Lord Sefton's dog has also got stouter stock than 'Judge,' some of them being perfect gluttons, as for instance 'Sweetbriar' and 'Sapphire.' 'Senate,' bred by the late Earl of Sefton, has left his mark in the kennel of the present lord, and in that of Mr. Jones, whose 'Junta' was by him; he was also sire of 'Wanton,' the dam of 'David,' so that his name must not be omitted. Still it is to the union of Mr. Borron's 'Beacon' with Mr. Campbell's 'Scotland Yet,' that we must look for the great run of victories achieved by 'Canaradzo,' 'Coorooran,' 'Sea Foam,' 'Sea Pink,' and 'King Death;' and as 'Beacon' can also claim to be the sire of another Waterloo Cup winner in 'Roaring Meg,' his fame is not in that instance shared with Mr. Campbell's bitch. I must therefore offer his portrait as that of the most successful stallion in Lancashire of late years, though only half of Lancashire blood, the remainder being Scotch.

There can be little doubt that the speed of the old Lancashire greyhound was very great, perhaps even greater than that of our modern dogs; but if we look at the hind-quarters of 'Blacklock,' whose portrait is the only one left sufficiently well executed to be depended on, we shall see that there is not enough power in the back and thighs to maintain the speed. Nothing can be more

'BEACON.' *

beautiful than the fore-quarters of this dog, and with the head of a 'Jason,' and the hind-quarter of a 'King Cob,' perfection in the greyhound might be anticipated. But though, with his low hocks

* For pedigree, see Appendix.

and long thighs, he could get fast to his hare, it is scarcely possible for such a conformation to enable a dog to 'go on,' nor should I expect it with such a tall weak form as he is shown to have possessed. Besides this, his muscular development must have been generally low, since he only weighed 53 lbs., though standing 26 inches high, whilst 'Mocking Bird,' standing very little, if at all, higher, and a bitch, weighed more than 60 lbs. I have seen a very fast son of his, of the same shape too, burst himself, and reduce his pace to a canter, in little more than three hundred yards. 'Senate' and 'Oliver Twist,' when united with 'Emperor,' 'Streamer,' or 'Bachelor' blood, and more especially when good Newmarket strains have been superimposed, seem to have been useful. To the former class belongs 'Judge,' while in the latter may be included the greater part of Lord Sefton's kennel, 'Riot,' 'David,' and 'Jacobite,' *cum multis aliis*. But to 'Bugle,' and his sister 'Stave,' in combination with 'Streamer,' most of the best Lancashire greyhounds of the present day may be traced; and from this source come 'Beacon' and 'Blackcloud,' to which dogs I have already alluded. On the other hand, 'Senate' when put to bitches of strains not remarkable for true running has done no good, and the best running dog thus bred, Mr. Jones's 'Junta,' has proved to be a source of great mischief, which not even the care and judgment of Amos Ogden has been able to neutralise.

The Scotch Greyhound was brought to great perfection by Dr. Brown, 'Lord' Eglinton, Mr. A. Graham, Mr. Sharpe, Sir Jas. Boswell, Mr. Wilson, Mr. Jardine, and Mr. Gibson. It can scarcely be considered as a distinct variety, for its sub-varieties are as numerous as the names of the above gentlemen, and even more so, since I have been obliged to omit several who have almost

'DAVID.'

equal claims to our notice. Of the above sub-varieties Dr. Brown's dogs were perhaps the most distinct, and among them ' Heather Jock ' was in himself a host, both as a winner, and as the sire of numerous successful litters. His peculiarity of ears, which he transmitted to many of his descendants, was always against his appearance; but there can be no doubt that he was a first-class

'MONARCH.'

greyhound, as were also his progeny, 'Rufus,' 'Bessy Bell,' &c. Lord Eglinton's name has only to be mentioned, in order to conjure up the *names* of 'Waterloo,'* a wonderful runner, but

* I much regret that I am unable to give portraits of 'Waterloo,' 'Heather Jock,' and other Scotch dogs.

238 PECULIAR CHARACTERISTICS OF VARIOUS STALLIONS.

apparently not capable of transmitting his prowess to his progeny. Mr. A. Graham's fame cannot so clearly be traced to any one particular dog, but a long list of victories must be accorded to

'HUGHIE GRAHAM.'

him; most of his celebrities have been more or less crossed with the old rough greyhound. Mr. William Sharpe's 'Monarch' will always connect his name with the early dogs of coursing, and his 'Hughie Graham' with the generation just past; but the first is of pure English blood, and the second very nearly so; and, what is very remarkable, they were both fawns, though of different shades, of entirely different blood, and certainly of totally opposite forms. No shape can be conceived, in my opinion, more efficient than that of 'Monarch;' and by a reference to the list of his stock, it will be seen that their successes correspond with this opinion. 'Liddesdale,' sire of 'Hughie Graham,' was also sire of Mr. Henderson's 'Larriston,' one of the best greyhounds that ever ran, and successful as a stallion, being sire of 'Effort,' 'The Brewer,' and Woodman,' all well-known stallions in the South. But if the above dogs are to be connected with the names of their respective owners, that of 'Jason' must not be mentioned without the name of Sir James Boswell, who may well be proud of his descendants, if not of the dog himself: he also is in great measure of English blood.

Most of the true Scotch dogs are a little wider across the ears than is *often* seen in the South, and possess more destructiveness in proportion, though perhaps a little more intellect with it than is desirable. They very soon enter to their game, and require very little practice before being perfect in their parts. They are very hardy, and have not that bareness of hair about the cheeks and thighs which the high-bred English greyhound so often displays. They run with great fire and speed in their puppyhood, but soon learn to take liberties if used too often or too long. They do not run slack like the Lancashire, it is true, but they soon begin to 'cheek' their hare and worry her to death, instead of driving her with that venom which we all like to see. This is particularly the case with those descended from Dr. Brown's 'Chance' through 'Heather Jock,' 'Haphazard,' and 'Rufus,' and also in those which claim his dog 'Sport' as their progenitor—viz. 'Jamie Forest' and 'Bravo.' Lord Eglinton's and Mr. A. Graham's kennels have been so intermixed with the Newmarket and Lancashire blood, that they can scarcely be said to be true Scotch; and the old rough greyhound is nearly extinct as a public performer, while indeed the genuine Scotch greyhound is almost equally extinct.

Lastly. The YORKSHIRE greyhound must be alluded to as a distinct breed, though, like the others I have mentioned, he is now nearly extinct. He might perhaps more properly be denominated the 'North Country' dog, as he is not confined to Yorkshire, but the breed extends to Cumberland, Northumberland, and indeed to all the northern counties. I know very little of the history of this variety, but anyone who has seen 'Young Cedric,' 'Dalton,' 'Assault,' or 'Rattler' fifteen years ago, or 'Black Cap' more recently, will be satisfied that they are as distinct as the Lancashire from the Scotch or Newmarket breeds. Their chief peculiarity in appearance resides in the head, which is very long with a tendency to a Roman nose. Their speed is very great: indeed, I believe 'Dalton,' 'Assault,' and 'Young Cedric' to have been as fast as anything I ever saw run. In working powers they are perhaps inferior to the Lancashire, and their stoutness has always been disputed, even their best supporters being obliged to be silent on that score. At present I believe there is no public kennel of any high form in which this breed is kept up, with the exception of Mr. Thompson's, whose 'Truth' was remarkable for stoutness, as is perhaps her sister 'Tirzah,' but it is common enough among the local coursers who patronise the north-country meetings.

SUMMARY.

SUCH are the chief varieties from which the public greyhound of the present day is descended; for, as I before remarked, very few are left in their original purity. Since the death of 'Judge' no Lancashire sire of any note has remained, 'Skyrocket,' and indeed all of Lord Sefton's breeding, being more or less crossed with Scotch or Newmarket strains. It is useless therefore to make a selection from these five breeds, as they cannot be said to exist, and the young public courser must now look to individuals, or at all events to particular kennels. Taking public running as a guide, there can be no doubt that 'Bedlamite' has been the most fortunate in getting winners, and his descendants should therefore be chosen, taking care that his good qualities are not neutralised by crosses with inferior blood. But with the exception of 'Jacobite' (also dead), none of his sons seem to have done much service at the stud— 'Ranter,' 'Gipsy Prince,' 'The Wizard, 'Black Adder,' and 'Black Eagle,' having been put to many excellent bitches without getting anything of very superior form. His blood is perpetuated however in the following public stallions, either on the dam's side or on that of the sire's, viz. 'Cardinal York,' 'Picton,' 'The Wizard,'

'Kingwater,' 'Forester,' 'Regan,' 'Referree,' 'Seagull,' 'Spencer,' 'Gipsy Prince,' and 'Gipsy Royal,' 'Ranter,' 'Rienzi,' 'Railroad,' 'Effort,' 'The Brewer,' 'Derry,' 'Rebel,' 'Ringleader,' 'Windermere,' 'Bosphorus,' 'Bright Chanticleer,' 'Ajax,' 'Blackadder,' 'Baffler,' 'Buckshorn,' and 'General Havelock.' From 'Figaro,' through other dams than 'Bessy Bedlam,' come 'Lablache,' and 'Little Wonder,' 'Mechanic' (son of 'Mocking Bird'), 'Jeffrey,' and 'Ingomar' (son and grandson of 'Mœris'), and 'Belligerent' (through 'Weapon,' another son of 'Figaro'), besides some others whose names do not occur to me. Going still further back to 'King Cob,' we have 'David' and his sons 'Lapidist,' 'Little Wonder,' 'Gabriel,' and 'Colchicum,' and no doubt 'Patent' as soon as he has had another spin for the Waterloo Cup. 'Little Wonder' has three lines of 'King Cob,' adding one through 'Figaro' to the two in 'David,' obtained from 'Sam,' and 'Tollwife.' It will thus be seen that there is plenty of 'King Cob' blood in the market, and that there are few stallions at the service of the public without one or more lines of his blood. As our public greyhounds are thus rendered nearly all of the same breed—for the descendants of 'King Cob' and those of 'Beacon' and 'Scotland Yet' comprise a very large proportion of them,—there is not now the chance of any one strain distinguishing itself, as happened when 'King Cob' and 'Foremost,' followed by 'Figaro' and 'Bedlamite,' made their appearance as public sires, and carried nearly all before them in their respective days. Besides these strains, there are some few descendants of Sir Jas. Boswell's 'Jason' through 'Vraye Foy' and 'The Curler,' but

SUMMARY. 243

though for a time this blood seemed likely to rival that of 'Figaro' and 'Foremost,' it has now nearly died out in the male line—'Colchicum' (son of 'The Cure' by 'Lopez') being the only sire advertised in England, and 'Murder,' another son of that dog, in Ireland. Mr. Price's 'Patent' is however descended from him on the female side, as also is Mr. Lister's 'Chloe,' the former being a great grandson of 'Egypt,' and the latter a grand-daughter of 'Lopez,' which two dogs were sons of 'Vraye Foy.' Add to these the true Lancashire blood of 'Judge' and 'Skyrocket,' and the combination of Lancashire and Scotland in 'Beacon' and 'Blackcloud,' and the list is nearly exhausted.

It appears therefore that most of our best, or at all events of our most fashionable, modern sires, are descended from 'King Cob,' either through 'Figaro' and 'Kentish Fire' in the male lines, or through 'Sam,' who was a grandson on the female side. Next to these strains come the Scotch lines of 'Waterloo,' 'Monarch' and 'Bowhill,' exhibited in 'Scotland Yet,' 'Beacon' and 'Blackcloud,' and in the descendants of 'Larriston' through 'Effort,' 'The Brewer' and 'Woodman.' The success of 'Weapon,' chiefly through 'Pugilist,' as shown in 'Belligerent' and 'Emilia,' may also be attributed to the combination of 'Figaro' and 'Waterloo' blood, 'Ruby,' the dam of 'Weapon,' being by 'Moses,' brother to 'Waterloo.' Beyond the variously combined strains of these dogs, it would be scarcely safe for the young courser to go; in proof of which it may be alleged that for some years past no large stake has been won by a greyhound bred in any other way. 'Judge' and 'Beacon,' with the aid of 'Skyrocket' and 'Junta,' have monopolised the Waterloo Cup and the chief Lancashire stakes; while 'King Cob' 'Larriston,' 'Skyrocket,' or 'Blackcloud,' may be credited, either directly or indirectly, with all the large stakes in the south.

It is not, however, to be supposed that the above named greyhounds are the only ones which I should select—since I consider that one brother is nearly as good as another for the purpose of getting stock, until proved otherwise; for, after trial, the matter is totally different. No one can say of two brothers or sisters which shall produce the best litter: indeed very often the worst runner of a family begets the best descendants. And, therefore, as it would be absurd to do more than suggest the principles which should guide the selection, I have not gone into an extended list. But with these broad outlines the young breeder, after obtaining his brood bitch, may easily take upon himself to select the particular dog which he will cross her with; and after all that may be written or said, that choice must to a certain extent be considered a lottery, since the utmost efforts of the most successful have too often ended in disappointment.

In the preceding remarks on the choice of a stallion, I have been supposing the breeder to have selected a bitch of some one of the above breeds, possessing the properties I have alluded to; but with regard to the choice of the stallion for the particular breeds from which I have advised him to choose his brood bitch, the task is much more difficult. The only safe plan is the following: viz. to consider the bitch herself, both individually and as connected with her family. Then to select such a stallion as shall not only suit her individually, but whose blood is likewise suitable, and, if possible, one whose blood has made 'a hit' in some litter, the produce of a bitch collaterally allied to the one in question. Then again, he must consider whether her blood is very pure and unmixed, or whether she is much crossed with other breeds. If the former, nothing but an equally pure stallion will have much effect; whilst, if crossed, care must be taken that she is not put to a very pure greyhound, unless it is wished to obtain all his peculiarities rather than to retain hers. It is often the case that a much-crossed bitch will answer best if put to a good and pure stallion dog, because the produce will almost entirely resemble him; but if the bitch can be procured of unexceptionable blood, it is better to depend upon her producing her own likeness, and then to find a stallion as like her in all her good points as possible, and as pure in blood. The result of this would be that the produce would be like both parents, and would inherit all their good qualities.

'VRAYE FOY.'

CHAPTER XI.

Advantages or otherwise of the Bulldog Cross—Best Age of Sire and Dam —Table of the Ages of the Sires and Dams of the Winners and Runners up of the Six principal Stakes run in England during the last Ten Years.

BULLDOG CROSS.

THERE is still one point which must be considered in the selection of the cross, namely, whether it is advisable or not to use those breeds which are notoriously crossed with the bulldog. In the early days of public coursing, Lord Orford, Lord Rivers, Mr. Etwall, Mr. Raimes, Sir James Boswell and Mr. Fyson all adopted this cross, and their example was followed in more recent times by Mr. Lawrence, who, like Mr. Etwall with ' Egypt,' used his brother ' Lopez' at the stud with success. These two dogs had a double strain of the bulldog, taking one through their sire ' Vraye Foy,' who was twelve removes from the bulldog, and another from their dam ' Elf,' the ninth in descent from that breed. But though ten years ago it looked as if the stock of ' Vraye Foy ' would rival that of ' Figaro ' and ' Foremost,' yet it is now apparent that the son of ' King Cob ' has almost extinguished them both, and that the bull- dog strains exhibited in ' The Czar,' ' Egypt,' and ' Lopez,' have not been so successful as I formerly anticipated. ' Blue Hat,' ' Patent,' and ' Chloe,' are the three best modern instances of greyhounds in which the bulldog cross is exhibited, and they all possess it very remotely, the first getting it through the ' Czar,' who was descended from Mr. Etwall's ' Eurus,' on the side of his dam, the second from ' Egypt,' and the third from ' Lopez'—these three, however, speak strongly in favour of the strain; but Mr. Hanley, of the 1st Life Guards, who has persevered in trying the experiment to the sixth remove, has as yet done nothing to show its advantage. Commencing with a granddaughter of ' King Cob,' which he put to ' Chicken,' a thoroughbred bulldog, he has successively put the produce to ' Blunder ' and ' Preston,' bred by himself, but without very illustrious parentage; then to ' Bedlamite ' and ' Brightsteel,' and since then to his dog ' His Grace,' but as yet the produce have shown none of the properties of a first class greyhound, except in appearance, one of them, 'His Excellency,' having taken the first prize at the dog show held at Islington in May 1864. It may be alleged that there has not yet been sufficient time to test the experiment, or that Mr. Hanley was unfortunate in selecting his early greyhound crosses, and this latter point may probably have had something to do with his failure, if such is to be the result of so much pains and expense; but certainly as yet the produce have not come up even to the form exhibited by the dog which he used. At present, therefore, the experiment may be considered a failure, but there is no knowing what indefatigable perseverance may accomplish. My own belief is that the bulldog cross developes the animal courage, and that it also somewhat increases the mental faculties, so that the dog is inclined to run cunning but not slack. This point should therefore be considered; but as I fancy it will be found that the increase of jealousy and courage will almost always overpower the tendency to lurch, the advantages will more than counterbalance the disadvantages to the public courser. I am inclined to believe that the bulldog cross will in most cases prevent a greyhound from running well through more than two seasons. The puppy has more tact, and soon comes to his best; but that state is not so long maintained, for as soon as he becomes careless of his game, and finds that he has no difficulty in killing, he loses his zest more rapidly than the true-bred greyhound. I much doubt, therefore, whether this cross is so well adapted to private coursing, or to the use of those who expect their dogs to run through as many seasons as 'Sandy,' 'Emperor,' or 'Cerito' have done. To those who are contented with two seasons, the blood of those above mentioned is, I believe, the best now out, and may be resorted to with the greatest confidence.

BEST AGE IN THE SIRE AND DAM.

The next point to consider is, the best age to breed from, both in the sire and dam. This, like the last, is a much-vexed question, and in order to settle it I constructed the following table ten years ago, which gives the ages, as far as I could ascertain them, of the sires and dams of the first and second dogs in the five principal thirty-two dog stakes run in England in the ten previous, and also the first dogs in the Waterloo purse and Altcar stakes. In this table, therefore, you have the ages of the sires and dams of four of the most successful dogs in each of the three chief coursing districts in England during the ten years between 1843 and 1853. In the earlier years there are some deficiencies, but still we have the age of the sires of one hundred and thirteen dogs, and that of the dams of ninety-eight, which numbers are quite sufficient for the purpose in view.

Nothing is so likely to lead to error as the attempt to generalise from too small a number of facts, and there would also be a great objection to any *selection* of examples of good dogs got by their sires at particular ages, since we know how prone we all are to form a theory upon insufficient data, and then to support it by cooking up examples telling in its favour. To avoid these errors, and with a view to get at the real state of the case, the table was constructed at the cost of some hours, in searching the back volumes of Thacker, and in corresponding with those who would be likely to give me the information sought. The result will I hope be considered sufficient to settle the question in a satisfactory manner.

Stake and Year when won or run up for	Names of Winners		Names of their Sires		Names of their Dams		Age of Sire when got	Age of Dam when got
Season 1843-4.								
Druid Cup	Spring	1841	Glider	1836	Snail	1837	5	4
Ditto, run up	Billy go by'em	1841	Stumptail	1830	Mirth	1835	11	6
Great Western	Crape	1842	Lopez		Bombazine.			
Ditto, run up	Blue Banner	1842	Valparaiso		Black Bess.			
Newmarket, All Ages	Kizzie (pup)	1842	King Cob.	1838	Bashful	1835	4	7
Ditto, run up	Saffron	1841	Blucher		Zinc.			
Newmarket Puppy Stakes	Kotzebue	1842	King Cob.	1838	Kathleen	1839	4	3
Ditto, run up	Traveller	1842	Charles XII.	1839	Madame	1839	3	3
Waterloo Cup	Speculation	1841	Sandy	1838	Enchantress	1838	3	3
Ditto, run up	Dressmaker	1841	Hector	1835	Lill	1835	6	6
Waterloo Purse	Rowena	1841	Exciseman	1839	Lovely		2	
Altcar Stakes	Cantrip	1841	Waterloo	1838	Clara	1839	3	2
Season 1844-5.								
Druid Cup	Nell	1842	Ion		Theon			
Ditto, run up	Benevolence	1842						
Great Western	Agitation	1843	Emperor	1837	Mavourneen	1840	6	3
Ditto, run up	Walburga	1843	Waterloo (W's)	1841	Gip		2	
Newmarket, All Ages	Kizzie	1842	King Cob.	1838	Bashful	1835	4	7
Ditto, run up	Farmer	1842	Kenwigs	1837	Fairy	1839	5	3
Newmarket Puppy Stakes	Knabella	1843	King Cob.	1838	Knab	1839	5	4
Ditto, run up	Golden Crocus	1843	Fantail	1839	Crucifix	1839	4	4
Waterloo Cup	Titania	1842	Driver	1835	Zoo	1839	7	3
Ditto, run up	Sherwood	1853	Kenwigs	1837	Sarah		6	
Waterloo Purse	Screw	1842	My Lord	1836	Princess Royal	1840	6	2
Altcar Stakes	Kizzie	1842	King Cob.	1838	Bashful	1835	4	7
Season 1845-6.								
Druid Cup	Regina Victoria	1843	Westwind	1839	World's End	1840	4	3
Ditto, run up	Fly (Holes)	1843						
Great Western	Pilgrim	1844	Glider	1836	Proserpine		8	
Ditto, run up	Fan	1844	Marquis (S's.)	1842	Fly (Powney's)	1842	2	2
Newmarket All Ages	Probity	1844	King Cob.	1838	Kate	1839	6	5
Ditto, run up	Dewdrop.							
Newmarket Puppy Stakes	Seidlitz (late Fan)	1844	Marquis	1842	Fly (sister to Nell)	1842	2	2
Ditto, run up	Figaro	1844	King Cob.	1838	Frederica	1839	6	5
Waterloo Cup	Harlequin	1842	Emperor	1837	Lady		5	

BEST AGE IN THE SIRE AND DAM.

Stake and Year when won or run up for	Names of Winners	Names of their Sires	Names of their Dams	Age of Sire when got	Age of Dam when got
Season 1845-6.					
Waterloo Cup, run up	Oliver Twist . 1844	Sadek . . . 1840	Sanctity . . 1839	4	5
Waterloo Purse . . .	Derwent . . . 1843	Priam . . . 1839	Beauty . .	4	
Altcar Stakes	Original . . . 1844	Hyson . . . 1839	Empress . . 1837	5	7
Season 1846-7.					
Druid Cup	Magic 1844	Marquis . . 1842	Fly (sister to Nell) . . 1842	2	2
Ditto, run up	Bessy Bell . . 1844	Heather Jock 1840	Blackbird . 1840	4	4
Great Western . . .	Auchinleck . . 1845	Jason . . . 1841	Rosebud . . 1839	4	6
Ditto, run up	Juverna . . . 1845	Fop 1843	Swallow . .	2	
	Magic 1844	Marquis . . 1842	Fly	2	
Newmarket, All Ages	Highland Lassie 1842	Chieftain . . 1839	Flora M'Donald 1839	3	3
Ditto, run up . . .	Miles 1844	King Cob . . 1838	Minerva . . 1839	6	5
	Mawworm . . 1844	Musquito . . 1838	Midsummer . 1838	6	6
Newmarket Puppy Stakes	Daisy 1845	Defiance . . 1840	Here I am again 1842	5	3
Ditto, run up	Thoresway Lass 1845	Chieftain . . 1839	Fancy . . . 1842	6	3
Waterloo Cup	Senate . . . 1844	Sadek . . . 1840	Sanctity . . 1839	4	5
Ditto, run up	Flirt 1843	Marquis (Webb's) . 1839	Coquette . . 1840	4	3
Waterloo Purse . . .	Harriet (Hampsen's) . . . 1845	Hotspur (*his*)	Handy (*his*).		
Altcar Stakes	Tricksey . . . 1844	Scythian . . 1842	Zoe 1839	2	5
Season 1847-8.					
Druid Cup	Wildfire . . . 1845	Waterloo (W's.) 1841	Whirlwind . 1842	4	3
Ditto, run up . . .	Lord George . 1845	Billy go by'em 1841	Orange . . 1841	4	4
Great Western . . .	Merry Lass . . 1845	Kotzebue . . 1841	Lady . . .	5	
Ditto, run up . . .	King Canute . 1846	Jason . . . 1841	Queen . . .	5	
Newmarket, All Ages	Fire Office . . 1845	Cecrops . . . 1838	Perfection . 1841	7	4
Ditto, run up	Daisy 1845	Defiance . . 1840	Here I am again 1842	5	3
Newmarket Puppy Stakes	Cinneraria . . 1845	Foremost . . 1841	Faith . . . 1842	5	4
Ditto, run up . . .	Cactus . . . 1846	Marquis (S.'s.) 1842	Spotless . . 1843	4	3
Waterloo Cup	Shade 1846	Nonchalance 1842	Margery . . 1839	4	7
Ditto, run up	Smut 1846	Sam 1844	Lucy . . .	2	
Waterloo Purse . . .	Tom Bowling . 1845	Tom Tough . 1843	Titania . . 1842	2	3
Altcar Stakes	Blueskin . . . 1845	Snowball . . 1841	Scut . . .		
Season 1848-9.					
Druid Cup	Royalist . . . 1846	Marquis . . 1842	Spotless . . 1843	4	3
Ditto, run up	Czar 1846	Foremost . . 1841	Catch'em . . 1843	5	3
Great Western . . .	Brilliant . . . 1847	Chieftain . . 1839	Ruby . . . 1842	8	5
Ditto, run up	Leeway . . . 1847	Westwind . . 1839	Laura . . . 1842	8	5
Newmarket, All Ages	Amina . . . 1846	King Cob . . 1838	Kate . . . 1839	8	7
Ditto, run up	Roulette (pup) 1847	Young Cecrops 1843	Win if I can 1841	4	6
Newmarket Puppy Stakes	Locomotive . . 1847	Son of Musquito 1846	Wideawake . 1843	1	4
Ditto, run up	Turquoise . . 1847	King Cob . . 1838	Madró . . 1842	9	5
Waterloo Cup	Magician . . . 1846	King Cob . . 1838	Magic . . . 1841	8	5
Ditto, run up	Forward . . . 1846	Foremost . . 1841	Catch'em . . 1843	5	3
Waterloo Purse . . .	Duke 1846	Squire . . . 1842	Agitation . . 1843	4	3
Altcar Stakes	Crenoline . . 1846	Senate . . . 1844	Brenda . . 1836	2	10
Season 1849-50.					
Druid Cup	Fan 1847	King Cob . . 1838	Nell 1842	9	5
Ditto, run up	Bridesmaid . . 1846	Briton . . . 1841	Lady . . . 1841	5	5
Great Western . . .	Achilles . . . 1848	Marquis . . 1842	Fly (Holes) . 1843	6	5
Ditto, run up	Alacrity . . .	. . . . .	. . . . .	6	5

BEST AGE IN THE SIRE AND DAM.

Stake and Year when won or run up for	Names of Winners		Names of their Sires		Names of their Dams		Age of Sire when got	Age of Dam when got
Season 1849-50.								
Newmarket, All Ages	Bridesmaid	1846	King Cob	1838	Here I am again	1842	8	4
Ditto, run up	Rattler	1847	Velox	1840	Alice		7	
Newmarket Puppy Stakes	Renown	1848	Rocket	1846	Spotless	1843	2	5
Ditto, run up	Pathfinder	1848	David Deans	1842	Pamela	1844	6	4
Waterloo Cup	Cerito	1848	Lingo	1845	Wanton	1842	3	6
Ditto, run up	Neville	1848	Scot	1842	Grace	1845	6	3
Waterloo Purse	Well I never	1847	Foremost	1841	Flirt	1843	6	4
Altcar Stakes	Lady Mary	1847	Highflyer	1844	Mayflower	1844	3	3
Season 1850-1.								
Druid Cup	Ebb	1848	Westwind	1839	Enford Lass	1845	9	3
Ditto, run up	Compact	1847	Cataract	1843	Countess	1842	4	5
Great Western	Puzzle'em	1849	Jason	1841	Puzzle	1845	8	4
Ditto, run up	The Nailer	1849	Caliban	1844	Judy		5	
Newmarket, All Ages	Mocking Bird	1848	Figaro	1844	Malvina	1843	4	5
Ditto, run up	Merchant	1848	Figaro	1844			4	
Newmarket Puppy Stakes.	Trotzig	1849	Figaro	1844	Twilight	1845	5	4
Ditto	Triste	1849	Foremost	1841	Madré	1842	8	7
Waterloo Cup	Hughie Graham	1849	Liddesdale	1845	Queen of the Way	1844	4	5
Ditto, run up	Staymaker	1848	Foremost	1841	Dressmaker	1841	7	7
Waterloo Purse	Wicked Eye	1847	Foremost	1841	Flirt	1843	6	4
Altcar Stakes	Dalton	1848	Spanker	1843	Lady Easby	1844	5	4
Season 1851-2.								
Druid Cup	Mocking Bird	1848	Figaro	1844	Malvina	1843	4	5
Ditto, run up	Merry Lass	1847	Foremost	1841	Fly	1843	6	4
Great Western	Impudence	1850	Czar	1846	Pink Eye	1847	4	3
Ditto, run up	Rhoda	1850	Foremost	1841	Ruby	1842	9	8
Newmarket, All Ages	Dunkeld	1849	Doron	1842	Destiny	1843	7	6
Ditto, run up	Jester	1849	King Cob	1838	Edith	1846	11	3
Newmarket Puppy Stakes	Tendresse	1850	Foremost	1841	Madré	1842	9	8
Ditto, run up	Bedlam Bess	1850	Figaro	1844	Bessy Bedlam	1846	6	4
Waterloo Cup	Cerito	1848	Lingo	1845	Wanton	1842	3	6
Ditto, run up	Larriston	1850	Liddesdale	1845	Hannah	1845	5	5
Waterloo Purse	Neville	1848	Scot	1842	Grace	1845	6	3
Altcar Stakes	Lopez	1849	Vraye Foy	1845	Elf	1847	4	2
	Cricketer	1849	Old Nick	1838	Castle		11	
Season 1852-3.								
Druid Cup	Bedlamite	1850	Figaro	1844	Bessy Bedlam	1846	6	4
Ditto, run up	Merlin	1850	Czar	1846	Havoc	1843	4	7
Great Western	Miss Hannah	1851	Sam	1847	Tollwife	1847	4	4
Ditto, run up	Whirlwind	1851	Gaper (Burgess')		Haidée (Hill)			
Newmarket, All Ages	Tendresse	1850	Foremost	1841	Madré	1842	9	8
Ditto, run up	Bona Dea	1849	Snowball		Wish you may got it	1844		5
Newmarket Puppy Stakes	Trafalgar	1851	Miles	1844	Twilight	1845	7	6
Ditto, run up	Thyme						7	6
Waterloo Cup	Cerito	1848	Lingo	1845	Wanton	1842	3	6
Ditto, run up	Movement	1849	Foremost	1841	Fairy	1843	8	6
Waterloo Purse	Miss Hannah	1851	Sam	1847	Tollwife	1847	4	4
Altcar Stakes	Zurich	1851	Liddesdale	1845	Bride	1849	6	2

BEST AGE IN THE SIRE AND DAM.

TABLE II.

Number got by Sires at	1 year		Number produced by Dams at	1 year	
,, ,,	2 ,,	12	,, ,, ,,	2 ,,	7
,, ,,	3 ,,	8	,, ,, ,,	3 ,,	25
,, ,,	4 ,,	30	,, ,, ,,	4 ,,	20
,, ,,	5 ,,	17	,, ,, ,,	5 ,,	21
,, ,,	6 ,,	20	,, ,, ,,	6 ,,	12
,, ,,	7 ,,	7	,, ,, ,,	7 ,,	9
,, ,,	8 ,,	9	,, ,, ,,	8 ,,	3
,, ,,	9 ,,	6	,, ,, ,,	9 ,,	0
,, ,,	10 ,,	0	,, ,, ,,	10 ,,	1
,, ,,	11 ,,	3	,, ,, ,,	11 ,,	0
		113			98

From this table it results that four years is the best age for the sire, and three for the dam; and what is very remarkable, both the dog and bitch seem suddenly to arrive at their best at each of these ages, since in the dog the second year seems to be better than the third, in which year only eight were begotten by their sires, and in the second year of the bitch only seven of the whole number were whelped; after the third year in the dog, and the second in the bitch, the numbers suddenly increase in the dog to thirty and in the bitch to twenty-five, and then very gradually fall off for three years in each, when the change is again sudden, and then gradually falls off as before for three years, after which a very limited number were produced. So that in round numbers it would appear that, rejecting the first year of puppyhood, the dog's productive age may be divided into three cycles of years of three each, the first and last of which are comparatively bad and the middle one only to be relied on. In the bitch very nearly the same rule applies, but she seems to come to her best one year earlier.

This result of statistical inquiry is in entire opposition to Mr. Thacker's theory, which was that the great proportion of good dogs were begotten by old sires, and out of old dams; and it shows the folly of jumping to conclusions, and of suiting your facts to preconceived theories, as we most of us are too apt to do.

But there is another reason for the preference of young sires and dams, namely, that their employment will hasten the maturity of the young animal, so that the puppy of eighteen months old, if begotten by a young sire, will be better furnished and developed than the son of an older dog. This is now well established, and from a knowledge of the fact, breeders of sheep have succeeded in producing mutton at twelve or fourteen months old, of as good size and fatness as used formerly to take double or treble the time, and though, perhaps, not quite of equal flavour, as compared with an old wether, yet superior by far to mutton of the same age as formerly bred. As a proof of this fact in the greyhound, may be cited the cases of 'Kizzie' and 'Hughie Graham,' which are the only *puppies* that have won any of the great *all aged* stakes of late years, and they were both got by their sires at four years of age, and out of young dams. 'Locomotive,' also, is an extraordinary instance of a very large puppy (said to be 75 lbs. running weight) winning good puppy stakes early in the season, and his sire was only one year old when he got him. But I am bound to admit that there is also another reason for this early maturity, namely that our puppies are better reared, and more carefully attended to in their infancy, though I think this does not exert so much influence as the above practice.

DURATION OF PREGNANCY.

The bitch is said by naturalists to go with young sixty-three days, reckoning from the time of warding. This is no doubt the average period, but it cannot be reckoned on with certainty. I have myself had two bitches whelp on the same day though a week had intervened between the two days of warding. From careful records kept by Mr. Gibson and other experienced coursers, I am strongly of opinion that the nine weeks must not date from the access of the dog to the bitch, but from the middle of her heat. Most bitches are more or less 'in season' twenty-one days, which may be divided into three periods of nine days each. In the first nine days there is only a little swelling and heat of the external organs; in the second there is great swelling, and in the early part a slight discharge of blood, which is replaced by a flow of yellow mucus, continuing to the end; the third period resembles the first, except that the symptoms of heat &c. are on the decline instead of the reverse. The bitch will not usually admit the dog during more than four or five days, but sometimes this is extended to the whole of the middle period. When a bitch has been warded twice the puppies generally come sixty-three days after the middle of the interval between the two wardings. The following table gives the periods of fourteen pregnancies carefully calculated by Mr. Gibson, who was the first to suggest the explanation which is here afforded, of the difference in pregnancies so often found to exist :—

	Warded	Pupped	Duration of Gestation
			Days
Foremost bitch	Nov. 25	Jan. 25	65
Sybil	Dec. 1 and 10	Feb. 5	67 or 57
Cleopatra	Jan. 26	March 31	64
Bonnet Blue	Jan. 27	March 31	63
Bessy Bell	Feb. 13	April 17	63
Gratitude	Feb. 14	April 19	64
Black Bonnet	Feb. 24	April 28	63
Delaval bitch	Feb. 27	May 2	64
Bashful	April 4	June 5	62
Nancy	April 5	June 9	65
Shepherdess	April 9	June 13	65
Sylon	May 28	Aug. 1	65
Syringe	June 13	Aug. 18	66
Surety	June 22	Aug. 25	64

'MAID OF ISLAY.'

CHAPTER XII.

In-and-in Breeding—Examples of Success in adopting the Practice—Best Time of the Year for Breeding—Management of the Brood Bitch—Foster-Nurse.

THERE is a prevailing objection to what is called breeding 'in-and in,' not only among greyhound breeders, but also among breeders of neat cattle, horses, and sheep. It is, I believe, generally

s

admitted that, by this plan, you do not deteriorate your stock in elegance of shape, but it is supposed that there is a great falling off in size and stoutness, and more especially in the substance of the bone, which, however, is a desideratum, rather than otherwise, with cattle and sheep-breeders, although with the greyhound-breeder bone is a great object. On the other hand, Mr. Thacker, the great advocate of this plan, maintains that though in the greyhound there are certainly some exceptions, stoutness can only be insured by 'in-and-in' breeding, and that a decided cross will be assuredly prejudicial to that quality. As an instance of this theory, he brings forward, in his 'Breeder's Guide,' the case of 'Hour-glass,' and 'Harriet Wilson,' which were well known to be remarkably stout, and yet very much in-bred. In the fourth volume of his 'Annual,' he also adduces Mr. A. Graham's 'Screw' as an instance of stoutness in an animal much bred 'in-and-in.' Some parts of that pedigree, however, are incorrect, and therefore though I have little doubt that she was so bred, yet, as part is undoubtedly wrong, the whole *may* be, and consequently no great stress can be laid upon this example. Mr. Welch also has adduced Mundy's 'Wonder,' the 'Nottingham Violet,' Dr. Scott's 'Sparrowhawk,' Robinson's 'Streamer,' and Mr. A. Graham's 'Agitation,' as all 'in-bred,' and all stout.

A remarkable case of stoutness, combined with 'in-and-in' breeding, is that of Sir James Boswell's celebrated litter, composed of 'Vraye Foy,' 'Auchinleck,' 'The Curler,' 'Sweetheart,' 'Polka,' and 'Rosa,' which were not only stout runners, but have perpetuated this quality in their stock, 'Lopez,' 'Egypt,' and

'Brighton,' having been more particularly celebrated for their endurance.

From an examination of their pedigree as given in the Appendix, it will be obvious that 'Jason' and 'Rosebud' were first cousins, once removed as regards 'Butterfly,' and twice removed as regards 'Majesty.' Mr. Randell's celebrated bitch 'Rival,' as stout a greyhound as ever ran, was by a grandson of 'King Cob' out of a daughter of that dog; and Mr. Sharpe's 'Maid of Islay,' whose portrait (taken by photograph) heads this chapter, is another illustration of success attending this mode of breeding, she being by 'Jason,' a grandson of 'Monarch,' out of 'Molly Malone,' a granddaughter of the same dog, and she also has plenty of bone. Mr. Long's 'Lizzie' again may be quoted, being a large and bony bitch, yet out of an aunt by her nephew. 'Motley,' and his sisters 'Kitty Brown,' 'Miss Hannah,' and 'Moneytaker,' were also in-bred and have been of great use at the stud, especially the two first named, to which we are indebted for 'David' and his numerous winning progeny, and for 'Chloe,' the winner of the Waterloo Cup last year. All the litter were, however, small, but as 'Tollwife,' their dam, was a diminutive bitch, and had a strain of the Italian greyhound, no conclusion can be arrived at on that score. 'Mustard,' sire of 'Monarch' and other good greyhounds, was three times in-bred to 'King Cob,' yet he possessed great size and enormous bone, and his son 'Monarch' resembles him in both these particulars. As one of the strongest modern instances of close in-breeding without loss of constitution, size, or bone, I append his pedigree, which is the more remarkable from the fact that 'Matilda Gillespie,' and 'Vraye Foy,' were also much in bred.

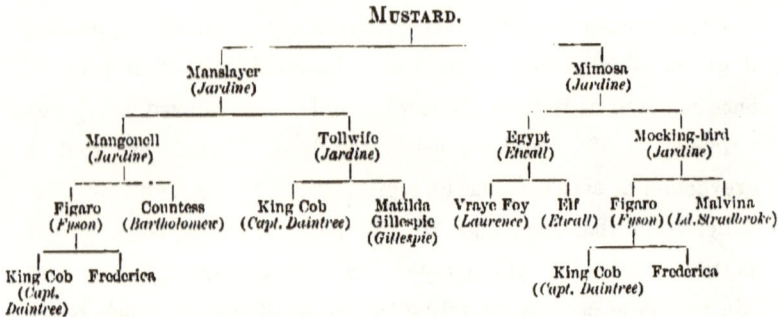

Numerous other examples of winning dogs possessing three lines of the same strain might also be adduced, including 'Patent' in the south, and 'Windermere' in Lancashire, each of which dogs has three lines of 'King Cob' and certainly neither is deficient in stoutness; but the argument that in-breeding, when not carried too far, is advantageous, is now so generally admitted that it is a loss of time to support it by facts. Mr. A. Graham's rule of 'once in and twice out' is perhaps the most prudent course to pursue; but 'twice in and once out,' is, in my opinion, not carrying in-breeding too far when the out-crosses are decided.

BEST TIME OF THE YEAR FOR BREEDING.

As the fashion has now set in strongly for produce stakes to be run in September, October, and November, it is important to breed puppies as early as possible in the year preceding, more particularly as far as dog-puppies are concerned. Of course a dog-puppy whelped in January or February has a great advantage over another produced in July, or even in May or June; but this is not equally applicable to bitches, for they are amenable to other laws besides those connected with their powers of endurance. It is frequently the case that the bitch-puppy, if whelped early in the year, is 'at heat' about July or August in the following year, which materially interferes with her running in the early part of the season; whilst the May or June puppy is very likely to go on till a much later period without that disheartening result. It is well, therefore, to be more careful of early dog-puppies than of the bitches, and *vice versâ* with the later litters. As the bitch goes with young about sixty-three days, it is not safe to put her to the dog earlier than the end of the first week in November; but it is not often that a favourite will be so accommodating to her master as to select that particular week; on the contrary, it more frequently happens that she fixes upon October and April as the months for displaying her sexual propensities. The former of these is of course out of the question if in breeding for puppy stakes, and the latter will produce a litter in June. All things considered, I should prefer breeding in March or April to an earlier period, because the whelps born in those months are not so likely to be chilled and stopped in their growth, which is a worse defect even than want of age.

MANAGEMENT OF THE BROOD BITCH.

Having, then, made up your mind as to your choice of a stallion, and having, as far as practicable, obtained a bitch 'at heat' at such a season as will suit your purpose, the next step to be taken is, to see that she is put to the stallion dog by some person upon whom dependence can be placed. This is of great consequence where the dog is a great public favourite, for I am afraid that it sometimes happens that the kennelman in charge mistakes some younger and more vigorous animal for the veritable Simon Pure, whose powers are reserved for some one else, more alive to the many tricks which are passed upon inexperienced breeders.

The best time for the confluence of the sexes is when the usual term of nine days is just going off, say about the seventh or eighth day, which may be known by the cessation of the usual bleeding from the vagina. When this ceases, no time should be lost, as the bitch will very soon refuse the dog. As soon as the bitch is able to take her usual exercise, without fear of annoyance, she should be taken out regularly, or suffered to be at large. Nothing is of so much consequence as this. You can never expect a healthy offspring from a fat, dyspeptic mother, and confinement will as surely produce disease in the dog as in the human subject. This exercise should be continued as usual up to the end of the seventh week, after which time care should be taken that the bitch is not induced to overleap or strain herself by following others in their play. It is better, therefore, to lead her in a strap, if with other dogs, or to give her her entire liberty by herself in some quiet farm-yard or cottage garden.

It generally happens that towards the end of her time the bitch becomes very thin; she should then be better fed than before; but it is more desirable that she should be somewhat low in flesh than too fat, as this only leads to fever, and consequently to a stoppage in the secretion of her milk.

If possible, she should have a roomy loose box, or some similar place, for her *accouchement*, and she should be separated from other dogs for the last week, for fear of injury by fighting. There should be plenty of clean straw, and, if convenient, a boarded floor for her to make her bed on, as the whelps are sure in sucking to scratch all the straw away, and afterwards lie upon the bricks or stone. If, however, a boarded floor is not to be had, get a piece of old carpet, and put it on some litter, and then more straw upon that, by which means you prevent the whelps from scratching away more than that lying above the carpet, and they are consequently kept dry and warm. Care should be taken that the bitch's bowels are regularly open, and, if they are not, a little castor oil should be given, with plenty of broth afterwards. As the milk begins to fill the teats some days before whelping, it is well to give more sloppy food than usual, and a portion of milk, if easily obtained, is of service, as it is highly desirable that the secretion of milk should be fully established by the time the whelps are born. To do this effectually, the food should be nutritious and sloppy, but not so heating as to produce fever. In making this change, regard should be had to the previous diet of the bitch. If she has been fed upon much flesh, it will not do to take it away entirely and substitute milk and flour; but whatever the food has been, let your change be somewhat to a lighter, a more nutritious and a more liquid kind. For instance, if much flesh has previously been given, then substitute good meat broth for a part of it, taking care to thicken the broth with the same kind of meal she has been accustomed to. It is astonishing how often the health of greyhounds is upset by a thoughtless change of food, as, for instance, at the beginning of training, dogs, which had previously been living upon barley-meal and greaves, are often at once put upon a pound of flesh a day. Instead of improving in condition, and 'training on' no wonder that they 'train off,' and the same will apply to the time of whelping.

There is seldom much necessity for interference with the process of parturition. The greyhound puppy is generally so small in proportion to the mother that the passage into the world is 'as easy as a glove,' and as soon as they take the nipple the whelps may be considered safe if there is plenty of milk, a warm bed, good food, and a good mother. The three first of these requirements are mainly dependent upon the kennelman; but the last depends upon the temper of the animal—some bite their puppies severely, some lie upon them, and some great awkward bitches tread upon their offspring;

but these are not common casualties, and if they occur more than once are sufficient to induce us to destroy any but a very great favourite. For the first ten days it is only requisite to feed the mother, which should have her food lukewarm till the third day, and to give plenty of clear litter to the whelps. The bitch should be encouraged to come into the yard and empty herself two or three times a day, but it is not requisite to induce her to go out for more than a few minutes. The drain upon the constitution of suckling will keep up the digestive powers for so short a time; but after the first ten days she should be led out for an hour a day. It is necessary to lead her, because she will seldom leave the whelps so soon without compulsion.

FOSTER NURSE.

The greyhound frequently produces a greater number of whelps than she can well rear, and it becomes a question what is to be done in such a case. Many advise their all being left with her, believing that she can support them for a week or ten days, that is, till they can lap—but if the number exceeds six or seven, I should strongly advise either that the weakly ones be destroyed or that a foster nurse should be procured. I am so convinced of the superiority of those well suckled over the puny whelps which have shared the milk with nine or ten brothers and sisters, that I should not hesitate for a moment to destroy all above six or seven, if no nurse could be procured. A bad greyhound is worse than useless, and one good one is therefore better than a dozen bad ones. Now, every breeder knows how much the after growth of the puppy depends upon his size and strength at weaning time, and it is impossible to make up by any care and attention for the check given by an insufficient supply of mother's milk. The next question to consider is, the propriety of selecting any nurse for your whelps which is not of the greyhound breed. This is a much-vexed question, many breeders supposing that the mental and physical qualities of the nurse are imbibed with her milk. I have, however, seen so many instances of first-rate greyhounds suckled by sheep-bitches, bull-terriers, spaniels, and even pointers, that I do not hesitate to recommend my readers to take the first good nurse that comes to hand, regardless of breed. But it must be remembered that though a little terrier will do for a brace of puppies well enough for two or three weeks, yet after that time the milk does not come fast enough for the power and size of their mouths, and therefore they fall off in health and strength rapidly. A larger bitch, say of 20 lbs. to 30 lbs. weight, is therefore desirable if possible, and will suckle as many as an ordinary greyhound-bitch, if her milk is of the same age.* It has been proposed to go on supplying fresh nurses as fast as the milk of the first becomes dry; but the teeth of whelps at five weeks old become so sharp, that no

---

* Among the numerous examples of winning greyhounds reared by foster nurses of other breeds, may be adduced 'King Death,' winner of the Waterloo Cup of 1864, who was brought up by a bull bitch.

bitch will allow them to suck much after that age. In all cases it is best to muzzle the foster nurse for at least 24 hours. Some of her own whelps should be left at first together with the young greyhounds, and withdrawn, one by one, as she gets accustomed to them. In this way there is seldom much trouble in getting her to take to the new lot, even if her own whelps are a fortnight old, after which the milk is not so well adapted for newly-born puppies.

If the litter is more than four or five, it is necessary to begin to feed as soon as possible, in addition to the mother's milk; and as soon as the whelps can see, they may be induced to lap by dipping their mouths into warm milk once or twice a day. They soon begin to lick their lips, and, liking the taste, learn to take it out of the saucer. At a fortnight old the milk may be given regularly, and it is better to sweeten it a little, and at three weeks to thicken it with a very little *fine* wheat-flour boiled in it till it turns, or if the whelps are at all purged, with arrowroot or well-boiled rice. As soon as the litter has reached the fifth week, it will be necessary to begin with some mutton broth made from sheeps' heads, having some small portions of the meat well broke up, and, thickening with flour to the consistence of cream, take the precaution to avoid tape-worms mentioned at page 167. This may be given twice a day, or, if the number exceeds five, three times. After the fifth or sixth week the bitch had better be removed entirely, and the weaning begins, which will commence another division of our subject, viz. the rearing of the greyhound.

During the whole of her suckling the bitch must be well fed, and will require one or two quarts of new milk per day. After all danger of fever is gone, that is, by the third day, she should have as much flesh well boiled as she was accustomed to before her delivery, and plenty of good broth, well thickened with meal. This should be given her in the middle of the day, and a quart of milk with bread, and, if possible, a little trotter jelly night and morning. It sometimes happens, in spite of good feeding, that a delicate bitch is unable to continue her suckling; she becomes emaciated, and has a fit, followed often by entire loss of appetite. When this is the case to any extent, it is better to take the puppies away, and wean them, if old enough, or, if not, substitute a wet nurse. If, however, the attack is only slight, a gentle dose of castor oil, followed by a pill containing 2 grains of quinine and 1 of ginger twice a day, will often restore the powers of the system: or, if very low, an ounce of the decoction of bark with a drachm of Huxham's tincture and 30 drops of sal volatile, will be still more efficacious. But it is a proof of delicacy of constitution, sufficient to condemn her afterwards as a brood bitch.

CHAPTER XIII.

Rearing the Whelps—Best Time to choose them—Question as to Rearing at Home or 'at Walk'—Time and Mode of Feeding—Necessity for Change of Diet—Teething—After Twelve Months of Age, require only Feeding once a Day—The Evening the best Time to Feed—Necessity for Daily Exercise—Plenty of Bones should be given—Table of the Weights at various Ages—Undue Severity deprecated—Best Diet for the Greyhound—Flesh and Bread—Mode of making Bread without Barm—Other and cheaper Diets sometimes used—Removal of Dew Claws.

THE young courser must not now hug himself with the idea that his task is happily ended because he has obtained a beautiful litter of whelps, six weeks old, and the produce even of the best blood in England on the side of both sire and dam. They have yet an ordeal to go through, in which, without good management, and, what is more, good luck, all his hopes will be disappointed. That ordeal is the process of rearing, with its many attendant risks, at the time of weaning, or from distemper or worms, or from the numerous accidents to which so fragile an animal is subject. One of the most anxious periods is that of weaning, when the young stomach has to be accustomed to other food than that provided by nature. But by commencing to give thickened milk and broth at the third week, as already described, much of this difficulty will be overcome, as the stomach is gradually prepared for the change. I have already directed that at the sixth week at latest the bitch should be entirely removed, and the whelps fed four times a day, viz. at six in the morning, again at eleven, at four in the afternoon, and again at nine in the evening. If not fed so often as this they soon fall away in flesh, because they are so voracious at the time of feeding as to overload their stomachs, causing all sorts of mischief, such as flatulence, diarrhœa, and all the other concomitants of disordered nutrition. It is well to feed them at six and four with new milk, thickened with oatmeal, and with a very little sugar in it, or, if at all relaxed, with rice boiled in it for at least two hours instead of the oatmeal, and at the other two periods with sheep's head boiled down to form good broth, and thickened with fine wheat flour to the consistence of cream, adding a little salt, which all animals are the better for having. One head per day will make about enough broth for six whelps till they are nine or ten weeks old. Up to this time, whether in town or country, a loose box is the best place for the whelps, and there is no occasion to do more than keep them rigidly clean, taking care that the whole box is well littered down with short straw, which should be changed partially every day where required, and entirely once a week. Cleanliness is one of the most important points, at all stages of the greyhound's life. If the whelps keep in good condition, feeding well, and though not covered with 'milk fat,' yet hearty and strong, they may

CHOICE OF WHELPS. 271

be considered well through the danger attendant upon their weaning time at ten weeks old; at which period the dogs ought to weigh from 18lbs. to 20lbs. apiece, and the bitches somewhat less.

Now is the time to decide upon the whelps to be retained; it is true that the breeder should have already noticed the best-shaped whelps at the end of the first week; but if these have not been well weaned they should be rejected, choosing in preference those which have stood that ordeal, without *loss of shape*. I do not here allude to mere loss of flesh; it may so happen that an accidental cold or diarrhœa will pull down one of the very best of the litter for a short time; but this is picked up again in a few days, and is not of the slightest consequence. If, however, a whelp looks staring in his coat, grows round in his back, or shows decidedly bad feet, I should certainly set him on one side, particularly if his elbows are out or in too much. At this time the feet begin to show their form, and you may make a very good guess as to their future shape, which you cannot do while in the nest. But with regard to the shoulders and the general length of the frame, I think there is no time equal to the first week after birth, when, if by taking the whelp up by the tail, he brings his fore legs well over his head, and shows good back-ribs and sufficient length of body, you may rely upon it that, if he keeps his health, he will at full growth display these points again, even if, during his puppyhood, they have apparently been obscured. There is, however, great difficulty in making such a selection when the litter is pretty level; and, under the most favourable circumstances, the best judge will often reject the future winner, and choose some useless animal in preference. Some old hands will recommend the largest whelp; some, again, the smallest, or the last born; but from some experience in my own kennel, and a careful comparison with that of others, I know of no rule upon which dependence can be placed, except the hints I have already given. In this, as in almost every stage of the courser's career, 'good luck is better than a good dog,' as I have often been told by the most successful. Still good luck requires good management at its back, and happy is the man who can reckon upon both. Many successful breeders use artificial warmth in the rearing of early whelps, and no doubt it brings them on very fast, and, if not subsequently checked, they are all the finer and the better grown for it; but if they are kept very dry, and have a bordered stage to lie upon, which should be protected also from the wall, they will do very well without it, except in very severe frosts. Care should, however, be taken that they are not submitted to any draughts of cold air, but that whatever ventilation is necessary should be managed from the upper part of the loose box. It is astonishing what a deal of exercise whelps of this age will take in a box of the ordinary size, after which they retire to their warm corner, and by lying all together keep up warmth sufficient for health; still, in a severe spring, a January-born litter of puppies is very liable to be chilled in a hard frost, and if a loose box, opening into a warm stable, can be placed at their disposal, it will materially aid their growth. But if reared with this adventitious aid, which is much better than stove heat, because more regular, they require extra care if removed to a walk at a farmer's, or to other quarters, at ten or twelve weeks old; and it is well at this stage to consider what is the best mode of proceeding upon this point. That is to say, it is better to send the whelps out into the country 'to walk,' as it is termed, or to keep them at home in kennel? My answer to this question is this, that anything is better than confinement in a close unhealthy box or yard; but that if an airy situation can be selected where the whelps can have the run of a yard or other inclosure twenty or thirty feet long, they had far better remain under the eye of the breeder, and for the following reasons:—In the first place, few farmers or butchers really take any interest in the greyhound for its own sake, they only rear them as a favour to the party giving them in charge. Secondly, if any disease attacks the puppies, much time is lost before the proper remedy can be applied. Thirdly, the food is not given regularly, and seldom of sufficiently good quality, and it is not carefully boiled, from which cause tapeworm is so common among dogs reared 'at walk.' Fourthly, they are liable to all sorts of accidents from kicks, &c. Fifthly, they lie about in the wet and cold, contracting thereby rheumatism, and also from cold habitually setting up their backs till they grow into that form called the 'wheel-back.' Sixthly and lastly, they are always getting into mischief and receiving severe punishment for so doing, by which their spirit is broken, and they lose that fire

T

which ought to be carefully preserved. On the other hand, if retained at home, or near home, they should never be more than six, or, what is better still, four in one yard, and they should be let out into a field or paddock for a quarter of an hour before each time of feeding. After they are six or seven months old, whether at home or 'at walk,' greyhound puppies, I am quite satisfied, should not have their entire liberty. They only become lazy, never gallop as they do when just let out, and get so fat as to be an incumbrance to themselves; and they are very apt to accompany the farmer's sheep-dog, and assist him in finding hares, rabbits, &c., by which many a well-bred dog learns to run cunning. From the third to the sixth month whelps should be gradually accustomed to a liberal allowance of flesh, boiled in water, and mixed with their meal; and the milk should be entirely, but gradually, discontinued, and its place supplied by broth. My reason for this is practical rather than theoretical, as, judging from its analysis, milk ought to be equal to anything as a food for young dogs. I am, however, quite satisfied that dogs fed on milk, though they look fat and healthy, are not likely to turn out so well as those fed on good broth and meal, and they are frequently deficient in bone. This change should be made gradually, keeping at first to the mutton broth as before described, and gradually substituting for it oatmeal stirabout, with flesh cut up, or, still better, torn up, and mixed well in it. The stirabout should be made by stirring into the *broth in which the flesh has been boiled* enough oatmeal and *undressed* wheat flour to thicken it, so that

BEST DIET FOR WHELPS.

when cold it shall be capable of being cut with a knife without sticking to it much, for if too adhesive they do not eat it so well as when somewhat drier, always remembering to add a little salt to all their food. The wheat-flour should be boiled about ten minutes, and the oatmeal about fifteen, as a longer time makes the stirabout too sticky. The proportions of oatmeal and wheat-flour should be varied according to the *consistence* of the *fæces* passed, using more than half oatmeal if too hard, and less when the dog is too loose; the quantity of flesh should also be regulated by the *colour* of the *fæces*, which become quite black when the flesh is in too great a quantity; after six months, an average puppy ought to have one pound of flesh daily. Care should also be taken that the liver is acting properly, which may be known by the presence of the colour of 'gingerbread' in the motions. This is the healthy colour, and so long as you have this present, without diarrhœa or costiveness, you may be satisfied there is not *much* the matter. The flesh used should also be frequently changed, and the good kennelman may be known by his constantly looking out for 'slink' calves or lambs, as well as for sheep dying an accidental death. It is well also occasionally to stop the meat altogether for a day or two, substituting slops of some kind. The puppies' stomach, like that of man, requires constant change of diet, without which not only does the appetite suffer, but the blood becomes foul.

In order to satisfy myself upon the advantage or otherwise of a milk diet, I have divided a litter, and reared one part upon an unlimited supply of new milk, with an occasional allowance of flesh, and the other, as I have here recommended, upon porridge and boiled flesh, with trotters, &c. Up to three months old, the milk-fed puppies looked the best, but between four and five the others rapidly went by them, and looked in every way superior—being more muscular, more racing like, and more loose and bony, and weighing 4 or 5lbs. apiece more than the others, though not so at. A remarkable fact is, that the milk-fed puppies were at least a fortnight behind the others in shedding their teeth, and had not so fine and strong a set. It appears, from this, as if the meal has the property of encouraging the growth of enamel as well as bone.

If sheep's trotters can be procured, they are a great addition to the puppy's diet, and should be prepared as follows:—They should be first put in scalding water for an hour, then scrape the wool off, and take off the hoofs, after which, they are to be simmered in one quart of water to every dozen trotters, till they tumble to pieces. The small bones are then to be carefully picked out, and the whole put by to get cold. A good spoonful of this is a great addition to each ration, and should be mixed up with the stirabout, or the dog will pick it out, as well as the meat, and leave the meal untasted. From three to six months old the whelps should be fed thrice a day; from six to twelve months twice, and after that, if they have been treated as I have described, they will have reached their full size; and feeding once a day, with a mouthful or two in the morning, is quite enough. Until dogs go into training, my opinion is that they are better fed at night, giving them just a mouthful in the morning, and exercising them twice a day—viz. morning and evening. They thus tire themselves out the last thing at night, after which they get their bellyfull, and then they rest quietly all night. Whereas, if fed in the middle of the day, they get restless and quarrelsome at night, and the kennelman has to use his whip to keep them quiet.

One of the most important points in rearing the greyhound is, to give him a daily supply of bones, which are not only requisite to keep his teeth clean, but, in order that he may, in gnawing them, give rise to that due secretion of saliva which his health demands. Dogs do not chew their food like man, but they require saliva to digest it, as much, or more than he does, and the only way to produce this secretion in sufficient quantity for digestive purposes is, to keep their jaws at work by the gnawing of bones. But, besides this, during the growth of their limbs, a large supply of phosphate of lime is required to build up the skeleton or framework, and, though the mineral element is partly found in the oat and wheat flour, still bones supply it in a condition more easily taken up by the absorbents of their alimentary canal. Another important point is, to give them occasionally potatoes or vegetable food of some kind, as cabbage, French beans, turnips, or carrots, once or twice a week. By so doing you will rarely require to physic your puppies, unless they happen to get worms, distemper, or other extraordinary aliment.

Between the fourth and fifth month, the set of milk-teeth are shed, and the permanent teeth come through the gums. In whelps which have been well reared, the teething is effected by the beginning of the sixth month, without any inconvenience greater than a slight loss of appetite and flesh; but in those which are badly fed, or brought up in dark confined places, this important process is later, and is often attended with fits, or diarrhœa, and general fever. This feverish state is often mistaken for true distemper, and will even go on to produce it if neglected. The best remedy is change of air, plenty of good food, not too heating, and an occasional dose of oil. If the liver does not act, or diarrhœa comes on, the remedies already ordered for these complaints should be administered.

During the course of the first nine or ten months it is satisfactory to know that your favourites are growing as fast as you could wish, but as they increase in size and weight in a very different ratio at different ages, it is only by experimental weighing that the old hand knows that he is going on well in his breeding stud. If, then, he finds that his whelps do not turn the weight he thinks they should do, and they have had no drawback, he concludes that they are not thriving, and either alters his plan of feeding, &c., or gets rid of them as unlikely to prove profitable to him. The best way to get at the weight of whelps, less than five or six months old, is to put each in a canvas bag (of which the weight can be easily ascertained and deducted), and then hook them by the string of the bag to a pair of steelyards. After six months the same plan may be adopted as with full-grown dogs, which are weighed by different people in different ways; but the following plan answers the best, and most people have the articles required ready to their hands :—The dog is to be suspended by a pair of horse-girths, one of which should be six inches shorter than the other, and their weight must of course be deducted. The short one should be passed under the dog's belly and the long one under his chest, between the fore-legs, so as to prevent its slipping backward. The four buckles may then be connected by a string, and suspended to the hook. By this plan the dog is rendered quite incapable of resistance, and generally lies as quiet as possible.

I have already given the weight at ten weeks old. The following table will give the weights from that age to ten months, when puppies generally weigh, if tolerably fat, the same as they afterwards do when fit to run.

	DOGS lbs.	BITCHES lbs.
At Three Months Old	23	22
At Four ,,	32	28
At Five ,,	40	34
At Six ,,	50	41
At Seven ,,	53	44
At Eight ,,	58	48
At Nine ,,	62	51
At Ten ,,	65	52

Some allowance may be made for drawbacks in the shape of distemper, &c., and also for the degree of fatness of the puppies, as I have calculated these weights on the assumption that they are fat, but not unwieldly; but with that proviso it will be found that by as much as the whelps fall short of the weights specified at the various periods of growth, by so much will they fall short of the top weights when full grown. There are certainly some breeds which take a longer time to fill up, but in ninety-nine cases out of a hundred the above rule will hold good, that is, if the whelps are as well reared as I have recommended.

With regard to the amount of exercise required during this period, I should say that as soon as they will follow well, which is generally at about four or five months old, they should be taken out for an hour night and morning, not confining them entirely to the road, which should be as unfrequented as possible for fear of accidents, but occasionally allowing them to play in a field or common for a few minutes; they should, however, always get some road work, to harden their feet, and keep the nails short enough, and they should not be taken out in greater numbers than four or five at one time, as more than that number cannot be managed without the use of the whip to such an extent as to destroy their courage. Towards nine months old three hours a day, divided in two portions, will not be too much; and this amount of exercise is sufficient till they go into training, and should keep them about five or six pounds above their probable running weight; but I should recommend up to this time that they should not be taken out with a horse, as they require constant supervision to prevent their attacking poultry, sheep, or cats. It is astonishing how full of mischief a puppy is, fed as highly as I have recommended; and yet your object should be to do as little to repress that love of mischief as is consistent with the avoidance of absolute murder of your neighbour's poultry or sheep. Do not, therefore, keep your favourites at your heels while out, but allow them to range freely, unless you see them show any symptoms of insubordination, when, if the voice is not sufficient, the whip must be used, proportioning its severity to the peculiar temper of the individual offender, but recollecting that one good sound thrashing is better than a dozen trifling ones. Many puppies are irretrievably ruined by the constant use of the whip, so that when slipped at a hare they do not know whether to give chase or to slink behind their master's heels. This feature in the puppy always detects a bad rearer of the whelp, and if I found it the case I would never trust the same individual to rear greyhounds for me a second time. In fact, if you can only stop your puppies short of doing actual injury the less you interfere with them the better. But I believe that the art of rearing them is truly a gift, like that of teaching children, in which few of us have attained the happy knack of procuring subordination without destroying the spirit of the individual by undue severity. If very mischievous, so as to be quite beyond control without extreme severity, I find it answers better to take the puppies out with a muzzle on, than to use the whip too much; many dogs are most determined cat-killers, and with them the muzzle is almost a *sine quâ non* where they are exercised in such situations as to meet with many of these animals. Others are inveterate runners of sheep, and though they will at first attempt to do the same with the muzzle on, they soon find out their powerlessness to do mischief, and give up the chase. There is also an advantage connected with the muzzle which has hitherto been overlooked, namely that it prevents the dog wearing it from getting hold of improper food, and then becoming infested with worms as shown at page 165. Up to the commencement of training there is not much use in dressing the puppies with the rubber or wisp daily, for which the dog's tongue is a good substitute, though I have no doubt they would be all the better for it. But if they come in thoroughly wet, either from rain or from galloping through water, they should be rubbed tolerably dry, except in the height of summer, when it is of no consequence.

Many good kennelmen give their puppies brimstone in their water, which, by the way, should be always within their reach, but I do not know that there is much good in it unless they are deprived of flesh as an article of diet. It should be carefully boiled for the reason given at page 167. Others touch their noses and sides with tar occasionally, which the dogs lick off and swallow. The only thing, however, which I have found to be generally necessary is the liberal use of neat's-foot oil in the summer, in order to kill the fleas, which are in some kennels a perpetual torment to the dogs. I have already specified the various applications needful in the eruptions to which the dog is subject; but *all* are liable to fleas, and I have described the several plans necessary to get rid of these parasites at pages 174, 175. In small numbers they do little harm, but when they swarm in the skin, as they sometimes do in hot summers, they interfere with the rest, and must be got rid of.

Such is the plan I have myself adopted, and would recommend to all those who intend to run in public for good stakes. It is true that it occasions a good deal of trouble and expense, but if you are to risk heavy stakes and travelling expenses, you are penny wise and pound foolish if you are niggardly of your purse in rearing. This plan also, or one more expensive even, is adopted by most of those who are successful at the present time, and therefore, to compete with them, you must do as they do.

But you not only want boldness and strength in the greyhound, you also want the respiratory or breathing process well established. In other words, you want a good winded dog, and to effect this purpose, flesh is utterly useless as an article of food; at least, it would require an enormous quantity to produce the same effect as a small proportion of flour. It is now ascertained beyond the possibility of doubt, that all articles of food in omnivorous mammalia must be divided into two classes, one of which serves for the true nutrition and reproduction of the solid parts of the body, whilst the other ministers both to the performance of these processes, and also to the production of animal heat, which is mainly effected by the agency of the heart and lungs. If, therefore, the two processes are not both equally attended to, you will have either, on the one hand, in the dog reared on flesh alone, a great overgrown muscular frame with small chest, weak heart and lungs, or, in the flour-fed animal, a fat, unwieldy, hippopotamus-like dog, without muscular developement or animal spirits, but generally of good wind. It is well known that the dog *may* be reared and fed upon either of these classes of food; but experience teaches the advantage, and science shows the reason of their due admixture. Those who require further proof may obtain the information they seek in the Lectures of Professor Liebig on Chemistry. The annexed table shows the proportion of the two classes of elementary materials in the following articles of food : —

	Materials used in building up the bones, muscles, &c.	Materials used in the respiratory process, and in forming fat.
Cow's milk contains for	10 parts of the above	30 parts.
Fat mutton	10 ,, ,,	27 to 45
Lean mutton	10 ,, ,,	19
Beef (lean)	10 ,, ,,	17
Horseflesh (lean) . .	10 ,, ,,	15
Hare and rabbit . . .	10 ,, ,,	2 to 5
Wheat flour	10 ,, ,,	46
Oatmeal	10 ,, ,,	50
Barleymeal	10 ,, ,,	57
Potatoes	10 ,, ,,	86 to 115
Rice	10 ,, ,,	153

A reference to this table will show why a horse fed on potatoes gets fat, but can do little work, why barley is better than potatoes for working purposes, and why oats are still better than barley, because the proportion of muscle-making matter in them is greater than in barley, and nearly double what it is in potatoes. So in regard to the dog, it will be seen that the building-up power of flesh is, on an average, nearly three times as great as that of wheat or oatmeal, the former exceeding the latter in a slight proportion. Cow's milk contains about the same proportion as would be found in an equal mixture of flesh and meal, and upon it dogs will thrive; but they fall off when first put upon other food. The peculiar characters of flesh are exemplified in a remarkable manner in the flesh of the hare, which contains only two parts of respiratory materials in twelve. This will account for the wonderful muscular powers of the animal, and the extraordinary development of its propulsive hind quarters in proportion to its chest and fore quarters.

The mode of rearing which I have described, is in my opinion undoubtedly the best; but there are various articles of food in addition to those I have mentioned, which are in common use among the owners of greyhounds. One of the most common, and at the same time the most unfit for the purpose, is composed of barleymeal and greaves; now, either of these alone is bad enough, because of their tending to produce fat instead of muscle; but why the two should be combined, I am at a loss to know. The reason given me by a friend of mine who adopts the plan is, that there ought to be a great difference made between the ordinary food of the greyhound and that which he gets when in training. Now, if this is correct in principle, then undoubtedly the plan is a good one, for nothing except rice is more unfit for training purposes than barleymeal, but the principle itself is bad, and is just as absurd as would be the rearing of thorough-bred colts without corn, in order that they should also feel the difference when put in training. And yet we know that they are fed upon corn, with the happiest results, from the earliest period at which they can be persuaded to chew it. I have also been told that barleymeal and greaves must be good, for dogs will often run better upon it than they afterwards do when in training upon mutton and bread. This also I do not dispute, for I am quite sure that dogs accustomed to *any* food, no matter what, run better upon it than upon its very opposite, and therefore barley-fed dogs will be in better health, and consequently more fit to run while continuing to eat what their stomachs are accustomed to, than when fed upon mutton and biscuit, if given them without preparation. But I have never known a really good dog reared in this way, though I know two large kennels in which it is used for both young and old, while out of training, with the most unfortunate results in both cases. Many of their puppies have shown good shape, and their skins have been as fine as satin, but their muscles were round and soft, without full development, and there was no mischief brewing in their eyes, nor were they looking as I like to see greyhounds, ready to jump out of their skins on the slightest provocation. My friend (one of the above) assured me that his dogs were always in good health, and were so good-tempered that his kennelman could easily manage thirty at one time out of doors. 'Then,' said I, 'I would not give you thirty pence for the whole lot, for either they are cowed by the whip, or there is nothing to cow.' And so it turned out: they would gallop most elegantly in their play, but when put in slips, as many ran from the hare as to it, and those which did join in the course had no fire in their style of running, so that he never got beyond the first tie in any stake in which he was engaged. This was not the fault of the blood, as no expense or pains had been spared in getting the best in England.

Buttermilk thickened with flour is another very similar article of food, but it is something better, inasmuch as the buttermilk contains a considerable quantity of the nutritive matter of the milk, varying according to the peculiar process adopted in making the cheese. It is, however, very little better than barleymeal and greaves, and is only useful in default of better articles of diet. These are the most common mistakes made in giving too little animal food; but the opposite error is even worse, since it leads to the production of a great overgrown, mastiff-looking greyhound, heavy and bulky about the shoulders, yet with a small chest, and not wind enough to follow the butcher's cart, which is generally the accompaniment of a dog fed in this way. I allude to the dog reared at a butcher's, and fed upon offal, and nothing else in the shape of meal. Most of these dogs die in the rearing; they get diseased, generally in the form of dysentery, and die complete skeletons. But if the butcher has had experience in rearing greyhounds, he adopts a plan which saves him trouble and expense, and also the lives and health of the puppies which he has to rear. It is true that this plan is not so good as the mixture of meal with the offal, but still, after they become accustomed to it, it agrees very well, and is the best as well as the cheapest substitute for the flesh and meal plan with which I am acquainted. This mode is the following:—Instead of cleaning the entrails and paunches, the whole should be preserved, that is, the whole of the vegetable food contained in the stomach and intestines, taking care to reject those lower entrails in which the food has become impacted in the sheep, and all nourishment extracted. This *may* be given raw, and dogs soon eat it eagerly, taking care to mix it altogether, by cutting the entrails and stomach into small pieces; but it is much better to boil it all up together, stirring it the while, and mixing a *little* flour the last thing, to thicken it. Of course the smell precludes the boiling of this unsavoury mess in any inhabited house; but if a boiler can be obtained in an open outhouse, it may be used for this purpose. Dogs reared at a butcher's are almost sure to be infested with worms, so that it is useless to take any precaution against them.

There is one other point upon which I have known old hands to disagree, viz. as to the propriety of giving dogs raw meat at any time. Many experienced persons keep their horseflesh in a tree or other airy place till it is dry and as tender as possible, and then they allow their puppies to gnaw at it, and tear it from the bones without any kind of dressing. I am bound to admit that I have known good dogs result from this mode of treatment; but I never tried it, and therefore I cannot speak from personal experience. I am, however, very averse to the use of raw flesh without being kept till tender, as I have myself experienced the ill effect in my own kennel in former years.* With regard to the kind of oatmeal and wheat flour which I should recommend, I have no doubt whatever that the coarse Scotch oatmeal is the best, and also the most free from adulteration. It is to be bought now almost throughout England, and will go nearly twice as far as the ordinary English meal. Whether this difference is due to the grain only, or to adulteration with cheaper meal, I cannot say,

* Mr. Randall lost his celebrated bitch 'Riot,' from eating the flesh of a horse which had been just killed, and to which she had gained access by accident. There was no reason to suppose that the animal was poisoned, and the death of the bitch, as well as 'Blackcloud,' who also died from eating the same flesh, must be attributed to the fact that it was only just killed.—J. H. W.

but that there is this difference a long experience justifies me in asserting without fear of contradiction. With regard to the use of undressed wheat flour, I am of opinion that it contains much more nourishment, and agrees with the dog better than fine flour; that is, after the age of eight or nine weeks, before which time it irritates the bowels and causes diarrhœa. The flour should be ground tolerably fine, but should contain all the bran and pollard. Red wheat is, I think, better than white, but I do not speak confidently on this point. The celebrated French physiologist, Magendie, found by experiment that a dog fed on fine wheaten bread alone, died after forty days; while another dog fed on brown bread lived on without any disturbance of his health (Millon, *Comptes rendus*, xxxvii. p. 40).

From the age of nine or ten months, till training begins, the food may be as already described for the puppy, or the flour may be made into bread, according to circumstances and the convenience of the master. It should, however, never be forgotten that the dog requires change of diet, and that every month he should be fed on slops for a day or two. Many use the ordinary dog biscuits as usually sold, but I should not recommend them, as they are made of all sorts of flour, generally of a damaged quality. The meal may be made into bread in the ordinary way with barm, or, better still, as follows:—

To MAKE BROWN BREAD WITHOUT BARM.—Take of flour 12 lbs., bicarbonate of soda 2 ounces, mix them well together with the hands or by sifting through a fine sieve; then mix 2 ounces of muriatic acid with 8 pints of water, stirring it well with a glass or earthenware rod; afterwards stir the acid and water quickly into the flour, using the same rod or a wooden spoon for the purpose. The dough should then be quickly put into common earthen flower-pots, filling them about two-thirds full, and baked immediately in a quick oven, *rather hotter than for common bread.* In this method there is no loss or change by fermentation, and the acid and soda combine to form common salt, so that there is nothing pernicious to the dog, and yet the bread is light enough to soak well. It has an agreeable natural taste, and keeps moist and good for ten days, if in an airy place; it is also easily prepared, not taking more than a quarter of an hour from the commencement to the putting into the oven. There is also a saving of 10 per cent. in the weight. In the common process the saccharine part of the flour, with a portion of the gum and the gluten, is lost by being converted into carbonic acid gas and spirit, which are driven into the air by heat, and this waste is incurred solely to obtain carbonic acid gas to raise the dough. In the soda and acid process the gas is obtained in a much more simple way, without loss and without decomposition of the nutritive materials existing in the flour. Wheat and oatmeal may be mixed in any proportion which may agree best with the dogs, and which varies a good deal in different districts, according to climate, soil, and warmth.

DEW CLAWS.

Many Wiltshire coursers invariably remove the dew claws, and in very flinty countries it may admit of a doubt whether this practice should be adopted. In all others it is certainly unnecessary, since these claws are undoubtedly useful in the turn, if not cut by the flints, when of course they become sore, and interfere with, rather than assist, the act of turning. If removed, it should be done at about the third week, with a pair of sharp scissors, drawing the skin well up the leg and from the claw, so as to remove as little of that integument as possible. If they are at all loose they are always better off, but my own opinion is that, if firm and sitting close to the leg, they are in all countries better on than off. It is true, they sometimes get injured, but so do all other parts, but I question whether they do not often save the leg itself from cuts, and thereby serve a useful purpose. Besides, unless really required, no humane man would lend himself to so barbarous an operation, and, therefore, we should be satisfied that the balance is much in favour of the operation before having recourse to it.

CHAPTER XIV.

Leading—Accustoming to the Muzzle—Entering to his Game—Kennels—Kennel Management—Dressings for Fleas &c.—Physic—Expenses of Rearing and Training.

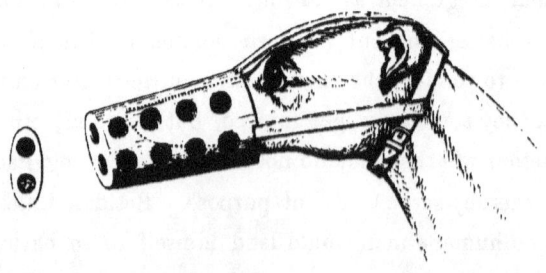

THE DOG has now been brought to a period when he must be treated somewhat differently to what he has been hitherto, for not only must his body be attended to, but his education should begin —that is to say, he should be allowed to see other dogs in pursuit of their game, and he should be accustomed to be led in the field, and the sooner after six months the better, if a bold, fearless dog. If, however, at all shy, it is better to defer the commencement to a later period, but I should never wait beyond the twelfth month. A high-couraged dog fights tremendously the first time he has a collar on, and should be taken into a grass field before it is put on. Do not take any notice, but let him have his fling, of course holding the strap the while, and, when he has tired himself, go to him, and pat him with the hand, and encourage him by the voice. After this, try and persuade him to follow, by gentle pulling at his neck-strap—he generally begins to fight once more, after which most dogs give in a little, and follow more or less cheerfully. This should be continued till the dog follows without pulling, when he may be encouraged by voice and hand, and set at liberty. In a few days he will lead well, but he should be taken out into the coursing field, and led about for a day or two with other dogs before being put into slips. By these precautions you get your dogs handy in the slips, they know what to expect, and yet do not strain at their collars, as the badly-broken dog so often does, thereby tiring himself before his course begins. The young dog generally strains at first, from being led behind other dogs, or more frequently from seeing his master in advance, and if the leader resists steadily, he tugs as steadily at the strap, and would soon be qualified for a dog-cart. Instead of resisting, the man in charge should jerk the dog's leading-strap with a sudden check, which brings him back, and, by repeating this' as often as required, he soon leaves off the trick. If, however, it once becomes a habit, it is most difficult to break, and, therefore, it is better to be careful at first. It is also well to accustom your puppies to wear the muzzle, for it will be found more easy to do so at an early age than later, and if not wanted to be worn during the cure of injuries, it is often required, as I shall by and by show, at the time of running, and then, if put on for the first time, it makes the dog uneasy, just when every discomposing cause is of consequence. The neck-strap should be at least two and a half inches wide, with a swivel ring. If narrower, as in ordinary couples, it is apt to cut the dog's neck, and also to slip over the head, to prevent which it should be buckled as tight as the dog can bear it without choking—especially in the Newmarket or Yorkshire bred dog, whose head is so narrow as to allow the strap to slip over his ears, unless very tight. The muzzle should either be made of leather, perforated with holes punched about the size of a shilling, or of wire, which may be obtained at Mr. George's, saddler, Long Acre, London. It should be long enough to extend three or four inches beyond the nose, so that the tongue may be protruded, the muzzle being made to fit loosely round the jaws just below the eyes. Two side straps, and one between the eyes, should then lead up to the strap which encircles the throat, close behind the ears. If this is made of stiff leather, and fits nicely, the dog can even take his exercise in it, and plays nearly as freely as without it. (See Fig.) If the dog is so savage as to require one to be constantly worn at exercise, it should be made very wide at the nose, and the end should be entirely open, so that he can put his tongue out, without difficulty. But this form is not so good for other purposes, as the dog can then pick up with his tongue any injurious food which is soft enough to adhere to it.

With regard to clothing, I do not recommend the use of it before the commencement of training, except while standing about on the coursing ground for the purpose of making the puppy handy, when, if the weather is very cold, it is better to put a cloth on.

During the summer months I have found that the practice of swimming the dog through a river or the sea is highly conducive to health, and may be adopted every day; the dogs always play freely after it, and in the warm weather they hardly do so sufficiently without it. It also braces them, and I think renders them much less likely to catch cold in the severe exposures to which they are subject at the public meetings in the following winter.

There is a great difference in the various breeds as to the fondness for water, some disliking it to such an extent as to refuse to follow their master through a small river if obliged to swim—whilst others will go in and swim about like a water spaniel; and even in the severe weather of a cold winter cannot be kept from galloping in any shallow water which may come in their way in the meadows in which they are exercised.

In one of the letters of 'Scrutator' on hunting, that gentleman writes strongly against allowing hounds to swim, and I have no doubt that he is quite correct, because, of course, a pack of fox hounds will not, and cannot, be allowed to play about, as greyhounds should be encouraged to do. The consequences, therefore, of getting wet, would be bad, since the hounds would merely walk or lie about and get chilled, which would be the sure forerunner of rheumatism, either in the form of kennel lameness or chest-founder ; whereas, with greyhounds, a good gallop in their play dries them in a few minutes, and no ill consequences result, so that there is a great advantage, without any attendant evil, in adopting the plan of swimming them in the summer months.

ENTERING TO HIS GAME.

With regard to the time at which the greyhound puppy should be entered to his game there is a great difference of opinion; one party maintains that it is better to let the *sapling* learn his trade, whilst the other holds that this only does harm, and that it is better to wait till he has arrived at *puppyhood*. I should here remark, for the benefit of the tyro, that the young greyhound is called a sapling till he is a year old, after which he becomes a puppy till two years old, or till the end of each season respectively. My own opinion is, that puppies reared well and of moderate size are fit to see a hare—if bitches, at ten months old, and if dogs at twelve; but the best test of the fitness of the dog is the cocking of the leg upon urining. As soon as he begins to do this he is acquiring the fire and strength of the adult animal, and is fit to exert himself in a moderate course without injury; but prior to this his joints are unset, his muscles are soft and flabby, and he only injures himself without gaining any advantage, not generally being able to get blood from want of strength and tact. Care should of course be taken to prepare the sapling for his trial of strength, though if exercised, as I have advised, twice a day, he will run himself into pretty good condition; still some greyhounds are naturally so hardy that nothing will keep them from putting on fat but a limitation of food, and in such a case it is better to reduce them in a moderate degree before showing them a hare. If, however, the ribs are tolerably apparent, you need be under no apprehension of any mischief, but in any case care should be taken that the course is not likely to be very severe, and the hare should, if possible, be found at such a distance from covert that it will not fatigue the sapling too much for his strength. It is also a question whether to put him down with another of the same age, or to pair him with an older companion; the former is the best plan, I think, for even a sapling likes to have the hare to himself, and if he does little with her, still he likes to find that he can do that little as well as his fellow. Greyhounds, of all dogs, ought to feel jealous of each other, and the moment that feeling is extinguished, either by hopelessness or carelessness, the animal will not exert himself. But at twelve months old a sapling well reared and well bred will often knock his hare about, and kill her too, and this is particularly the case with forward bitches; indeed, I have known many bitch saplings run better in April than in the October following. As soon as the sapling understands what he is doing, and finds that he has a chance with his hare, especially if he is lucky enough to get a kill, all that is required has been done, and he should be reserved for the following season. By this early entrance to his sport the young greyhound is encouraged to start well from the slips next season, because, as he is patted and made much of after his course, which he never yet has been when running sheep, cats, &c., he finds that there is some game at which his master permits him to exert his propensities, and they are, consequently, concentrated upon it. On the other hand, if a sapling is entered before his frame is set, and before he has become bloodily inclined (which inclination comes to different breeds at different ages), much harm is done, for the young animal plays with his hare instead of trying to kill her, and this tenderness is apt to be continued to an inconveniently late period; but I have seldom seen this when the puppy has been properly reared. I have known some dogs which never could be taught to kill their hares, even by the example of others, and yet were good enough to win many courses in good company; but I have no doubt they would have been still better if with more devil in their compositions.

Nothing more is necessary to be done with the puppy before the commencement of his puppy season, in which he will be placed in the trainer's hands, and the description of which will come under the head of Training. Towards the end of the summer, however, the puppies ought to be exercised two or three days a week on the road, their keeper being either on foot or horseback, but in either case going from 10 to 15 or 20 miles at a moderate pace. This is to harden the feet, and get them ready to stand their work in training, and it should be given in the cool of the morning or evening. It is, however, well to caution the young courser against mixing the puppies and aged dogs together, either in kennel or in their exercise. In kennel the old dogs domineer over the puppies, and never give them any peace, whilst at exercise they are too lazy themselves to lead in their gallops, and yet too jealous to allow the puppies to lead. They therefore immediately rush up and bite the puppies the moment they start off, so that all chance of good strong exercise is prevented. On the road this is of no consequence, and a man on horseback may take out a dozen dogs with him of all ages, without inconvenience, because then they have only to follow, and as there is no scope for play, so they do not quarrel with one another. But the moment they are let into a field, the play begins, and, like children's play, soon leads to quarrels, in which the puppies are bullied and cowed by the old dogs, so that if old dogs and puppies are of necessity taken out together, they should each be coupled while the other is let loose to play.

KENNELS.

A very material part of the management of the greyhound, as indeed of all dogs, is the proper construction of the kennel. It should be at once airy and warm, dry and clean. If a large kennel of dogs is kept, there is generally no necessity for keeping them in one yard, which is always injurious to them, even if divided into small lots. No animals thrive when too thick upon the ground. Even sheep, as the farmer well knows, when they are stocked too thickly, soon become diseased, and this is the case with hares, pheasants, grouse, or partridges. It is difficult to say why this is the case, but that it is so is now well known. So fully is the principle acknowledged in Paris, that the children in the Foundling Hospitals are nearly all sent out to nurse in small detachments, though a branch hospital in the country would not cost half so much. It is probable that in kennels and hospitals much depends upon the deterioration of the air in breathing, but this cannot be the case with sheep, hares, &c., which are entirely in the open air. However, we need not investigate the cause—the effect is well known; and I have rarely seen a healthy kennel where the number exceeded a dozen, and they are not very often in blooming health where they exceed six or eight. It is better, therefore, to divide your kennels into pairs, distributing them over your domain at intervals of not less than 100 or 150 yards—just as you would hovels for mares and colts—indeed nothing makes a better kennel than a good hovel with its yard, if the walls are high enough, and if not, they are easily raised. An ordinary-sized hovel, divided into two by a brick wall, will accommodate from six to eight dogs well. If, however, the kennels are to be built from the foundation, I should recommend the yard as well as the sleeping-room to be covered over; greyhounds are very susceptible of wet, and yet require for cleanliness' sake a yard to run into. It is therefore better to roof in the whole building, and then divide it into sleeping-rooms and yards. It is now generally agreed that a clay soil is the best for dog-kennels, but this is not of so much consequence in greyhounds, because in any case the floor of the yards, as well as the sleeping-rooms, should be laid in cement with glazed tiles—even slate absorbs too much, and should be rejected—the tiles, being glazed, do not absorb either urine or water, and are consequently soon dry after being washed down; whereas brick floors, if washed, are not dry for many hours in winter, and are also constantly impregnated with urine. Asphalte forms also an excellent material for kennel floors when properly laid. There is a reason for the selection of clay soils for kennels which has never yet, that I am aware of, been made known, and has only lately been discovered in the researches now going on in agricultural chemistry. It has been proved by Mr. Way, and the experiments have been published by him in the *Journal of the Agricultural Society*, that clay absorbs ammonia in a remarkable manner, and also several other salts contained in manure, and that it not only absorbs these salts, but combines with them, and most probably destroys their injurious effects upon animal life. Hence it is highly probable that whatever excrementitious salts of the dogs' urine, &c., are suffered to percolate into the soil, are rendered harmless in the clay substratum, whilst they are retained and allowed to putrefy and become a constant source of mischief, in the sandy or gravelly foundations which used to be selected.

The greatest number of separate kennels which I would ever advise under one roof would be three, which would require a building altogether about twenty-five feet long by fifteen feet wide; this should be bricked up at the back and half the ends. The front should be of brick for about three feet from the ground, as also the front half of the two ends; above these dwarf walls open wire-work or wooden laths should be carried up to the eaves of the roof, which need not be more than seven feet from the floor. This building may then be divided by brick walls into three compartments, each eight feet wide and fifteen feet long, doors of course being left at convenient places. The partition walls should be carried up to the roof, and will prevent the necessity of any principals, which materially reduces the expense. About six feet may then be partitioned off from each compartment for a sleeping-room, and the whole paved, as before directed, taking care either to drain each into a central, well-trapped drain, or to slope them gradually towards the front, in which an opening should be left to allow the escape of the washings into a drain outside. A door should of course be provided in the wall of the sleeping-room, and a window, which should be capable of being opened or shut with a graduated slide, for the purpose of ventilation. There should also be an aperture, capable of being opened or shut, in the back of the sleeping-room, to allow of a thorough draught in warm weather. The best aspect is a south-east or south-west, as the sun is very essential to the health of dogs, except in very hot weather indeed, when a canvas awning is required, if there is no shade from trees. With regard to the bricks used in the walls, care should be taken that they are of the hardest and least absorbent kind; or, if at all soft, they should be cemented for three feet from the ground, and whitewashed every year. The only thing now left to describe is the sleeping bench. These are better made in the form of a trough, eight feet long, nine inches deep, and three feet wide, to fit the end of the sleeping-room opposite the door; but they should be made in a movable form, so that they can be raised or lowered at discretion; or, at least, one should be so, as it is often wanted very near the ground for dogs injured by accidents, or for young puppies. For grown dogs they should be fixed so that the front edge (which should be rounded off smoothly) should be about three feet six inches from the ground. This is higher than the usual height, but it keeps the dogs well out of the damp; and I think, also, they like to be high in the world, at all events they seem to thrive better the higher they are from the ground. The roof may be either of tiles, felt, or slate—thatch is objectionable from the harbour for fleas which it affords. The first material is, I think, the best, but the dearest; the second is equally good, but does not last so long; whilst slates are too hot in the summer, and are also cold in the extreme in the winter. Neither of the two former require a ceiling to the sleeping-room, but slates certainly both in summer and winter require that protection. A kennel of this form and size for nine or twelve dogs, may be put up for from 30*l.* to 40*l.*, according to the locality in which it is situated, and the materials used. A very good form of kennel is described as follows, with the aid of the annexed engravings, the first of which is the ground plan, and the second the elevation.

Let a square brick or stone building, *a b c d*, be put up,

twelve feet wide in each direction, and divided by inside walls into four lesser squares, each of which forms a separate lodging-room, and will hold from three to five dogs. Round this is a covered yard, *e f g h*, bounded by open pales, or wire netting, above the height of two or three feet. The yard should be separated into four by sliding doors, made to lift, by which there is no chance

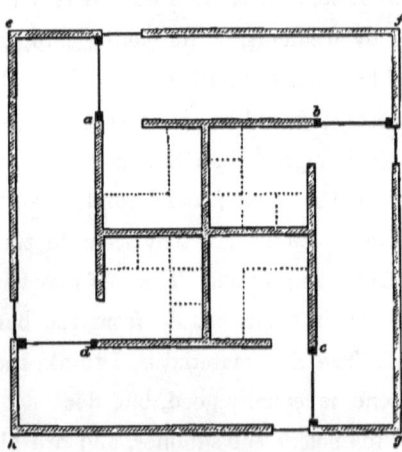

Ground Plan of Greyhound Kennel.

of catching the dog as he runs through, and each division should have a separate entrance from without, and also into the corresponding lodging-room. In this way each lot of puppies may be let out into the whole area of the yards, and will thus take a great deal of exercise by galloping round and round it, which on wet days is a great advantage. A central ventilator, as shown in the elevation, keeps all sweet.

The floor, as in all kennels, should be impervious to wet, and the draining carefully attended to.

Elevation of Greyhound Kennel.

KENNEL MANAGEMENT.

It is of great importance to health that the kennel should be kept scrupulously clean; the kennelman should, therefore, wash it down every morning, and mop the floor as dry as possible afterwards. In the cold weather of winter, it is a good plan to strew sawdust on the floor, or to cover it with straw, but I prefer the former; wheat straw is the best for litter, and should be shaken up daily, and renewed twice a week. Where fleas are very troublesome in the summer, deal shavings are a good substitute for straw. If it is cold, the door of the sleeping-room must be

x

closed at night, and, when very severe, by day also. Some trainers cut a hole in the door, and nail loosely over this a piece of carpet, which allows the dog to pass in and out without admitting too much air, and is an excellent plan except in very cold weather.

When ticks have once infested a kennel it is often very difficult to eradicate them, and even brimstone burnt with closed doors fails to do so. In such a case dissolve an ounce of corrosive sublimate in a pint of spirit of wine, and brush over the walls and woodwork with the solution. Then whitewash with quicklime and water, and when all is dry the dogs may be admitted with impunity. Fleas retreat into the roof, so that they cannot be destroyed in the same way, and the only remedy is to sprinkle turpentine over the litter and up into the crevices of the roof.

PHYSIC.

With regard to physic during puppyhood, I should never give it, as a regular thing, without cause; and the causes are as numerous as the diseases of the dog. No harm, however, can arise from an occasional mild dose of castor oil; indeed, I am in the habit of directing a dose whenever the puppy shows, by his dulness or want of appetite, that he is slightly off his feed. This occasional use of oil is only substituting one vegetable irritant (the oil) for another and more natural one, the grass, which the dog takes whenever amiss.

EXPENSES OF REARING AND TRAINING.

Many young coursers may like to know the outlay which must be incurred in order to bring a small stud of greyhounds into the field. For their information, the following table of expenses is added, premising that it is the lowest possible calculation, in accordance with the directions given in this book, and on the supposition that success attends upon each particular litter:—

	£	s.	d.
To one quarter of the value of brood bitch, reckoning that she will last four years, and cost 20*l*.	5	0	0
To travelling expenses and stallion .	6	10	0
One year's keep of bitch, and tax on ditto	3	10	0
Rearing six puppies till eighteen months old at 10*s*. 6*d*. a week, for food and litter only — flesh 3*s*. 6*d*., meal 5*s*. 6*d*., trotters 1*s*., straw 6*d*.	37	16	0
Tax on ditto for one year	3	12	0
Man to exercise and feed ditto, reckoning one-third of his time, at 12*s*. per week — this is on the supposition that he can be occupied in other work .	14	8	0
	£70	16	0

This sum, divided by six (the full average number of a litter), will make the cost of each puppy, when ready for training, in round numbers, 12*l*.

You may thus fairly calculate upon each of your greyhounds standing you in about 12*l*. or guineas at his first appearance, and this with the best luck, and on the calculation that you rear six good greyhounds out of each litter. But every old courser will know how much this is above the average. It is not every one who has a 'Mocking Bird,' a 'Scotland Yet,' or a 'Riot,' nor has every master the good management of Messrs. Davy, Campbell, and Randell. I could mention many who rear from twenty to fifty every year, and are content with one or two winners out of that number. Now what can these 'one or two' cost? Even if sent out to walk among friends or tenants, the mere charge for brood bitches and sires must be enormous, and is sufficient to deter any person who has a limited income from embarking in such an extravagant sport. But I believe that this want of success is mainly owing to the extent of the speculation. Greyhounds cannot safely be accumulated in this way, and the very excess of care in trying to get a good choice by having a large stock of puppies to select from, leads to disappointment. My advice, therefore, has been given on the principle of doing a little, but doing that little well; and on this plan I fancy a good manager, and a real lover of the animal, who will take some trouble himself, and see that his dogs are in good health, daily or every other day, and that they have proper exercise, may calculate upon success in a much greater proportion than the owner of a large and unmanageable stud. Of course I do not for a moment suppose that he can expect to rear three or four first-rate dogs out of every bitch, but that he may fairly hope to have in each (if the blood is unexceptionable and the parents healthy) three or four greyhounds good enough to win a stake or two during the season, with an occasional first-rater among them. And I firmly believe that, by adopting the principles which I have endeavoured to make clear, he will have a better chance of avoiding failure than by any other mode; and the more I see of rearing greyhounds, the more convinced I am of the truth of these opinions.

CHAPTER XV.

Maximum and Minimum of Work in Training—First Preparation of the overfed Dog; of the Bitch in Season—Modes of Reducing Fat—Directions for Feeding—Private Trials—Final Preparation—Management at Meetings and after Running—Receipts for Cordials.

MAXIMUM AND MINIMUM OF WORK IN TRAINING.

SOON after the publication of the first edition of 'The Greyhound,' an opinion was very generally expressed by coursers that the amount of work directed by me was too great, and that many greyhounds would be ruined by following out strictly the rules which I had laid down. Mr. Temple was particularly strong in his censures, and indeed may be said to have originated the exaggerated idea which was formed of them. At his instigation, I believe, Mr. Welsh obtained from six celebrated public coursers accounts of the mode of training adopted by each, and published them in the sixteenth volume of 'Thacker's Annual,' whether with or without the knowledge and consent of the writers is a matter of no importance to my present purpose. Suffice it that they were published, and that the experience of these gentlemen, however gained, will always be of the utmost value to the young courser. I am not going to follow Mr. Welsh's example, and insert these letters without authority, much as I should like to do so; but I cannot resist the temptation to refer to Mr. Jones' letter, in which he states that 'Amos (his experienced trainer) calculates that "Jael's" work averaged thirty miles a day' when in training for the Wiltshire downs, where she ran remarkably well. Now the utmost distance that I ever advised is as follows:—'For the first ten days or a fortnight the dogs should have *three days a week* from *fifteen* to *twenty-five* miles a day of fast work, following a man on horseback, *trotting one-half, galloping* at best pace *a mile and a half or two miles*, and *walking* the remainder. As much as possible of this should be upon turf, as the more the feet are saved the better. After this work on the Monday, Wednesday, and Friday, the dogs should be well washed from dirt, and then dried with a cloth, &c. . . . On the Tuesday, Thursday, and Saturday, they should be taken out by the trainer on foot, accompanied by a man or boy who is a stranger to them. They may be suffered to play about in the fields for an hour, taking care that they do not stand or lie down. This should be done on the way to good training ground, which should be a hill side of at least half a mile long, or as much more as practicable, and of good grass if possible; but if the dog is to run over arable land, then of land of a similar quality. The assistant, when near the foot of the hill, should take up all the dogs, and running a stirrup leather through the ends of the leading straps, buckle it round his waist, for fear of their snatching themselves out of his hands, and also in order to leave both his hands at liberty to unloose their straps. The trainer should then walk briskly up the hill, pursuing the same course which he intends the dogs to follow, and when arrived at half a

AMOUNT OF WORK NECESSARY.

mile off or more, if they still see him, should commence shouting and whistling to the dogs. Upon this the assistant should let loose the one which is the most lively, and inclined to run to the trainer, when he will immediately exert all his powers to run up to his master. The other dogs should be one at a time let loose, &c. . . . When the nature of the ground will admit of it, it answers well for the trainer to be on a pony, and gallop off up the hill as soon as the dogs get good sight of him, &c. . . . After the trainer has carried their exercise as far as he thinks right, the dogs should be walked back to kennel,' &c. . . . In these extracts are embodied the whole of the directions which I gave for regulating the amount of work, and although I confess that subsequent experience has convinced me that there are some breeds which will not stand this extent of work, especially if the dogs have been allowed to lie idle all the summer, yet that there are others in which it will be borne with the greatest advantage; and in this view I am supported in particular by Mr. Jones' letter published by Mr. Welsh, and generally by all the other five, though not certainly to the same extent. Many large stakes have been won by dogs either wholly untrained or only partially so; but, on the other hand, it would be difficult to say how many have been lost for the want of a sufficient preparation. Even at Altcar it is seldom that a large stake is won without a severe course or two in going through it, and every one must remember instances in which all chance of the stake has been lost by the best dog in it from this cause. I do not contend that any preparation will entirely do away with this element of risk, but that it will greatly reduce its extent no courser of experience will dispute. The principle is clear enough which should regulate the amount of work—namely, to carry it out to such an extent as to reduce superfluous flesh, and improve the wind and stamina, without at the same time making the dog slow or slack, and carefully avoiding the injurious effect which is so well known as 'over marking.' To do this requires the practised eye of the trainer, and indeed there are very few men who can be trusted fully to alter the amount of work according to circumstances. I have myself had dogs brought out to perfection by the same man who, with another lot, differently bred, trained them to death's door. With regard to the use of a horse in training, there can be no doubt that it can be dispensed with if the trainer is an active man and can walk from sixteen to twenty miles on end. But there are few who both can and will do this, and hence I prefer the use of the horse, which few trainers are industrious enough to eschew. *Slow* roadwork I am satisfied does good in every way, hardening the feet, strengthening the nails, and in this way preventing many of the accidents likely to occur in the coursing field. *Fast* roadwork, that is, carried to the extent of galloping, will injure the speed; but a steady trot has no such effect, as is proved by the fact that 'Barrator' was trained by Mr. Briggs entirely in this way, and that Mr. Dixon's flyers, 'Deacon' and 'Dalton,' did most of their work on the road. No doubt if a greyhound is confined to his kennel, or to a small grass paddock, for months, during which his feet become unaccustomed to friction, he will be made footsore, and his muscles shaken, by at once putting him to travel long distances on the road. This would be an abuse of the plan, and not the proper use of it, and no one but a tyro would dream of such a practice. If a man has only four or five dogs in training, he can manage to bring them out well enough for any country without a horse, but if he has more it will be better to find him one; and the extra cost incurred, which need not be more than from ten to fifteen shillings per week, will be reimbursed by the superior success of his dogs, if they are intrinsically good. No training will make a bad greyhound into a good one; and unless a man has a prospect of possessing the right sort of stuff, he may as well keep down his expenses, but if it appears that his dogs are worth the outlay, no expense should be spared.

FIRST PREPARATION OF THE OVERFED DOG.

In the directions which I have given for rearing the puppy, he has been kept in a state which renders him always fit to go into severe work. A fortnight or three weeks' final preparation is all that he requires even for the most severe country, and a week or ten days ought to fit him for average coursing. But the majority of puppies are not thus taken care of. Instead of being only from four or five pounds too heavy, they are ten or fifteen pounds above their proper running weight, and being loaded with fat inside, they would be permanently injured if they were put either to fast work in training, or allowed to run a course. Such a dog is generally in every way unprepared for running, the pads of his feet being generally very thinly covered, his muscles and heart being loaded with fat, and his nails often so long as to rattle as he trots about his kennel. When an animal is in this condition, no attempt should be made to get him fit to run in less than five or six weeks, and even that time will not suffice in many cases.

The first thing to be done is to get the overfed dog into the same state as he would have been if he had been reared and kept as I have recommended in Chap. XIV. To effect this care should be taken that his stomach is not disordered by a change of food, nor his lungs and heart deranged by being put to a severe strain while still overloaded with fat, nor his feet made sore by friction on the road before they are gradually hardened and their pads accustomed to secrete fresh cuticle as fast as it is worn away. In the first place the trainer should weigh his dog, and carefully consider how much he has to get off him before he will be fit to run. To do this some experience is necessary—partly gained by observing at what weight most dogs run well, and partly by regarding the condition of those who run badly. It should be remembered that the dog must not only be rendered capable of bearing hard work with impunity, but that his spirits must be kept so high that he will be willing and anxious to do it. In this last respect consists the greater difficulty of training the grey-hound over that incurred in bringing out the horse. The latter animal need only be considered as a machine, which, if in order, can always be made to do his best, by whip or spur; but no such aids can be brought into play with the greyhound, who often

PREPARATION OF THE OVERFED DOG.

throws away his chance by looking on when he has success within his grasp. In him the will must be regarded as well as the power to defeat his antagonist, and whilst the trainer of the horse may feed and work him up to the highest point which his constitution will bear, only taking care that he neither makes his legs and feet stale, nor 'overworks' him, thereby destroying his pace and stamina, the greyhound trainer must, in addition, be careful that he keeps plenty of fire in his dogs, so that they are ready and willing to exert themselves to the uttermost. In reference to this subject a great difference of opinion exists, and many successful coursers maintain that the overfed and neglected dog may be got fit to run in a fortnight or three weeks, beyond which no good can be done, and if kept longer in training he will go off instead of improving. Against this doctrine I strongly object, and it is manifest from the repeated successes of such greyhounds as 'Riot' and 'Rival' in Mr. Randell's kennel, and others nearly though not quite so remarkable, that the greyhound can be kept fit to run for months together, taking care to let him down for a few days occasionally. Thus, by a reference to 'Riot's' performances given in the Appendix, it will be seen that she ran once, and sometimes twice, a month during each season, from October 1854 to March 1858, with the exception of about two months in each year, when she was either 'in season' or breeding. It may be said that she was an exception to all rules, but this does not apply to her constitution, and her case shows plainly enough that health may be maintained for months together without throwing the dog out of training. The chief cause of the dog being upset in training consists in the danger of disordering the stomach by overfeeding, or by keeping him too long upon highly stimulating food. This is far more likely to do mischief than work, which in a healthy animal is soon forgotten. Worms, and other causes, affecting the stomach and bowels, are a fertile source of 'upsets,' and it behoves the trainer to guard against them in the most careful manner. When free from these complications, and if the dog is of a hardy sort, the amount of work laid down in these pages will never make him slow. Such a result would show that the trainer had made a mistake in his estimate of the necessary quantity, which, as I before remarked, must be carefully graduated according to its apparent effects. When a dog is too tired to leave his bed after work, on being called by his trainer, he will speedily become fresh again if in a healthy condition, and allowed a day's rest. My object is not to bring him into the coursing field jaded and spiritless, but, on the contrary, to prepare him so gradually that he scarcely feels his work to be severe, because, in proportion as it has been increased, his powers have *pari passu* gone on improving. On the other hand, if the dog is out of health, a single day's overwork produces a permanent impression which no rest will remove. The animal becomes flabby and wastes away, losing all spirit and appetite, and showing unmistakable evidence of being 'overmarked.' In such an unfortunate case there is nothing to be done but to throw the dog out of training for some months at least, and the owner will be fortunate if he ever recovers his powers altogether.

When the trainer has made up his mind as to what is to be done, the next thing is to proceed by giving a dose of physic, which should either be about three-fourths of a drachm of horse-ball composition, or a table-spoonful of castor oil, mixed with nearly that quantity of syrup of buckthorn and a tea-spoonful of syrup of poppies. Either of these should be given on an empty stomach early in the morning, two hours after which some broth should be given, and shortly afterwards he may be taken out to exercise, which will soon set the physic in operation. About twelve or one, when the desired effect is fully produced, he may be brought home and fed with a light meal, composed of bread sopped in weak broth—not exceeding altogether a pint and a half. Of course the trainer will notice if any worms have passed, and if any are seen provision must be made for their subsequent removal from his interior. Next day the dog should be exercised early in the morning, going five or six miles out and home, but whether his trainer is on foot or on horseback must depend upon circumstances. If a horse is used the pace need not exceed a gentle trot at any time, and the greater part of the distance may be walked, so as to occupy about three hours. On returning to the kennel let his feet and legs be washed with warm water and carefully dried, the feet being treated accordingly if they are sore from road-work; but to prevent this as much as possible the exercise should be on turf as far as is practicable. After this the trainer takes the dog between his knees, and rubs him all over with a pair of friction gloves, or a bag of horse-hair cloth made to fit the hand, commencing at the shoulder, passing thence along the muscles of the back and ribs, and finishing at the quarters and hind-legs. The dog may then be allowed to enter his bed, where he remains quietly till feeding time, allowing him a bone to amuse himself if he is alone, but this should not be given him if he has kennel companions, as it is sure to lead to quarrels, unless they can be carefully watched to prevent such a result. At one o'clock feed upon the quantity decided on as necessary for the reduction or increase of weight, according to circumstances, the average required being a pound and a half altogether, and composed of equal quantities of meat torn or cut into small pieces, and mixed with soaked bread or biscuit.

In deciding on the proper allowance of food, both as to quantity and quality, the trainer takes into consideration the previous habits and diet of the dog. If he has been well exercised and regularly fed, he will not at first require much alteration in his diet, and it is only by ascertaining what effect has been produced upon his weight that it is to be altered. When the dog has been fed upon greaves and barley meal, as is often the case, without tasting flesh, great care is necessary in gradually accustoming him to the latter kind of food, as, though it is always preferred by the canine race in all its varieties, it does not agree with their stomachs when given without a liberal allowance of farinaceous food, and this is especially the case where flesh is allowed in considerable quantity without gradually accustoming the dog to it. The greater the proportion of flesh to bread the more will the fat of the body be reduced, but this cannot be carried beyond a certain point without leading to indigestion and diarrhœa. After feeding, the dog is left in kennel till the next morning, but many trainers prefer to let him out for half an hour in the evening, and some give a small portion of food also at that time. On the following morning no roadwork whatever should be given beyond what is absolutely necessary to reach some grass land, where the dog should be allowed to play, being walked about there for three or four hours. After this he is taken home and treated exactly as before. On the fourth morning the trainer has to consider whether his charge is progressing as he wishes in point of weight, for which purpose he puts him on the scales, taking care to choose the same period of the twenty-four hours for the comparison as that on which he last weighed him. If about 2 lbs. have been lost he may come to the conclusion that he is going on well, and no alteration need be made; but there are some constitutions so robust that they refuse to give up their fat to ordinary measures, and over them castor oil has little or no effect, nor will any reasonable reduction of food produce what is desired. These cases are, however, exceptional, and I believe that there are very few dogs which cannot be brought out light enough by a fair amount of exercise united with a reduction in their food. Trainers in general have a great objection to starvation in their own persons, and hence perhaps they think it less cruel to their charge to physic them than to reduce their food, but it is a great mistake in every way. Occasionally, however, a dog of a gross constitution has made his feet too sore in his work to go on with it to a sufficient extent to effect the reduction in weight which is desired, even when due starvation is practised, and in such a case an active purgative like the following may be tried with advantage: —

Take of Powdered Jalap . . . . 10 grains
Carbonate of Soda . . . . 15 grains
Epsom Salts . . . . . ½ ounce
Tincture of Ginger . . . . 30 drops
Weak Chamomile Tea . . . 6 ounces
Mix, and give as a drench.

Or

Take of Barbadoes Aloes . . . . 1 drachm
Ginger . . . . . . 2 grains
Palm Oil . . . . . . ½ drachm
Mix into a bolus, and give as such.

Either of these doses will produce a number of watery evacuations, which will carry off two or three pounds of fat without seriously weakening the dog. Still I confess I do not like them to be used except as a last resource, since they tend to produce dyspepsia, and, if much used, lower the tone of the constitution considerably. Of course, if the liver is not acting, proper measures must be taken to set it going.

From this point in the preparation the work must be continued as before; the trainer, if he has a horse, taking the dogs out with it every alternate day for a distance gradually increased up to eight or ten miles out and back, and increasing the pace according to the strength, wind, and condition of the feet. It seldom is necessary to gallop more than a mile or a mile and a half at a stretch, choosing a piece of turf for this purpose. Five or six miles may be done on the trot, and the remainder on the walk. Should no horse be used the trainer trusts to the natural playfulness of his dogs for the gallop, but he should keep them going constantly for the time he is out (four hours) by walking briskly himself.

By attention to the previous directions and by the following which are chiefly abbreviated from them, most dogs may be brought to the required condition.

1. Give no more physic than is absolutely necessary, never using the stronger kinds while the feet are capable of bearing work.

2. Give as little bread, or other farinaceous food, as will keep the dog in health, which may be known by the colour of his fæces, too much flesh turning them more or less black or chocolate-coloured, instead of that resembling gingerbread.

3. Use as much and as prolonged exercise, either on foot or on horseback, as the constitution and feet will bear, carefully avoiding jading the dog, or carrying work to the extent known as 'over-marking.'

4. Use plenty of friction.

5. Watch the feet carefully, and see that the cuticular covering of the pads is not worn too thin, so as to make them sore. When this is likely to occur or has occurred, after washing them with water to remove all grit, bathe them with a saturated solution of alum, and when dry dress them with pitch ointment.

By attention to these rules, from 3 lbs. to 6 lbs. a week may be got off, and when the dog is within a pound of his contemplated running weight, he may be considered to have completed this first preparation, and to be ready to begin training in earnest.

It was formerly the custom in some kennels to send out dogs under heavy clothing, in the hope that it would have the effect of sweating them and thus reducing their weight. This plan is now exploded, as it is found that no such result takes place, the dog's skin being very little inclined to give out fluid, and practically he does not sweat to any appreciable extent, though on a very warm day fine globules of perspiration may be seen to collect on his coat, showing that, however trifling it may be, there is some sensible perspiration from his skin. I have known dogs sent out to exercise with three or four cloths on, but it only makes them slow and jades them; nor do I believe that, even in the most severe weather, training ought to be conducted with the aid even of one cloth. If the trainer moves briskly forward and does not stop to rest himself, his dogs will keep themselves warm enough in the coldest weather, and are far better unclothed. Where stove-heat is employed in the kennel, clothing may be necessary, and especially so when away from home; but otherwise I believe it is a mistake to use it at all until the dog leaves home for a meeting where he is about to run. Sometimes a very delicate animal may require a light cloth, and in wet weather a waterproof one, but these are exceptions which will seldom occur.

It is a great mistake to run a greyhound, either in public or private, while he is undergoing the course of medicine, work, and starvation, which are too often so hastily accumulated on him that he loses his spirits and strength to a very great degree. While in this state he feels no zest in the pursuit, and hence the slack style of running which so frequently disappoints both owner and trainer, sometimes reaching to the extent of stopping with the hare in view. When the preparation has been properly conducted, such a thing should never occur with a well-bred dog, and, however cunning he may become from constant practice, he should never run slack. Even in the most severe countries a well prepared dog, although he may be stale from a hard course or two, should always show fire enough; and if he does not, depend upon it there has been some mistake in his preparation, provided his breed is the right one.

PREPARATION OF THE BITCH 'IN SEASON,' OR AFTER BEING SO.

It is now a recognised fact among experienced coursers that very few bitches can be depended on for three months from the time they are 'in season.' Sometimes when this state first comes on, they will run very keenly, and even when bleeding they occasionally do so; but they are always more or less uncertain, and unless they are very much wanted, they are far better left at home than paraded in public when in this condition. It is not only that the bitch loses her course, but she is afterwards injured by it; for it either tends to reduce her subsequent zest for the sport, or when her bodily powers are upset it affects her constitutionally. As soon as 'the heat' is over, a tendency to lose muscle and to lay up fat is developed, indicating that the animal is in a state fit for breeding purposes rather than for running. This change varies considerably, and if the trainer finds that the muscle keeps up, and that his bitch is lively and well, as will sometimes happen, he may be justified in training and running her. Generally, however, bitches when 'put by,' even if they do not at once become flabby and fat, will yet waste away in training, and will not stand nearly the same amount of work as at other times. There is a condition of the whole system in which every function is rendered subservient to the formation and nourishment of the young, even when impregnation has been prevented. Animals when with young, become still more fat than when prevented from becoming so, and they also preserve their health to a much greater degree; for this reason the farmer puts his feeding cows to the bull, although he intends to kill them in the course of two or three months. At first, it would occur to everyone that the necessity for nourishing the embryo calf must take something away from the fat of the mother, but, on the contrary, it is found that up to a certain period the cow increases in weight more rapidly than she would do if not 'in calf.' On this principle many coursers, rather than 'put by' a bitch, and with the view of being enabled to run her for the next fortnight or three weeks, or soon after whelping, allow her access to a dog, and in the latter case destroy the whelps. It is still a doubtful point which is the better plan, and numberless cases of success and failure following each might be adduced. 'Riot' never ran better than when she won the Altcar Cup, in October 1857, after producing her first litter in the previous spring; and in March 1858, after rearing her second litter in January, she won two stakes at Tredegar Park, and divided the Caledonian Cup (32 dogs) with that excellent bitch 'Baffle,' after an undecided course. 'Tollwife,' improved in her running after her first litter; and many similar examples, though not perhaps quite so remarkable, might be adduced. Mr. Webb's 'Flirt' ran fourth for the Waterloo Cup when three weeks gone in pup to 'Foremost,' the produce of which was a litter composed of 'War Eagle,' 'Wicked Eye,' 'Wrestler,' and 'Well I never.' On the other hand, numerous instances could be adduced of bitches never recovering their form after whelping, and I am inclined to believe that the chances are very even as to the result. My opinion is that it mainly depends upon the number of the puppies composing the litter. 'Riot' had only six in her first, and seven in her second litter, and 'Tollwife' a still smaller number. Hence they were not much pulled down during pregnancy, and soon recovered shape and strength; whereas, when a bitch has a large litter of ten or twelve puppies, she never is restored to her maiden shape, nor does she recover her strength for a long time, and is seldom as fast afterwards as she was before. My opinion is that almost all bitches become more fiery, and run more stoutly, after one or even two litters, but in the majority of instances they lose speed. Probably a good deal depends upon their treatment during their 'heat' and subsequent pregnancy; for it often happens that bitches are kept in kennel almost constantly through these periods, and are not allowed sufficient exercise to maintain them in health. One thing is quite certain, namely, that the vast majority of bitches will run slack for two or three months from the time of going off their 'heat.' This may generally be reckoned to extend to the third or fourth week after their natural 'whelping time;' so that there is no saving of time in keeping them from the dog, for if the bitch is not much pulled down by a large litter, and does not suckle more than one or two whelps, she recovers herself completely in three weeks after pupping. When it is desired to run a bitch as soon as possible after having had a litter, it is better to keep one whelp on her for a fortnight, when she may safely be dried and at once put into slow work.

MODES OF REDUCING FAT.

I need scarcely inform my readers that fat is laid up in the body in store for future exigencies, and is of no *present* use whatever. Hence it is so much dead weight to be carried by the animal which possesses it, and it is one chief object of the trainer to get rid of it as far as possible, since it not only interferes with speed from its weight, but also by its direct pressure upon those important organs of circulation, the heart and lungs. There are three modes of getting rid of fat, all of which act by compelling Nature to fall back upon this substance, when she is called upon in an unusually sudden manner to find materials to supply waste of blood, or some of its component parts. These are: *first*, physic; *secondly*, starvation; and *thirdly*, work.

By physic is to be understood purgative drugs, which act by suddenly draining certain portions of the blood into the bowels. In this way a demand is made upon the storehouses of the body for the supply of material to fill up the void, and fat being the chief article contained in these receptacles, is at once absorbed into the circulation in considerable quantities. Hence this is doubtless the quickest way of removing fat, but it has many objectionable and inseparable attendants, including its lowering effect upon the digestive organs, and its tendency to cause the absorption of muscular tissue at the same time. For this reason it should be used with great care.

Starvation is much less objectionable than physic, because it merely limits the general supply of nourishment, calling upon the storehouse to render up its contents, and not actually wasting the muscular tissue until the supply of fat is exhausted. The dog, however, bears starvation remarkably well, and it does not injure his digestive organs, or lower his strength, as it does those of the horse. Indeed, the practice of an occasional act of starvation conduces to the health of all the *carnivora*, and in the *felidæ* is ever necessary to their health, while among the *canidæ*, though it is not so imperative, it is more or less desirable. The domestic dog instinctively supplies this want by eating grass, which makes him disgorge his food, and is therefore equivalent to starvation.

Work, however, is the grand means of reducing fat, and where the body is in a healthy state it should be mainly depended on for that purpose. For not only does it effect the object, but it does it without any injurious effects, and is accompanied by the good result of increasing the general health, and particularly that of the muscular system. Like everything else, it may be carried too far, and, as I have previously remarked, it is better to avoid the tendency to injury by reducing the food slightly, than by depending entirely upon work. A great many plans have been proposed for keeping down fat, not only in the dog, but in the human subject, and of late Mr. Banting has become famous for that carried out by him at the suggestion of Mr. Harvey. According to him, man can be kept in health upon a diet composed almost exclusively of animal food, two or three ounces of bread or biscuit per day being all that he allows. Time will show how far this theory is correct, but it is pretty clearly made out that it does effect a reduction of fat. With the greyhound no such good would follow, for we all know that there are very few of them which would keep in health if allowed fifteen ounces of flesh per day and only two or three ounces of bread. The experiment has been tried so often with failure as the result, that it is quite useless to repeat it, and 'Bantingism' will certainly not succeed in the kennel. Some years ago, Magendie, the great French physiologist, tried a series of experiments upon dogs by feeding them upon flesh from which the juices had been previously washed. He found, however, that they soon pined away and died, and that there is something more wanted to support health than the mere chemical elements composing muscular and bony tissue. So, also, in feeding dogs upon food too highly concentrated, it is found to disagree, and a diet composed of animal jelly and sago, which each contain the principal component parts of the body, is speedily found to disorder the system to an extent which is scarcely to be believed without actual observation. The reason of this is that jelly and sago, as well as washed flesh, are deficient in certain saline substances contained in the serum of the blood; and for the same reason, if dogs are fed upon boiled flesh, without giving them some of the broth in which the boiling has been carried on, they will soon become unhealthy. Hence it is necessary to avoid these mistakes, and to select such articles as are within a reasonable compass as to bulk, and yet contain the necessary proportions of neutral salts and phosphoric acid. Which then are these articles? 1st. In flesh we find the materials for supporting and developing the powers, and keeping up the tone of the muscular system; 2ndly, in bread is contained about one-fifth of the same materials as are found in flesh, together with starch and other carbonaceous matters, required for the respiratory process, and for sustaining the general health of the body; and 3rdly, in each are met with the salts of the blood, such as phosphoric acid in combination with potash and soda, alkaline earths, such as magnesia and lime, iron, and common salt.

DIRECTIONS FOR FEEDING.

In choosing the various articles of diet during training, regard should be had to their effects upon the muscular, nervous, and circulating systems, as well as upon the general health. Without full and strong muscles the pace necessary for outstripping his fellow cannot be developed or maintained in the greyhound and without a due amount of nervous energy and a full supply of healthy blood, the attempt will not be made. To be successful, he must be willing as well as capable of sudden and continued exertion.

Hence his muscles require fibrine and gelatine, his brain and bones demand phosphoric acids and phosphates in combination with various substances, and his blood must be made up of fibrine, albumen, and saline substances suspended in water. These substances are all found in bread and meat; but to keep the digestive organs in good humour a variety must be offered them, and some fresh vegetable matter must occasionally be added. Horseflesh, when free from drugs given for the disease of which the animal has died, is sufficiently good for training purposes; next to it comes beef; but better than either is mutton, on account of its suiting the stomach of the dog, and of its being less heating and stimulating. In training, therefore, these should be varied, the usual plan being to feed upon horseflesh or beef till the week before running, and then finish upon mutton. To these should be added a little jelly made from cow heels and sheeps' trotters. Thus in the lean flesh of one of the above animals joined to bread, jelly, and salt, will be found the best food for training purposes. They contain all that is wanted, they agree with the stomach, and they afford sufficient materials for the purposes of respiration.

During training, unless the dog is soft in constitution, the appetite generally keeps good; indeed, most animals would eat more than is given them. Some are, however, so delicate that their stomachs give way under work, and for such poor wretches all sorts of remedies have been devised, such as beefsteaks fried in brandy, sago and eggs, rabbits fried in onions, mutton pemmican, &c. Unless, however, there is some particular necessity for running a dog, as, for instance, when engaged in a produce stake, recourse should never be had to such unnatural food. It is, however, very desirable to change the diet continually, and the mode of cooking it, and for this reason the following variations are given:—

1st. Simple boiled lean mutton, beef, or healthy horseflesh, either of which will answer, but mutton agrees best with the stomach, and a greater quantity of it will be borne without injury. Whichever is used should be kept for at least a fortnight, and the broth should be used to soak the bread.

2nd. Either of the above chopped into small pieces, should be put into a saucepan, and just covered with boiling water, after which the whole should be just boiled up, carefully stirring it to prevent burning.

3rd. Either of the above should be put on a toasting fork, or in a Dutch oven, and done before a quick fire till the outside is brown, taking care that the inside is still what is called underdone; after this it should be cut in small pieces.

4th. A sheep's head is to be split and put into a frying-pan with a very little lard, so as to brown rapidly, with the aid of some flour. The meat should then be cut off and the fat picked out rejected. Dogs are very fond of this food, and it suits them well as an occasional variety.

5th. The bread which is used may be either that made without barm, as described at page 289, or common bakers' bread (brown if possible), or biscuits made specially of coarse wheat flour and oatmeal. These should be mixed in the proportion of about three parts wheat flour to one part of oatmeal, and the dough should be either made light with the acid and soda, or with barm. Captains' biscuits are generally full of weevils, and often musty, besides which they contain no oatmeal, and are made of fine flour. Loaves made of about the weight of 1 lb. each will keep well for ten days or a fortnight, which is quite long enough for all practical purposes. If kept beyond this time they become mouldy.

6th. I have advised that at all times the water should be boiled, for the purpose of preventing the development of worms, but even if not done with this view, it is better to do so when the dogs are in training, as by accustoming them to its use there is less danger of a change of water disagreeing with them.

7th. The hour for feeding when in training is usually from twelve to one o'clock, but when actually running it is not always possible to adhere to this rule.

PRIVATE TRIALS.

Before the greyhound is tested in public it is usual to see what powers he has, by trying him against some well-known dog in private, so as to prevent as far as possible the chance of disappointment which is so grievous to the courser.

Even with this precaution it too often happens that the anticipations formed by the owner are not realised, but this is dependent more upon defect in his judgment than upon the plan itself. Sometimes the private trial is not conducted in the same way as the public one. The slip is too short, or the ground is different, and in either case the result may be deceptive; but if no mistake of this kind is made, there is no reason why as much confidence should not be placed in a private performance as in a public one. It is true that the trial dog is not always to be depended on, and that greyhounds at all times are uncertain animals; but, on the whole, it may be concluded that the judgment of the owner or his servants is too often subservient to his hopes and fears, and that in this cause is to be found the seat of the disappointments which we so often hear of. There are other reasons for these private trials when the dog is a puppy, consisting in the fact that practice is required before he is capable of doing his best. Hence every dog should course a certain number of hares before he is brought out, and it is of little use at first to put him down with a trial dog, as it is only wasting the powers of the latter. So, also, I believe that every greyhound should occasionally see a hare, without which he loses his zest for the sport and becomes slack. For these several reasons every public courser should have the use of some ground for his private trials, and he should take care that, as far as possible, it should be of the same nature as that over which he intends subsequently to run his dogs in public.

On the day before the private trial, the greyhound should not have any fast work, beyond that which he takes at play, but he should be walked out for at least three hours upon meadow or down land. After this he should be dressed as usual, and then fed at about one o'clock, a little lighter than usual, his meal not exceeding three-quarters of a pound of flesh and the same quantity of bread soaked in broth or warm jelly. After feeding, he may remain in kennel till the evening, when he should be walked out for half an hour, and again dressed.

On the morning of the trial, walk the dog out for an hour, till he has thoroughly emptied himself, when he may be taken home and well frictioned, after which he is ready to take into the coursing field.

If the owner has not confidence in his own judgment, or in that of his trainer, he had better consult some more experienced friend, to assist him in this arduous task. He should remember how much inclined we all are to make allowances for the faults of our pets; and if his friend condemns his dogs more decidedly than he does himself, or than his trainer does, who is likely to be still more prejudiced in their favour, he should not be surprised. These private trials are almost more annoying to the owner than the public ones, because there is less excuse to be made for his dogs. If a dog has an accident in the trial, so long as it does not disable him, he may be put down again to another hare; but in public, when the judge has given his fiat, no second chance is allowed, and all sorts of excuses may be made by the owner for failures which, to the looker-on, are manifestly the fault of the animal. The young hand is, however, sometimes led to condemn his puppies without cause, fancying that they run cunning when they are only deficient in experience. Many young dogs will, for the first course or two, prick their ears and run behind their companions, because they really do not know how to take part in the fray, but only let them once get a chance, and, if their breeding is good, they will not repeat the misdemeanour. The experienced eye will readily detect the difference, but the tyro should be made aware that it does exist.

FINAL PREPARATION.

It is only with the puppy on his first entrance to his game, that the private trials occupy any portion of the time devoted to training, but at that period of the education it will often take a fortnight to complete them. During this time the feeding should be as already described, except on the day before the trials, when it should be lighter than usual. On the intervening days, the exercise and hill-slips should be continued, unless the courses have been very severe, taking the precaution to weigh the dog occasionally, so as to know that he is all right as to weight, and also to avoid severe work on the day before the trials. After they are completed it will be generally prudent to give the dog a dose of oil, working it off as usual with broth, but feeding at the ordinary time, and in the usual way. This will prevent any tendency to indigestion, which is very apt to occur in the greyhound if he is kept on high food for any length of time without vegetables or aperients of any kind. The former are scarcely suited for the diet of a dog in training, and so recourse must be had to the latter in the mildest form.

If it can be avoided, it is better not to run the dog within a fortnight, or at least a week, of the public meeting, for fear of accidents which are always likely to occur. Sometimes, however, such a cautious policy is impracticable, but in that case every courser ought to have two strings to his bow.

The last week but one prior to the public appearance should be devoted to the strongest and fastest work of which the dog is considered capable. If a horse is used he should be put to his utmost speed for three or four miles at a time on some good turf, but after all, this only develops a good long canter for the greyhound, unless the horse is a first-class thoroughbred, which is seldom the case. The hill work should also be increased slightly, but I must again repeat the necessity for the trainer to take care that he does not jade and 'overmark' his dogs. His object is to get as much flesh off as possible without this injurious and fatal effect, so that in the next week he may slacken his operations, and thus bring out his charge light and corky in spirits, yet perfectly free from internal fat, and with their muscles all wound up to 'concert pitch.' This is the perfection of the art, and it is only among the select few that it is ever fully acquired.

With regard to food, little change should be made, the chief one to be attended to depending on the fact that it often freshens the stomach to give a few boiled potatoes five or six days before running. In all other respects the diet may be as described at page 331.

During the whole of the last week there should be no road work whatever, as far as it is possible to avoid it. The pads are thereby allowed to cover themselves with their horny cuticle, and in this way less danger of cuts is incurred than when they are thinly clothed.

On the day before running no fast work whatever is to be allowed, but there should be at least three or four hours walking exercise; in fact, the treatment is the same as directed on the day before the private trial at page 333.

MANAGEMENT AT MEETINGS AND AFTER RUNNING.

With regard to the time when dogs should be sent to the quarters prepared for them at a meeting, much difference of opinion exists. Some trainers like to get their dogs accustomed to their new quarters for a week before they are brought out, while others think that it is the better plan to keep them at home to the last. Much depends upon the distance they have to travel, and upon other circumstances, such as the nature of their new quarters, &c. Timid dogs are much upset by travelling, while hardy bold animals take pleasure in it. Again, there are many which cannot be reconciled to a new kennel for a night or two, and will be so restless for that time as to deprive themselves and their companions of their accustomed rest. For these reasons it is always better, if good training ground can be found in the neighbourhood, to move the dogs to their quarters a week prior to the meeting, or perhaps even a few days earlier. They then become perfectly acclimatised in every way, and if they do go amiss they have time to recover from it, or if they are really rendered unfit to run they are not allowed to do so, and are not consequently disgraced. Many of the northern trainers, when they have only one or two dogs with them, keep them in their own bedrooms at night, and as this always makes them contented, there is the less reason for moving them from home earlier than necessary.

On the morning of the day of running, walk the dogs out in their clothing, which should now only be removed when they are put in slips, except for frictioning. This exercise should last about an hour, more or less, according to the distance to the ground and the mode of conveyance, but sufficiently long to induce the dog to empty himself. In case the stake is a good one, I should always advise the use of a muzzle, as it not only prevents all chance of wilful poisoning, but it also keeps the dog from picking up any carrion or other accidental matter which would do him no good. After this the gloves should be used, and the dog is ready.

A dog-cart should always be provided whenever the ground is more than two or three miles from the kennel, and in all cases it is necessary when the trainer has several dogs engaged. Without it, he may be obliged to keep his whole lot walking or standing about during nearly the whole of the day, in all kinds of weather, and in a state of excitement which does nearly as much harm as cold and wet. Provided with his card, the trainer knows exactly in what order his turn will come; but he does not know at what hour, for hares are not always found when and where they are expected, and the courser is often kept on 'tenter hooks' for hours, waiting till one is found. When his turn comes next the trainer should keep within a reasonable distance of the slipper and should at once go up to him when the last brace is slipped. Then loosing, but not taking off his cloth, he allows the slip-collar to be properly adjusted, still keeping his own neck-strap on till both dogs are in the slipper's possession, and then, removing both neck-strap and cloth, he should interfere no more unless his dog is so badly educated as to be awkward in the slips. A great deal of trickery is practised by cunning trainers in insisting upon the slip-collar being buckled very loosely, by which the slipper often

MANAGEMENT AFTER RUNNING.

bears the blame of letting a dog out of slips, whereas the trainer is really in fault. The object of this is to cause the one with the loose collar to get the advantage of his antagonist in the slip, and to effect this the trainer risks his getting his head out. This ought not to be allowed; the slipper is the proper judge of the requisite tightness, and no interference ought to be permitted. Many a time I have heard a trainer call out 'You are choking my dog!' when the collar was actually dangerously loose. Of course a practised slipper like Raper would not be induced to listen to such an attempt to mislead him, but there are others who are easily bullied into compliance with any remark of this kind, and upon such only is it attempted. In down countries a horse should always be provided for the trainer to take up his dog with, and many a stake has been lost for want of this assistance; the dog, already exhausted perhaps by a severe course, getting another hare before he is taken up. At Altcar and the other Lancashire meetings men are always to be found who know the ground, and will pick up the dog whichever way he goes; but in important stakes it is well to trust as little as possible to chance aid of this kind, as it sometimes happens that they are bribed to give something injurious to the animal before the trainer can get to him. As soon as he is reached his mouth should be sponged out, and he should be quietly led, without his clothing on, to a sheltered situation, where he should be well frictioned till he has got his tongue in, and is all right in wind, when he may be clothed and taken to his cart.

The following directions will apply to the various circumstances likely to occur at this time: —

1st. When only one course is run per day, and the dog is not distressed, do not interfere in any way, but use friction only, and feed as near the usual time as possible.

2ndly. When two or more courses a day are run, and the dog is not distressed, still do not interfere, but use a little friction just before each course.

3rdly. If the dog is much distressed, and after a few minutes does not recover himself, but is blue about the lips, with eyes of a deep red, take four or five ounces of blood; but if the blueness is not marked, and the distress not very great, give a tablespoonful or two of tea and brandy, mixed in the proportions of three parts of the former to one of the latter. This should be followed by a warm bath as soon as the dog reaches home, if the distress continues.

4thly. In every interval between courses, great care should be taken not to chill the dog; he should be clothed and wrapped up in one or more horse rugs if the weather is cold, and in any case it is better to err by keeping him too warm than to risk a chill.

5thly. Where the dog is distressed when about to run a third or fourth course, there is nothing so likely to relieve him as cold tea, mixed if necessary with brandy, in the proportions above mentioned. If, however, there is sufficient reason for desiring something still more supporting, recourse may be had to the following ball:—

SPICED MEAT BALL.

Take of Carraway seeds	10 grains
Cardamoms	10 ,,
Grains of Paradise	5 ,,
Powdered ginger	5 ,,
Lean knuckle of mutton, boiled	½ ounce

Bruise the seeds in a mortar, and then mix with the mutton to form a ball or bolus.

GENERAL REMARKS.

By the above method of training, the dog is fit to run as far as any ordinary hare will last before him before he is tired. If less work is given the hare often leaves her pursuer at the end of a mile, and the three go into covert at long intervals, or, as the trainers say, one, two, three. If the reader will only consider that the hare rarely has any fast work, and yet is always in training, he will see that it is because she is never confined all the year round. Hence he should remember that if he will follow the same plan, and never let the regular exercise of his dogs be neglected, there will be little necessity for anything but prolonged walking exercise, and all chance of over-marking will be avoided. When, however, this is not attended to, the training must be carried out to the extent I have advised; because fat has accumulated about the internal organs, and it cannot be got rid of by any means short of those I have described.

CHAPTER XVI.

National Coursing Club—Precedents established by it—Constitution and Bye Laws—Rules for the guidance of Coursing Meetings—Rules for the guidance of Judges in their Decisions of Courses.

NATIONAL COURSING CLUB.

Since the first edition of this book was published the National Coursing Club has been formed, chiefly by the exertions of the gentleman known to coursers as Mr. C. Jardine. As originally constituted in 1858, the members were to be elected by the subscribers to the Waterloo Cup, after the dinner on the evening before running. In 1862, however, it was decided to vest the election in public coursing clubs possessing twenty-four members and upwards, the change to be gradually effected by excluding ten members annually from the club by ballot. At present there are only twelve of the original members remaining; and in the year 1864 the probability is that the whole list will have been elected by clubs, or at all events there will only be two elected by the Waterloo Meeting.

The first act of the club was to draw up a code of rules for the regulation of meetings, which have since been universally adopted, subject to such modifications as may be necessary for the use of clubs.

A few alterations have from time to time been made in the original rules, and they now stand as printed in the following pages. At the Spring Meeting of 1863 the present code was formally adopted, and a select committee of three appointed to revise Mr. Thacker's rules for the decision of courses. These gentlemen accordingly proceeded to their task, and the result was that a simplified code was drawn up by them, and passed at the following Summer Meeting in London in 1863. It is useless to record all the doings of the club at their several meetings since 1858, but their decisions in cases submitted to them being of the nature of precedents, should be preserved, and I have accordingly collected them as follows:—

PRECEDENTS ESTABLISHED BY THE COURSING CLUB.

June 4th, 1859.—Case 1. In the Selby case, sent to the club at the previous meeting, it was decided 'that "Snowball" was only entitled to take his third share of the money to be divided between the three dogs left in; he not being entitled to the benefit of the bye till he had run it.'

February 21st, 1860.—Case 2. Captain Spencer brought before the club a case for their consideration which had been referred to him as one of the stewards of a meeting in the north. It appears that 'Iron King' had been bred by Mr. Brougham and given to a Mr. Hudson, who, considering him of no value, transferred him to Mr. Fisher. The latter ran him several times, paying all stakes and other expenses, without any claim being made; but on winning a stake, Hudson put in a claim for a share, and this was referred to Captain Spencer, who preferred taking the opinion of the club upon it. Mr. Fisher sent in a written statement, but though it was stated by Captain Spencer that Mr. Hudson promised to do so, none was forthcoming, and the club could only decide on this *ex parte* statement, backed by the opinion of Captain Spencer that he believed the facts as declared by Mr. Fisher to be substantially correct. On these grounds, therefore, it was unanimously 'resolved that, in the opinion of the club, the dog "Iron King" is the sole property of Mr. Fisher, and that Mr. Hudson is not entitled to any share of his winnings.'

February 19*th*, 1861.—Case 3. An appeal from Mr. J. Scott, of Dublin, against a demand for 10*l.* made upon him by the stewards of the Belleek Coursing Meeting under the following circumstances, which were stated in a letter from Mr. Scott, and confirmed by the oral evidence of Mr. Callan, who appeared for him, supported by a letter written by Mr. Owens to Mr. Scott. It appears that originally the Belleek Meeting was advertised to be held under the rules of the National Club, with the name of Mr. Owens as judge, but a few days before it came off that of Mr. Walker was substituted. Upon seeing this, Mr. Scott, who had taken two nominations, wrote to the secretary to decline keeping them, alleging that a breach of the thirteenth rule of the national code had been committed. The secretary, however, held him to them, and ultimately a demand was made upon him for the amount of the stakes, which sum Mr. Scott lodged with Mr. Bake, to abide the decision of the National Coursing Club. Evidence of these facts was given by Mr. Callan, who produced a letter from Mr. Owens, stating 'that he was not prevented by illness or any other unexpected cause' from judging at the meeting; and on these grounds it was decided unanimously 'that, as it appears from Mr. Owen's letter to Mr. Scott that he was not prevented acting as judge at the Belleek meeting, it is the opinion of this meeting that the stewards cannot call upon Mr. Scott to pay his entries, and Mr. Bake is therefore requested to return him the 10*l*. which he lodged in his hands, to abide the decision of this club.'

Case 4. This was laid before the club by the secretary of the Spelthorne Club, arising out of a decision of the stewards at a meeting recently held at Overton. The facts were stated simply by Mr. Dean (the secretary) as affecting A and B, but to render them intelligible I shall relate them as they occurred. In the first round of the Cup, Mr. East's 'Enjoyment' and Mr. Farnell's 'Farewell' were in slips together, when, a hare being started, in slipping the dogs 'Farewell' was held by a fault in the slips, while 'Enjoyment' got away single-handed and had a severe course. Mr. East then demanded that 'Farewell' should run a bye before the course was run out, which was resisted by Mr. Farnell, and ultimately laid before the stewards, who decided in favour of Mr. East; and the consequence was that 'Farewell' ran the bye, and then coming against 'Enjoyment,' was beaten by her, this bitch ultimately winning the stake. The club unanimously decided 'that the stewards were wrong in calling upon Mr. Farnell to run the bye, there being no rule to give them that power, and numerous precedents being against such a proceeding.' The secretary merely asked for an opinion on this point, and the question how far the stakes were affected was not entered into. Subsequently the matter was amicably arranged by Mr. East and Mr. Farnell.

Case 5. Mr. R. Anderson of High Felling, Gateshead, applied to the club to know if he was entitled to his entrance money back for a stake which, after a postponement, it was agreed by fourteen out of the sixteen nominators should be run off on a certain day, regardless of the weather. Resolved that, 'as the opinion of the majority in all such cases is binding on the minority, his claim be disallowed.'

June 1st, 1861.—Case 6. Mr. Smith, the secretary of the Somerville Aston Club, applied for the opinion of the National Club whether Mr. Partridge, of Hanbury, near Birmingham, was liable for a nomination to a stake run on February 18, 1860. It appeared that Mr. Partridge applied by letter for a nomination on February 12, which Mr. Smith wrote him on the 14th he could have, as was proved by the envelope of the letter, which bore the Evesham postmark of that date. Mr. Partridge declared that he did not receive this letter till the 18th, in the afternoon; but no corroborative evidence was given of this delay, and the club therefore decided 'that Mr. Partridge is liable for the nomination.'

Case 7. Major Beresford asked for an opinion whether he was liable for a nomination at the County Louth Champion Meeting held on March 6 and 7, 1861, the amount of which was claimed by the secretary, and deducted from the sum to which Major Beresford was entitled as the nominator of the third dog. Statements were put in by himself and his confederate, Mr. Douglas; and to support his side Mr. Callan, the secretary, appeared in person. From the evidence it was ascertained—first, that the conditions were, that the stake should consist of sixteen Irish against sixteen English and Scotch dogs, the draw to take place on March 8. Secondly, that at the Waterloo Meeting in February, Major Beresford and Mr. Douglas met Mr. Callan, and expressed a wish to have one nomination only instead of two, which had been allotted to them by mistake. Mr. Callan said that he had then twenty-two applications on the Irish side; but in the remainder of the conversation there was a difference in the statements. Thirdly, the conditions of the programme, and Mr. Callan's evidence, showed that he could not fill up the stake with Irish nominations instead of English until the time of the draw. Fourthly, a dog was finally entered in Major Beresford's name without his knowledge and consent. Under these circumstances it was decided by the club 'that Major Beresford is not liable for his second nomination, on the ground that, according to the conditions, only sixteen Irish nominations could be allotted before the draw, and even then the additional Irish nominations could only be given by general consent. The club are further of opinion that the secretary was not justified in entering a dog in Major Beresford's name without his instructions.'

February 18*th*, 1862.—Case 8. An appeal from Mr. Gunson, secretary of the late Whitehaven meeting, was laid before the club. It set forth that, in the first ties of a twenty-one dog stake, the bye was given by the stewards to the highest dog on the list, the lowest in the first round having previously had one. The Whitehaven meeting professed to be governed by the National code of rules, but no one on the ground having a copy, the stewards decided, they thought, in conformity with them, to the best of their abilities and memories. In the third ties another bye occurred, which was given to the middle dog, the lowest not having had a bye, which decision was protested against, and the bye was run under protest. The stake was ultimately won by the dog who obtained the bye in the first ties. The question put for the opinion of the club was, 'How the stakes should be given under the circumstances?' After some discussion it was decided, 'that as the order of running was altogether wrong after the first round, in consequence of the bye having been improperly given to the top instead of the bottom dog, the club are of opinion that the whole of the money should be divided amongst the eleven dogs standing in after the first round of the stake.'

May 27*th*, 1862.—Case 9. Mr. Randell brought forward a decision of the stewards of the Tredegar Park Meeting in March 1862, handing in a statement of the facts of the case, which were met by a counter statement of the secretary of the Tredegar Park Club. There was no difference as to the facts, which are shortly as follows :—Five sapling stakes were run for by nineteen dogs, and a cup was given by Lord Tredegar to be run for by their respective winners. Mr. Randell won two, Mr. Price two, and Mr. Evans one. Mr. Randell then claimed that his dogs should be guarded, on the principle that the stake was contested by the nineteen saplings.

The stewards, however, decided to the contrary, maintaining that it was a fresh stake, but instead of disturbing the original order of running on the card, and making a fresh draw, they adhered to the card, giving the bye to Mr. Evans, and compelling Mr. Randell and Mr. Price each to run their saplings together. Mr. Randell held that they were on the horns of a dilemma, and should either have guarded his dogs if they kept to the card, or else they should have drawn afresh. He asked the club, first whether the decision of the stewards was right, and, secondly, if wrong, what course ought to be adopted to make it right? After a short discussion, it was carried, 'that, in the opinion of the National Club, the stewards were wrong in their decision, inasmuch as that the cup itself formed part of the original entry of nineteen dogs, for which no new classification was necessary, and in which, therefore, two dogs belonging to the same owner were entitled to be guarded. And the National Club is further of opinion that the cup ought to be returned to the stewards, to be run for again by the five winners qualified under the National Club Rules as advertised.'

Case 10. A statement was made by Mr. Blanshard of the facts relating to the decision of the Coquetdale stewards in March 1862, compelling him to run his dog 'Baffler' single-handed for the Coquetdale Cup, to be run for by the four winners of the other stakes. In this instance there had been a fresh draw, and the National Club rules had been departed from so far by the only party interested, as to allow of Mr. Blanshard's two dogs being guarded, his third nomination ('Meteor') not being his own property. There was some little difference between Mr. Blanshard's statement and the official counter-statement of the secretary, but not in any essential point; the Club at once coming to the conclusion that the case rested simply on two points—first, whether an owner can at any time draw his dog, whether lame or not? and, secondly, whether there is any limitation to bye dogs except that of age? Mr Blanshard's statement was simply that 'Meteor' and 'Baffler' being drawn together, he drew the former as lame, and then put 'Wild Deer' in the slips to run the bye; but this was not allowed by the acting steward, who told him that he must either run 'Baffler' and 'Meteor' together, or run 'Baffler' single-handed. He submitted to do the latter, and now asked the opinion of the Club, whether the stewards had any right in the first place to attempt to coerce him to run 'Meteor,' and, in the second, to deprive him of the usual assistance of a bye dog? In conclusion he put in a certificate of Mr. Strangways, V.S., Edinburgh, that the dog was lame and unfit to run, and disclaimed any desire to upset the decision of the stewards, merely asking for the opinion of the National Club as a guide for the future.

Dr. Richardson and Mr. Foster, who appeared on the part of the Coquetdale Club, then each handed in a lengthy statement; but on being asked if they wished them read, they preferred making their own opinions known in a more conversational manner. Mr. Foster commenced by protesting officially against the question being entertained by the National Club, on the ground that 'Mr. Blanshard having refused to refer this dispute to the adjustment of the National Club when pointedly requested to do so at the time it happened, cannot now avail himself of any appeal to it. Without any right of appeal on the part of the complainant, the National Club is not competent to take any cognisance of the matter. He argued that the decision of the authorities of the Coquetdale meeting, right or wrong, is final and irrevocable, and the National Club has no judicial authority either in undoing or confirming the decision, and it is from the same cause incapable of giving any official opinion on the question.'

The President at once informed Mr. Foster that the meeting had decided to entertain the question, and the club was prepared to incur the responsibility thereby assumed. Dr. Richardson then argued the question 'on the ground that "Meteor" was fit to run, and that being so, his nominator had no power to draw him under the 24th rule of the National Code; that, in spite of this, Mr. Blanshard persisted in drawing him; but as the conditions of the cup required that it should be run for by the winners of the four stakes, they conceived that no other dog was qualified, and that no other could even run in the bye as an assistant. They therefore prevented Mr. Blanshard from using a fresh dog as an assistant to "Baffler" in the bye, and in this course they considered that they were fully justified by the analogy of puppy stakes, for which only puppies could run as bye dogs.' It was finally resolved 'that the National Club having fully considered the disputed case at the last Coquetdale Coursing meeting, which has been referred to them by Mr. Blanshard, and met by a printed statement from the committee of the Coquetdale Coursing Club, where the secretary has also been admitted to explain his own views, they are of opinion that there was nothing in the advertised programme of the Coquetdale Coursing meeting, in relation to the Coquetdale Cup, which debarred Mr. Blanshard, if he chose to exercise the right, from claiming under the present state of coursing law applicable to byes, to draw " Meteor " and substitute " Wild Deer " to run a bye with " Baffler." The club is therefore bound to declare that the decision of Dr. Richardson in the first instance, which was confirmed afterwards by the stewards and committee, was not in accordance with the rules of the National Coursing Club, and must not be admitted as a precedent in future. They feel it due, however, to Dr. Richardson and the stewards, to record their conviction that they only arrived at the decision which they came to from a strong desire to carry out the real equity of the case, and that they were actuated in their decision by a strict sense of impartiality. The National Club is sorry to add that they must express a very strong feeling of regret and surprise that the Committee of the Coquetdale Coursing Club should deny the competency of the National Club to enquire into a matter which has been properly brought before them, in order to ascertain their opinion on a difficult subject.'

February 17th, 1863.—Case 11. A charge of default standing over from the last meeting being gone into, it was resolved 'that the evidence on both sides not being quite satisfactory to the meeting, no decision could be arrived at, and no case of default was therefore substantiated against Mr. Bateman.'

Case 12. An appeal by Mr. Taylor against the stewards of the Border Club, for ordering a savage dog out of slips. Resolved, 'that, under Rule 6 of the National Club, the stewards of the Border Club had full authority to take what steps they might think necessary in regard to Mr. Taylor's greyhound while in slips.'

February 16*th*, 1864.—Case 13. An appeal made by Mr. Hyslop against the bitch 'Graceful' receiving the stakes as winner of the Puppy Cup at the late Brougham and Whinfell Meeting, asserting that she was not the *bonâ fide* property of her nominator, Mr. Jackson. In relation to this a letter was read from Mr. Brougham, one of the stewards, stating that he had received evidence on oath from several persons on this subject, but that it was of such a conflicting nature that he could not come to any .conclusion, and he therefore begged to lay the matter before the National Club. It appearing that the question of ownership lay between a Mr. Wood and Mr. Jackson, and the latter stating by letter that ' Graceful ' belonged to him, Mr. Wood was called in and examined. He said that the dam of ' Graceful ' belonged to him, and that Mr. Jackson owned the sire. It was therefore arranged that Mr. Jackson should have the bitch, allowing him to take what interest he pleased in any stake she might be engaged in. Mr. Jackson paid the tax and keep, as well as all entrance monies. On being asked whether he expected to receive any portion of the winnings at Brougham, Mr. Wood said, somewhat reluctantly, that he did, but he explained that he did not even know beforehand that ' Graceful ' was going to run there. She was given to Mr. Jackson on Carlisle Show day, in September. Mr. Hyslop, the appellant, being present, stated that his witnesses (who were examined on oath by Mr. Brougham) testified that both Mr. Jackson and Mr. Wood contradicted themselves in their statements, and contended that, being all disinterested parties, they ought to be believed in preference to Mr. Jackson, in whose name the bitch ran, and Mr. Wood, who admitted that he expected to receive a share of the stakes. After some discussion it was resolved, 'that the evidence produced fails to prove that Mr. Jackson was not entitled to run " Graceful " as his property.'

Case 14. An appeal upon an objection made by Mr. Hodson, the owner of 'Hylax,' against 'Macaroni,' the winner of the Northern St. Leger at the Scarborough Open Meeting in November last, in consequence of being wrongly nominated. Mr. Brown, the secretary of the Scarborough Meeting, produced the original entry from Mr. Simpson in which 'Macaroni' was described as by 'Bugle,' out of 'Sister to Riot,' and also showed his book in which he was so entered, though the name 'Wisdom' was afterwards substituted for 'Sister to Riot.' An affidavit was then read, which proved that 'Macaroni' was really out of 'Wisdom,' a daughter of the said 'Sister to Riot.' On this it was resolved that 'the pedigree given of " Macaroni " is proved to be incorrect, and he must be considered disqualified.'

Case 15. An appeal from Mr. Edgar Salmon, for the decision of the Club as to the validity of a contract for the sale of a greyhound, was withdrawn, being considered by the members to be beyond the province of the Club.

May 28*th*, 1864.—Case 16. An appeal made by Mr. Brougham against 'Blooming Daisy,' for not running a bye at the Brougham and Whinfell Meeting, in October 1863, in accordance with Rule 63. A letter was read from Mr. Brougham, detailing the nature of the case, from which it appeared that 'Blooming Daisy' ran a 'no course' according to the judge's decision, the reason for such decision being that a third dog, belonging to the owner of her competitor, had joined in immediately after the slip. 'Kitty Nicholson' was consequently disqualified, and the judge having given his opinion that, according to Rule 32, 'Blooming Daisy' had done sufficient to allow her to meet her next antagonist without running a bye, she ran the deciding course under protest. The question, therefore, submitted to the Club was, in effect, whether this was regular, or whether the stakes ought to go to 'Black Ball,' who was defeated by 'Blooming Daisy' in the deciding course. After some discussion it was resolved that, 'in the opinion of this meeting, "Blooming Daisy" had done enough, in accordance with Rule 32, to run the deciding course without running a bye.'

Case 17. An appeal from Mr. Chesshyre against Mr. Leighton receiving the stakes called the Oakley Stakes, for puppies, at the Cirencester Club Meeting in January last, won by his dog 'Lurlei,' in consequence of running a bye with an old dog without the consent of the stewards. The facts of the case were admitted to be, that three dogs only being left in the stake, Mr. Leighton's 'Lurlei' was entitled to the bye, which she ran with an old dog without the consent of the stewards being asked. She subsequently beat Mr. Chesshyre's 'Charles III.,' but on that gentleman's making the discovery that she had run the bye with an old dog, he claimed the stakes, and the matter was referred to the National Club. After a good deal of discussion, turning on the point that Rule 13 lays down no penalty for running a bye with an old dog, being in this respect the only exception in the code, it was resolved, that 'the bye in the third round of the Oakley Stakes at Cirencester not having been run in accordance with Rule 13, "Lurlei" cannot be considered to have gone any farther in the stake, and consequently is only entitled to the money given to the third dog.'

CONSTITUTION AND BYE-LAWS OF THE NATIONAL CLUB.

The National Coursing Club shall consist of not more than fifty members, of whom seven shall be a quorum. Ten shall go out by rotation, according to length of service, each year, at the summer meeting, and shall not be re-eligible for a twelvemonth. The gentlemen now composing the Club to be first on the list to retire, which, in their case, can be determined by lot; and new members coming in to be always placed at the bottom of the list, so as to mark the order of seniority. This rule not to apply to the President and Secretary, who shall be elected or re-elected annually.

The names of these ten members thus retiring shall be declared by the secretary of the National Club at the Summer Meeting in each year, and their places, together with any casual vacancies, shall be filled up with new members, who shall be selected by such established coursing clubs throughout the kingdom, of more than one year's standing, as may be composed of not fewer than twenty-four subscribers. These clubs to have the right of voting in alphabetical order, after due notification of their enrolment, from time to time, to the secretary of the National Club: and members thus selected to enter office at the May Meeting of the National Club.

That all coursing clubs throughout England, Scotland, and Ireland, composed of not fewer than twenty-four members each, shall have the right each to elect one or more members to the National Club in alphabetical rotation, and that before the 25th of March, in each year, they shall notify their enrolment and the list of their members to the secretary of the National Club.

The secretary of the National Coursing Club shall, after the Summer Meeting in each year, inform the several coursing clubs, in alphabetical order, which of them are entitled to fill the vacancies in the numbers of the National Club. Such clubs shall proceed to the election of representatives, whose names must be returned to the Secretary of the National Club before the 1st of January in each year.

It is to be understood that the alphabetical rotation is always to be followed in regard to the election by coursing clubs; and that, wherever the line is drawn in any one year, the next club in alphabetical order will head the list for the following year.

All complaints, of whatever description, or any matter in dispute connected with coursing, can be referred to the National Club for arbitration or adjustment; and no declaration or limitation by any body of men, which shall be intended to preclude such appeal, upon the occasion of an open meeting, shall be considered binding upon the subscribers to such open meeting, or upon the National Club.

Meetings for the despatch of business, and for the revision or alteration of rules, shall be held in London on the Saturday of the Derby week, at noon, and at Liverpool on the day of entry for the Waterloo Cup, at 3.0 P.M.; but the secretary, upon a requisition addressed to him in writing by any three stewards of a meeting, or by six public coursers, members of an established club, may summon a special meeting at the earliest convenient opportunity, at the most convenient place.

A month's notice must be given to the secretary of any business or proposed alteration of rules, before it can be discussed at the regular meetings of the National Club; and at any extraordinary special meeting nothing but the particular question for which that meeting has been convened can be entertained.

The National Coursing Club recommends that its code of laws shall be adopted universally, clubs merely adding such special or local regulations as may be required to adapt it to their own peculiar use; and as the principle of election to the National Club will henceforward vest in clubs consisting of not fewer than twenty-four members, they will be required annually to send a list of their enrolment to the secretary of the National Club, and to contribute their quota towards the expenses of the National Club, a statement of which shall be declared by the secretary at the Summer Meeting in each year.

Any club not having contributed its quota towards such expenses to be disqualified for returning a member to the National Club.

CODE OF RULES.

(1.) FOR THE GUIDANCE OF COURSING MEETINGS.

1. SECRETARY AND STEWARDS.—The Secretary of any proposed open meeting shall associate with himself a Committee of not less than three members to settle preliminaries. The management of the meeting shall be entrusted to Stewards and Field Stewards (in conjunction with this Committee), who shall be elected by the subscribers present the first evening of a meeting. No Steward to have a right to vote during a meeting in any case where his own dogs are interested. The Secretary shall declare, as soon as possible, how the prizes are to be divided; and a statement of expenses may be called for by the subscribers after a meeting, if they think proper.

2. ELECTION OF JUDGE.—The Judge may either be elected by the Secretary and Committee appointed under Rule 1, in which case his name shall be announced simultaneously with the meeting; or his appointment shall be determined by the votes of the subscribers taking nominations; but each subscriber shall have only one vote, whatever the number of his nominations. The appointment of the Judge to be published at the least two weeks before the meeting, and the number of votes, as well as the names of the voters, to be recorded in a book, which shall be open to the inspection of the Stewards, who shall declare the number of votes

for each Judge if called upon to do so by any of the subscribers. A fortnight's notice shall also be given of the day of voting, which shall be duly announced in the public papers. When a Judge, from ill-health, or any other unexpected cause, is prevented from attending a meeting, or during a meeting finishing it, the Stewards of the meeting shall have the power of deciding what is to be done.

3. POSTPONEMENT OF MEETING.—If a meeting appointed to take place upon a certain day be interfered with by weather which in the opinion of the Stewards is unfit for coursing, the Committee shall have power to postpone it, but not beyond the week. If, through a continuance of bad weather, the meeting be void, the subscribers shall be liable for their quota of expenses. This rule not to apply to produce meetings, which must take place as soon as the weather will permit.

4. TAKING DOGS TO SLIPS.—Immediately before the greyhounds are drawn at any open meeting, the place and time of putting the first brace of dogs into the slips on the following morning shall be declared, and the owner of any dog which shall not be ready to be put into slips at such appointed time and place, or in proper rotation afterwards, shall be fined 1*l*.; if not ready within ten minutes from such time, the absent greyhound shall be adjudged to have lost its course, and the opponent shall run a bye. If both dogs be absent at the expiration of ten minutes, the Stewards shall have power to disqualify both dogs, or to fine their owners any sum not exceeding 5*l*. each. No dog to be put into the slips for a deciding course until thirty minutes after its previous course, without the consent of its owner.

RULES FOR THE GUIDANCE OF COURSING MEETINGS. 361

5. DRAW.—No entry by a subscriber shall be valid unless the amount of stake be paid in full, when a card or counter bearing a corresponding number shall be assigned to each entry. These numbered cards or counters shall then be placed together in a bowl, and drawn out indiscriminately. This classification, once made, shall not be disturbed throughout the meeting, except for the purpose of guarding, or on account of byes. Dogs whose position on the card has been altered in consequence of guarding must return to their original position in next class, if guarding does not prevent it.

6. GUARDING.—When more than one nominator is taken by one person, the greyhounds, provided they are *bonâ fide* his own property, or the property of one person, shall be guarded as follows:—Two if more than a four-dog stake, three if more than a sixteen, four if more than a twenty-four, five if more than a thirty-two, six if more than a forty, seven if more than a forty-eight, and eight if more than a fifty-six. In produce stakes any number may be guarded. This guarding is not, however, to deprive any dog of a natural bye to which he may, in running through a stake, be entitled.

7. CONTROL OF DOGS IN SLIPS.—The control of all matters connected with slipping the greyhounds shall rest with the Stewards of a meeting. Owners or servants, after delivering their dogs into the hands of the Slipper, may follow close after them, but not so as to inconvenience the Slipper, or in any way to interfere with the dogs, under a penalty of 1*l.* Neither must they halloa them on while running, under the same penalty. Any greyhound found to be

beyond control and mischievous in slips may, by command of the Stewards, be taken out of slips and disqualified.

8. GREYHOUNDS OF SAME COLOURS TO WEAR COLLARS.—When two greyhounds drawn together are of the same colour, they shall each wear a collar, and the owners shall be subject to a penalty of 10s. for non-observance of this rule; the colour of the collar to be red for the left-hand side, and white for the right-hand side, of the slips. After the first round the upper dog on the card for the day will be placed on the left-hand, and the lower dog on the right-hand of the slips.

9. THE SLIPPER.—If through accident one greyhound gets out of the slips, the Slipper shall not let the other go. If the slips break and the dogs get away coupled together, the Judge shall decide whether it is to be a 'no course,' or whether enough has been done to constitute it an 'undecided course.' In any case of slips breaking, and either or both dogs getting away in consequence, the Slipper may be fined not exceeding 1l., at the discretion of the Steward.

10. RIDING OVER A GREYHOUND.—If any subscriber or his servant shall ride over his opponent's greyhound while running a course, the owner of the dog so ridden over shall (although the course be given against him) be deemed the winner of it, or shall have the option of allowing the other dog to remain and run out the stake, and in such case shall be entitled to half his winnings, if any.

11. GREYHOUND GETTING LOOSE.—Any person allowing a greyhound to get loose, and join in a course which is being run, shall

RULES FOR THE GUIDANCE OF COURSING MEETINGS.

be fined 1*l*. If the loose greyhound belongs to either of the owners of the dogs engaged in the particular course, such owner shall forfeit his chance of the stake with the dog then running, unless it can it can be proved to the satisfaction of the Stewards that the loose greyhound had not been able to be taken up after running its own course. The course not to be considered as necessarily ended when the third dog joins in.

12. IMPUGNING JUDGE.—If any subscriber openly impugns the decision of the Judge on the ground, except by a complaint to the Stewards according to Rule 32, he shall forfeit not more than 5*l*. or less than 2*l*., at the discretion of the Stewards.

13. BYES.—No greyhound shall run more than one natural bye in any stake, unless it should come to his turn a second time; and this bye shall be given to the lowest available greyhound in each round. When a dog is entitled to a bye, either natural or accidental, his owner or nominator may run any greyhound he pleases to assist in the course; provided always that in sapling stakes only a sapling may be used, and in puppy stakes none older than a puppy. But if it is proved to the satisfaction of the Stewards that no puppy can be found on the field, or otherwise in time to run an unexpected bye in the first class, the owner shall have the power of substituting an old dog. No dog shall run any bye earlier than his position on the card entitles him to do so.

14. ALTERATION OF NAME.—If any subscriber shall enter a greyhound by a different name from that in which it shall last have run for any stake or piece of plate, without giving notice to

the Secretary of the alteration at the time of entry, such greyhound shall be disqualified.

15. PREFIX OF *Ns*.—Any subscriber taking an entry in a stake, and not prefixing the word '*Names*' to a greyhound which is not his own property, shall forfeit that greyhound's chance of the stake. He shall likewise be compelled to deliver in writing, to the Secretary of the meeting, the name of the *bonâ fide* owner of the greyhound named by him, if called upon, and this communication to be produced should any dispute arise in the matter.

16. DESCRIPTION OF ENTRY.—Every subscriber to a stake must name his dog at or before the entry, and for all stakes must give the name of the sire and dam of the dog entered. The Secretary shall publish on the card the names of those who are subscribers, but do not comply with these conditions. These nominations shall not be drawn, but must be paid or. For produce stakes the names, pedigrees, ages, colours, and distinguishing marks of puppies shall be detailed in writing to the Secretary of a meeting at the time of entry. The subscriber must also state in writing, should he be required, through the Secretary, previously to or during the meeting for which such entry is made, the names and addresses of the parties who reared the puppies; and any puppy whose marks and pedigree shall be proved not to correspond with the entry given shall be disqualified, and the whole of its stakes or winnings forfeited. No greyhound to be considered a puppy which was whelped before the 1st of January of the year preceding the season of running.

17. OBJECTIONS.—An objection to a greyhound may be made to

the Stewards of a meeting at any time before the stakes are paid over, upon the objector lodging a sum of 5l. in the hands of such Steward or the Secretary, which shall be forfeited if the objection prove frivolous. The owner of the greyhound objected to shall be compelled to deposit equally the sum of 5l., and to prove the correctness of his entry. All expenses in consequence of the objection to fall upon the party against whom the decision may ultimately be given. Should an objection be made which cannot at the time be substantiated or disproved, the greyhound may be allowed to run under protest; but should the objection be afterwards substantiated, and the winnings have been paid over, the owner or nominator of the greyhound which may thus be disqualified shall return the money or prize, or be declared a defaulter. The money returned shall be divided equally among the greyhounds beaten by the particular dog thus disqualified; or if a piece of plate or prize has been added, such dogs alone as have been beaten in the several rounds by the greyhound objected to, shall have the privilege of contending for it.

18. TWO GREYHOUNDS REMAINING IN, &c.—If two greyhounds belonging to the same owner or to confederates remain in for the deciding course, the stake shall be considered divided, as also if the owner of one dog induce the owner of the other dog to draw him for any payment or consideration ; but if one greyhound be drawn from lameness, or from any cause clearly affecting his chance of winning, the other may be declared the winner, the facts of the case being clearly proved to the satisfaction of the Stewards.

19. THIRD AND FOURTH PRIZES.—When more than two prizes

are given, the greyhound beaten by the winner in the last class but one shall have precedence of that beaten by the runner-up. When only three dogs run in this class, then the greyhound first beaten of these three shall have the third prize, and the fourth prize shall be given to the greyhound beaten by the winner in the previous class, unless the winner had a bye in that class, in which case the fourth prize shall be awarded to the dog beaten by the runner-up in that class.

20. WINNERS OF STAKES RUNNING TOGETHER.—If two greyhounds shall each win a stake, and have to run together for a final prize or challenge cup, should they not have run an equal number of ties in their respective stakes, the greyhound not having run the sufficient number of courses must run a bye or byes to put itself upon an equality in this respect with his opponent.

21. DEFAULTERS.—No person shall be allowed to enter or run a greyhound in his own, or any other person's name, who is a defaulter for either stakes or bets.

22. JUDGE OR SLIPPER INTERESTED.—If a Judge or Slipper be in any way interested in the winnings of a greyhound or greyhounds, the nominators of these dogs, unless he can prove satisfactorily that such interest was without his cognisance, shall forfeit all claim to the winnings.

23. BETS ON AN UNDECIDED COURSE.—All bets upon an undecided course to stand unless one of the greyhounds be drawn. All bets upon a dog running further than another in a stake, or upon the event, to be p.-p., whatever accident may happen.

24. BETS ON STAKES DIVIDED.—Where money has been laid

against a dog winning a stake, and he divides it, the two sums must be put together, and divided in the same proportion as the stakes.

(2) FOR THE GUIDANCE OF JUDGES IN THEIR DECISIONS OF COURSES.

Rule 25. THE JUDGE who may be appointed at any Coursing Meeting shall be subject to the general Rules which may be established by the National Coursing Club for his guidance.

26. HE SHALL DECIDE ALL COURSES upon the one uniform principle that the greyhound which does most towards killing the hare during the continuance of the course is to be declared the winner. This principle is to be carried out by estimating the value of the work done by each greyhound, as seen by the Judge, upon a balance of points according to the scale hereafter laid down, from which also are to be deducted certain specified allowances and penalties.

27. THE POINTS of the Course are—

a. *Speed*—which shall be estimated as one, two, or three points, according to the degree of superiority shown. (See Definition below (a).)

b. *The Cote.*—Two points, or if gained when a greyhound is running the outer circle, three points.

c. *The Go-bye.*—Two points, or if gained on the outer circle, three points.

d. *The Turn.*—One point.

e. *The Wrench.*—Half a point.

f. *The Kill.*—Two points, or, in a descending scale, in proportion to the degree of merit displayed in that kill, which may be of no value.

g. The Trip.—Half a point.

DEFINITION OF POINTS.

a. In estimating the value of speed to the hare the Judge must take into account the several forms in which it may be displayed, viz.—

1. Where two greyhounds start evenly from the slips, and in a straight run-up a clear lead of at least fifteen lengths shall be gained by the one dog, or where a decided lead is taken by the dog running the outer circle, in either of which cases three points shall be scored.

2. Where a go-bye is made in the run-up, from one dog accidently hanging in slips, or starting slow and afterwards outstripping his fellow, for which two or three points may be scored, according to circumstances.

3. Where one greyhound leads the other, so long as the hare runs straight, but loses the lead from her bending round decidedly in favour of the slower dog of her own accord, in which case the one greyhound shall score one point for the speed shown, and the other dog score one point for the first turn.

4. Where only a slight lead is gained, one point to be scored for the speed, but the speed and the turn to be estimated separately. Under no circumstance is speed without subsequent work to be allowed to decide a course,

RULES FOR THE GUIDANCE OF JUDGES.

except where great superiority is shown by one greyhound over another in a long lead to covert.

b. *The Cote* is where two greyhounds start equal from a turn, and the dog which made the cast, by superior speed outruns his antagonist, and makes the next turn or wrench.

c. *The Go-bye* is where a greyhound starts a clear length behind his opponent, and yet passes him in a straight run, and gets a clear length before him.

d. *The Turn* is where the hare is brought round at an angle of 45 degrees from her previous line.

e. *The Wrench* is where the hare is merely bent from her line; but where she only leaves her line to suit herself, and not from the greyhound pressing her, nothing to be allowed.

f. *The merit of a Kill* must be estimated according to whether a greyhound by his own superior dash and skill bears the hare; whether he picks her up through any little accidental circumstances favouring him; or whether she is actually turned into his mouth, as it were, by the other greyhound.

g. *The Trip*, or unsuccessful effort to kill, is where the hare is thrown off her legs, or where a greyhound flecks her but cannot hold her.

28. The following ALLOWANCES shall be made for accidents to a greyhound during a course; but in every case they shall only be deducted from the other dog's score:—

a. For losing ground at the start, either from being unsighted or from a bad slip, in which case the Judge is to decide what amount of allowance is to be made, on the principle that the score of the foremost dog is not to begin till the second has had the opportunity of joining in the course.

b. For a fall while pressing the hare, when the next point gained by the other greyhound shall *not* count.

c. Where a hare bears very decidedly in disfavour of one of the greyhounds, after the first or subsequent turns, in which case the next point shall not be scored by the dog who may be unduly favoured, or only half his point allowed, according to circumstances.

d. Where a greyhound is ridden over, or disabled so that he cannot continue the course, such not being the fault of either of the owners of the dogs or their servants, in which case no subsequent points are to be scored, and the course shall end there.

29. PENALTIES are to be deducted from the score of the greyhound incurring them, and are as follows:—

a. Where a greyhound from his own defect refuses to follow the hare at which he is slipped, when he shall lose the course.

b. Where a dog wilfully stands still in a course, or departs from directly pursuing the hare, no points subsequently made by him shall be scored; and if the points gained by such greyhound up to this time be equal to those made by his antagonist in the whole course, he shall thereby lose the course; but where one or both dogs stop with the hare in view, through inability to continue the course, it shall be decided according to the number of points gained by each dog during the whole course.

c. *If a dog refuses to fence* where the other fences, any points subsequently made by him are not to be scored; but if he does his best to fence, and is foiled by sticking in a meuse, or where the fence is too high for him, the course to end there. When the points are equal, the superior fencer to win the course.

30. THE ORDER TO SLIP shall, where practicable, be given by the Judge, but the Stewards of a Meeting shall have power to depute this duty to some other person. The length of slip must necessarily vary with the nature of the ground, but should never be less than from three to fourscore yards, and must be maintained of one uniform length as far as possible throughout each stake. Whenever, from the nature of the ground, it is impossible for the Judge to be close at hand in the run-up, and the course is nearly evenly balanced, his decision need not be given till he has conferred with the Slipper, or person appointed to watch the slip.

31. IF A SECOND HARE be started during a course, and one of the dogs follow her, the course to end there.

32. A 'NO COURSE' is where sufficient has not been done to show superiority in either greyhound and must be run again; but where both dogs have a single-handed course, and where one is

agreed to be drawn, the Judge shall decide whether enough has been done for the other dog to remain in without running an additional bye. An 'UNDECIDED COURSE' is when the Judge considers the merits of the dogs so equal that he cannot decide; and the dogs shall be put in again after two courses unless one be drawn; but the owners must at the time declare to the Flag Steward which dog remains in; after an undecided or no course, and the dogs before being taken up get on another or the same hare, the Judge must follow and decide in favour of one if he considers that sufficient has been done to justify his doing so. After a 'no course' it shall be at the option of the owners either to run again immediately or at the expiration of two courses, the latter being fixed if they do not agree. If it is the last course of the day, fifteen minutes shall be allowed after both dogs are taken up.

32. THE JUDGE SHALL DELIVER HIS DECISION aloud immediately the course is ended, and shall render an explanation of such decision before the third succeeding course to the Stewards of a meeting, if required, through them, by the owner, or nominator, or representative of any owner or nominator, of a greyhound. The Stewards to express their opinion whether the explanation is satisfactory or not, and their opinion may be asked for in writing and published afterwards, but the decision of the Judge, once given, shall not be reversed.

APPENDIX.

APPENDIX.

PEDIGREES OF CELEBRATED BITCHES.

Mr. Bland's black bitch 'BELLE OF THE VILLAGE.'

BELLE OF THE VILLAGE

```
                    BELLE OF THE VILLAGE
          ┌──────────────────┴──────────────────┐
      Blackcloud                           Prizeflower
                                            (Purser)
   ┌──────┴──────┐                     ┌───────┴───────┐
Bluelight    Frolic                Paramount         Isis
            (Lord Eglinton)
 ┌───┴───┐   ┌────┬────┬────┐        ┌───┴───┐
Monsoon Stave Waterloo Florinda Idas   Pamela
(Col. Smart)  │                        │
    ┌─────┴─────┐                 ┌────┼────┬────┐
 Streamer   Bride            King  Kath- Son of  Daughter
                              Cob  leen  Stumps  of Baron
```

Mr. Borron's black bitch 'BLACKNESS.'
Sister to 'Belted Will.'

BLACKNESS

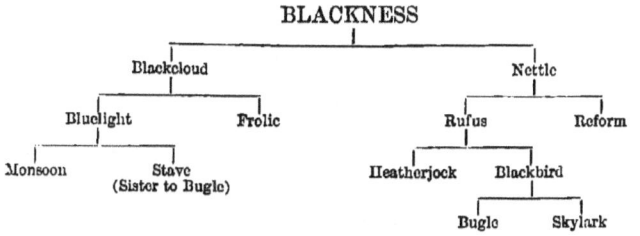

APPENDIX.

Mr. Randell's brindled bitch 'BRILLIANT.'
See 'Ruby.'

Mr. Brocklebank's, late Mr. Campbell's, white bitch 'CIOLOJA'

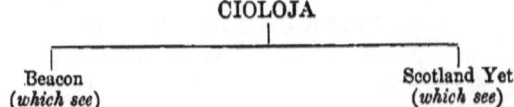

Broke her leg in a trial, and sold for 56*l.* to Mr. Brocklebank for the stud.

Mr. Swan's black bitch 'CINDERELLA.'
Sister to 'Staymaker,' which see.

Mr. Long's, afterwards Mr. Loder's, red bitch 'CACTUS.'
Sister to 'Figheldean' and 'Royalist.'
Whelped, 1846.—Height, 23 inches.—Weight, about 45 lbs.

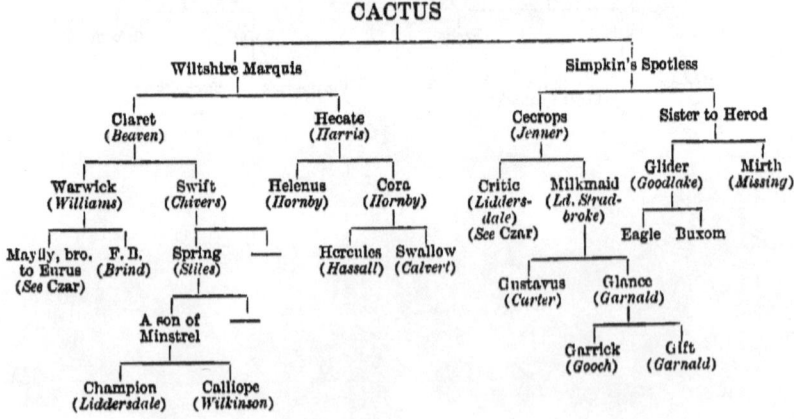

PERFORMANCES.

1847, Nov.—Was drawn in her second course for the Oaks at Everleigh. In the same month, was drawn in the deciding course for the Champion Puppy Stakes at Newmarket, the winner belonging to the same party.

1848, Jan.—Won three courses for the Fisherton Delamere Cup, at Deptford Inn; beaten by 'Wulston.'

Oct.—Ran third for the Druid Cup at Amesbury; beaten by her brother 'Royalist.'

Dec.—Won the Netheravon Cup.

PRODUCE.

In 1849, put to the 'Czar,' and produced eight whelps, most of which died of distemper. Three bitches were reared, one only of which distinguished herself, as 'Lullaby Baby,' afterwards 'Moss Rose.'

In 1853, put to 'Factotum.'

In 1856, put to 'Czar,' and produced Mr. Loder's 'Lady.'

Messrs. Cooke and Hinde's fawn and white bitch 'CERITO.'
Dam of 'Hopmarket,' and 'Speck,' sire of 'Railroad.'
Whelped, 1848.—Height, 25 inches.—Weight, 51 lbs.

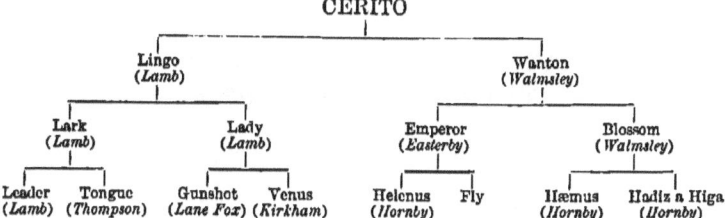

PERFORMANCES.

1849, in October, as 'Lucy Long;' beaten by 'Banker,' in first course for Cockerham Hall Cup.

1850, Feb.—At Broughton; beaten in her fourth course by the winner, 'Blueskin.'
Feb.—Won Waterloo Cup.
March 15.—Beaten in third course, at Altcar Club Meeting, by 'Sefton.'
Oct.—At Wiltshire Champion Meeting; drawn lame after first course.
Dec.—Won Ridgway Challenge Cup and Stakes.
1851, Jan.—Beaten in her fourth course for the Broughton Cup by 'Voltigeur,' the winner.
Beaten in her first course for Waterloo Cup by 'Jamie Forest.' Ran up with 'Dalton' for the Altcar Stakes.
Oct.—Beaten in her third course for the Londesborough Park Stakes, at Market Weighton, by the winner, the 'Three Blues.'
1852, Jan.—Won Crenoline Stakes and Picture, at Southport.
Jan.—Won Altcar Cup, at Club Meeting.
March.—Won Waterloo Cup.
Oct.—Beaten in the first course for the Scarisbrook Cup, at Southport, by 'Director.'
1853, Jan.—Won Altcar Cup, at Club Meeting.
March.—Won Waterloo Cup.

In all, 53 courses, winning 45; nett winnings, 1,000*l.*, besides the Ridgway Challenge Cup and Crenoline Picture.

Mr. T. T. Lister's white and black bitch 'CHLOE.'
Sister to 'Cresswell' and 'Liverpool.'

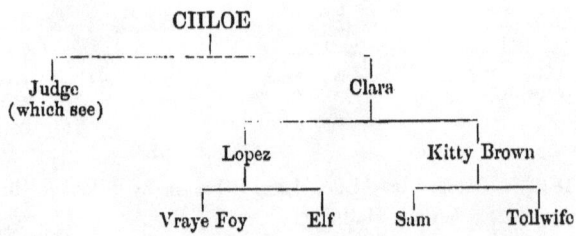

APPENDIX. 379

PERFORMANCES.

1861, Oct.—Ran up to 'Sapphire' for the Oaks at Ashdown Park; 32 dogs.
    Nov.—Beaten by 'Glory' in the first round of the Croxteth Stakes at Altcar.
    Same meeting, ran up to 'Ross' in the Hill House Stakes, 8 dogs, at Altcar.
1862, Jan.—Beaten by 'Band of Hope' in second round of the Members' Cup, at Altcar.
    Feb.—Beaten by 'Helvellyn' in first round of Ladies' Challenge Cup, at Ashdown Park.
    Same meeting, beaten by 'Helena' in first round of Ashdown Purse.
    Nov.—Won Altcar Club Cup; 16 dogs.
1863, Jan.—Beaten in first round of Members' Cup, by 'Retainer.'
    Same meeting, beaten by 'Honeymoon' in second round of Molyneux Stakes.
    Feb.—Won Great Waterloo Cup.
    Nov.—Won Altcar Club Cup; 22 dogs.
1864, Jan.—Beaten by 'Heiress' in third round of Members' Cup, at Altcar.
    Feb.—Beaten by 'Beadle of the Parish' in second round of Waterloo Cup, and by 'Sparkle' in second round of Plate.

In all, 38 courses, winning 27 and losing 11.

Mr. Clark's black bitch 'DRESSMAKER.'
Sister to 'Pleader' and 'Dart.'
Whelped, 1841.—Height, 25½ inches.—Weight, 56 lbs.

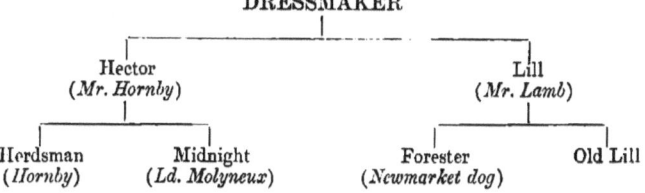

APPENDIX.

PERFORMANCES.

1842, Dec.—Won one course in Lytham Puppy Cup; 16 dogs.
1843, Feb. 8.—Won two courses in Clifton All-Aged Cup, Lytham; 24 dogs.
    Feb. 16.—Ran up with 'Zurich' at Southam, for the Cumberland Cup; 16 dogs.
    Oct.—Won Bendrig Cup; 15 dogs.
    Nov. 1.—Won Chatsworth Cup; 16 dogs.
    Nov. 15.—Won Clifton Stakes, Lytham; 24 dogs.
    Nov. 30.—Won the Cup, Streatham; 16 dogs.
1844, Feb.—Ran up with 'Speculation' for the Waterloo Cup; 32 dogs.
    Nov.—Ran up with 'Rocket' for the Chatsworth Cup; 16 dogs.
1845, Jan.—Won Scarisbrook Cup; 10 dogs.
    Feb.—Beaten by 'Brandy' in second course of Great Clifton Cup.
    Dec.—Beaten in first course for Altcar Cup.
1846, Dec.—Divided Lytham Champion Veteran Stakes.
1847, Feb.—Ran up with 'Old Nick' for Lytham Champion Veteran Stakes.
    March.—Drawn in third course of sweepstakes at Fleetwood.
    Thus winning 41 courses, and losing 7.

PRODUCE.

1848.—'Perseverance,' &c., by 'Marquis.'
1849.—'Staymaker,' 'Cinderella,' 'Waymark,' and 'Jingo,' by 'Foremost.'
1850.—'Worcester,' 'Widow Machree,' &c. by 'Briton.'

Mr. Fyson's 'FREDERICA' (*dead*).

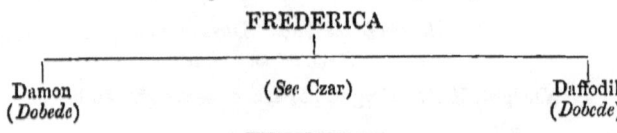

Mr. Webb's 'FLIRT' (*dead*), sister to 'HAVOC.'

APPENDIX.

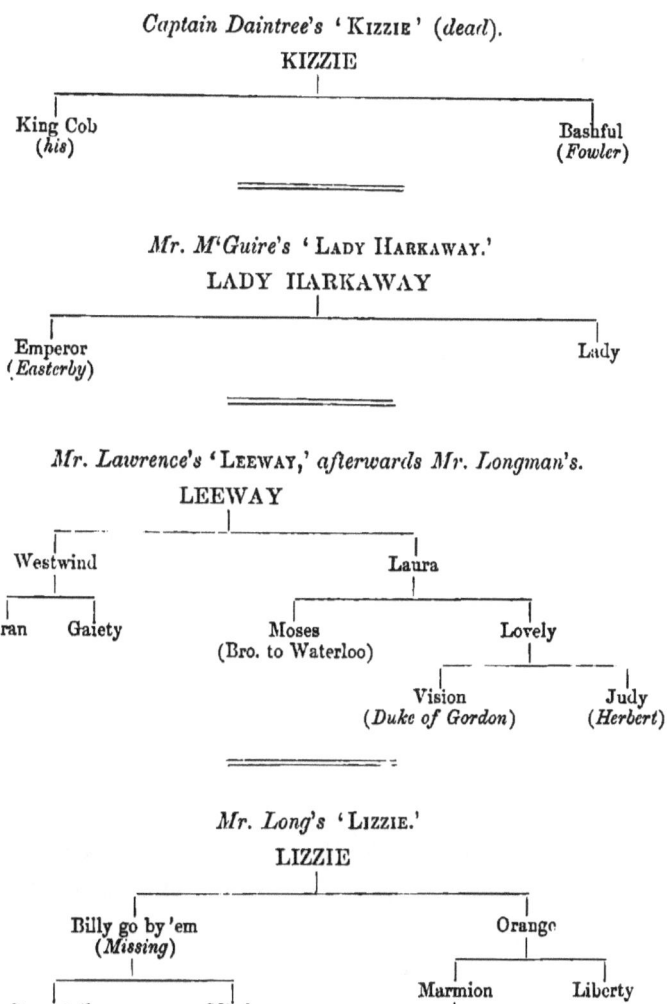

Captain Daintree's 'KIZZIE' (*dead*).
KIZZIE
— King Cob (*his*)
— Bashful (*Fowler*)

Mr. M'Guire's 'LADY HARKAWAY.'
LADY HARKAWAY
— Emperor (*Easterby*)
— Lady

Mr. Lawrence's 'LEEWAY,' afterwards Mr. Longman's.
LEEWAY
— Westwind
  — Bran
  — Gaiety
— Laura
  — Moses (Bro. to Waterloo)
  — Lovely
    — Vision (*Duke of Gordon*)
    — Judy (*Herbert*)

Mr. Long's 'LIZZIE.'
LIZZIE
— Billy go by 'em (*Missing*)
  — Stumptail
    — Rattlesnake
  — Mirth (*Missing*)
— Orange
  — Marmion
    — Major
    — Mirth (*Missing*)
  — Liberty

Mr. Lawrence's brindled bitch 'LANDGRAVINE.'

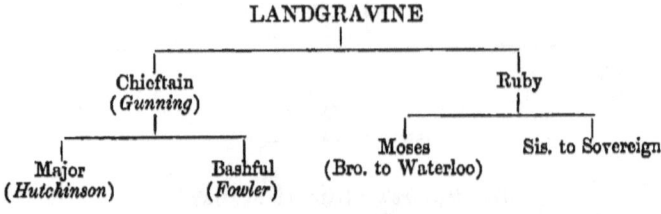

Mr. Sharpe's red bitch 'MAID OF ISLAY.'
Whelped, 1849.—Height, 25 inches.—Weight, 52 lbs.

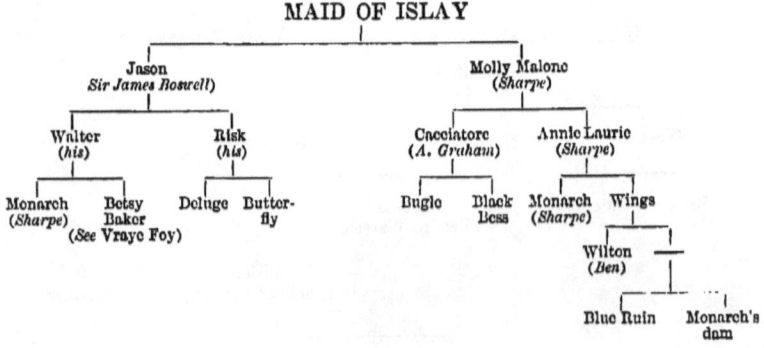

Mr. Marjoribanks' black and white bitch 'MISS HANNAH.'
Sister to 'Marmora,' 'Motley,' 'Captain Cavers,' 'Ancrum,' &c., &c.
Whelped, 1851.—Height, 23 inches.—Weight, 46 lbs.

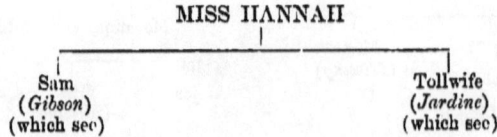

APPENDIX. 383

PERFORMANCES.

1852, Oct.—Won the Great Western Cup, at Amesbury.
1853, Feb.—Divided the Great Western with 'Marmora.'
March.—Won the Waterloo Purse.
Winning 12 courses and dividing one.

Mr. Marjoribanks' black bitch 'MOCKING BIRD.'
Sister to 'Humming Bird,' 'Marsh Harrier,' &c., &c.
Whelped, 1848.—Height, 26½ inches.—Weight, 61 lbs.

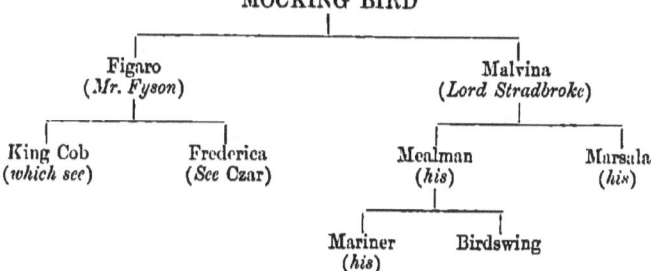

PERFORMANCES.

1849, Nov.—As Mr. Burton's 'Bonniveen;' was beaten in her second course for the Puppy Stake at Wolverhampton, by 'Patshul.'
1850, March.—As Mr. Holmes'; was beaten in her third course for the Baronet Puppy Cup, at Abington, by 'Wigan.'
In October, was beaten in her third course for the Druid Cup, by 'Ebb.'
Nov.—Won the St. Leger Stakes, 12 dogs, at Barton-on-Humber.
In the same month, divided the All-Aged Stakes, 20 dogs, with 'Merchant,' at Newmarket.
1851, Feb.—Won the Cup, 16 dogs, at Newmarket.
In the same month, ran third for the Waterloo Cup; beaten by 'Hughie Graham.'

1851, March.—Won the great North and South Stakes, 64 dogs, at Amesbury.
Oct.—Won the Druid Cup, 32 dogs, at Amesbury.
1852, March.—Was beaten in her second course for the Waterloo Cup, by 'Stanley.'
In November, was beaten in her second course at Ashdown Park, by 'Lizzie.'
1853, Jan.—Was beaten in her first course at Hornby Park, by 'Y. Champion.'
Running 41 courses, and winning 34—losing 7.

PRODUCE.

1852.—'Mansoor,' 'Mæris,' 'Mimosa,' 'Menes,' 'Moph,' 'Mehemet Ali,' 'Mummy,' and 'Mimic,' by 'Egypt.'
1853.—'Mountebank,' 'Minnesanger,' 'Morden,' 'Mandoline,' 'Marqueterie,' 'Motacilla,' 'Miniature,' and 'Masquerader,' by 'Motley.'
1854.—'Mechanic,' 'Momentum,' 'Malakoff,' 'Haymaker,' and three bitches unnamed, by 'Mathematics.'
1855.—'Mummy,' 'Medallion,' 'Mutiny,' 'Lord Mayor,' and black dog unnamed, by 'Ernest Jones.'
1856.—'Master Mocking Bird,' 'Bondsman,' and 'Mazourka,' by 'Lopez.'
1857.—'Mock Turtle,' and 'Mouthpiece,' by 'Junta.'

Mr. Randell's fawn and white bitch '**RUBY**.'
Whelped, 1842.—Height, 24½ inches.—Weight, 50 lbs.

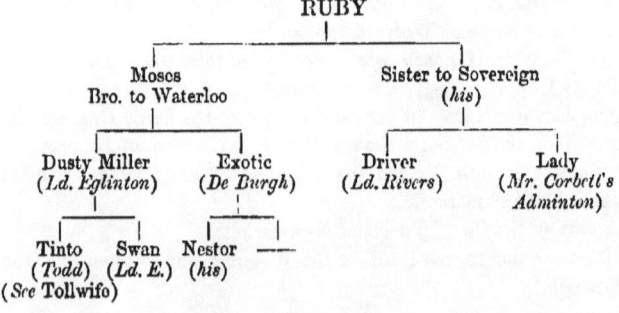

APPENDIX.

Mr. Randell's black bitch 'RIOT.'
Sister to 'Ranter,' 'Gipsy Prince,' Gipsy Royal,' &c.

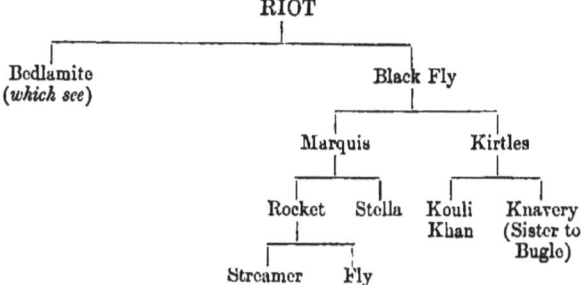

PERFORMANCES.

1854, March 10.—Won at Pensham; 4 dogs.
 March 14.—Won at Croome; 4 dogs.
 Oct. 24.—Beaten at Amesbury; 32 dogs.
 Nov. 9.—Won at Altcar; 16 dogs.
 Nov. 14.—Won at Newmarket; 24 dogs.
 Dec. 5.—Beaten at Barton-on-Humber; 8 dogs.
 Dec. 14.—Beaten at Altcar; 8 dogs.
 Dec. 27.—Divided at Burneston; 16 dogs.
1855, March 20.—Divided at Newmarket; 16 dogs.
 March 29.—Beaten at Biggar; 44 dogs.
 Oct. 24.—Beaten at Southport; 32 dogs.
 Nov. 13.—Won at Ashdown; 36 dogs.
 Nov. 27.—Beaten at Newmarket; 15 dogs.
 Dec. 11.—Divided at Kenilworth; 32 dogs.
1856, Jan. 9.—Beaten at Southport; 32 dogs.
 Jan. 18.—Won at Altcar; 12 dogs.
 Feb. 5.—Beaten at Newmarket; 16 dogs.
 Oct. 20.—Won at Amesbury; 24 dogs.
 Nov. 4.—Divided at Kenilworth; 28 dogs.
 Nov. 25.—Beaten at Sundorne; 16 dogs.
 Dec. 9.—Beaten at Newmarket; 20 dogs.
 Dec. 17.—Divided at Selby; 32 dogs.
1857, Oct. 28.—Won at Altcar; 12 dogs.

1858, March 11.—Won at Tredegar; 8 dogs.
March 11.—Won Cup at Tredegar; 2 dogs.
March 28.—Divided at Caledonian; 32 dogs.
Winning 74 courses, and losing 10.

PRODUCE.

1857.—By 'Barrator,' produced 'Regan,' 'Rioter,' 'Rebel,' 'Reckless,' 'Ringleader,' and 'Romp.'
1858.—By 'Blackcloud,'—'Rosymorn,' 'Refulgent,' 'Patience,' 'Mainspring,' 'Rainbow,' 'Riotous,' and 'Rough weather.'
1859.—By 'Judge,'—'Rienzi,' 'Referree,' 'Recorder,' 'Rhadamanthus,' 'Revolution,' 'Riot Act,' and 'Rebellion.'
1860.—By 'Bridegroom,'—'Master Leotaid,' 'Royalist,' 'Rapture,' 'Repentance,' and 'Resignation.'

Mr. Randell's fawn and white bitch 'RIVAL.'

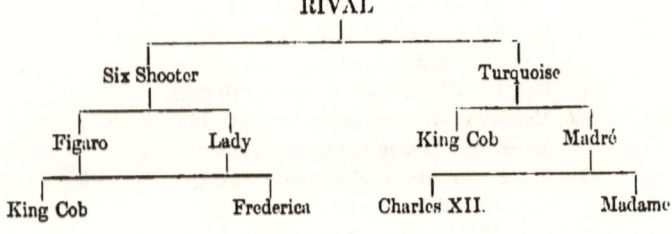

Mr. J. Campbell's white bitch 'SCOTLAND YET.'

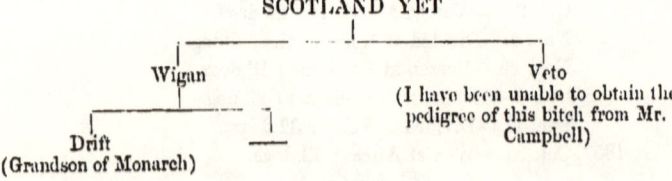

APPENDIX. 387

The Earl of Sefton's brindled bitch 'SAMPLER.'

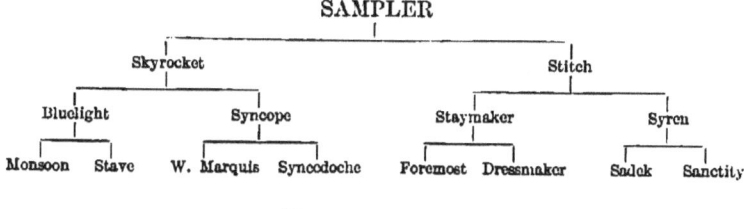

The Earl of Sefton's blue bitch 'SAPPHIRE.'

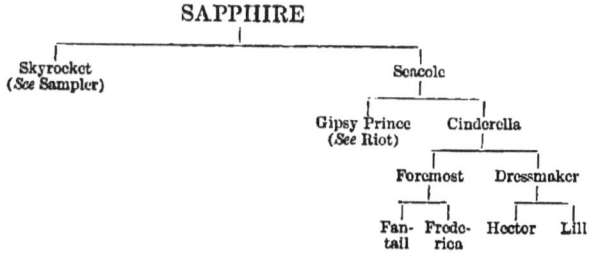

Mr. Spink's white and blue bitch 'SEA PINK.'

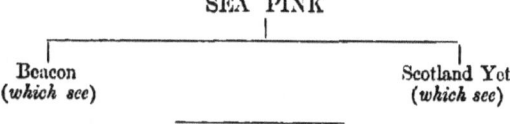

Mr. Bagge's black bitch 'TENDRESSE.'
Whelped, 1850.—Height, 23½ inches.—Weight, 52 lbs.

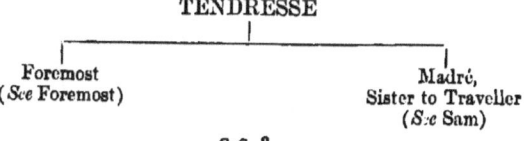

APPENDIX.

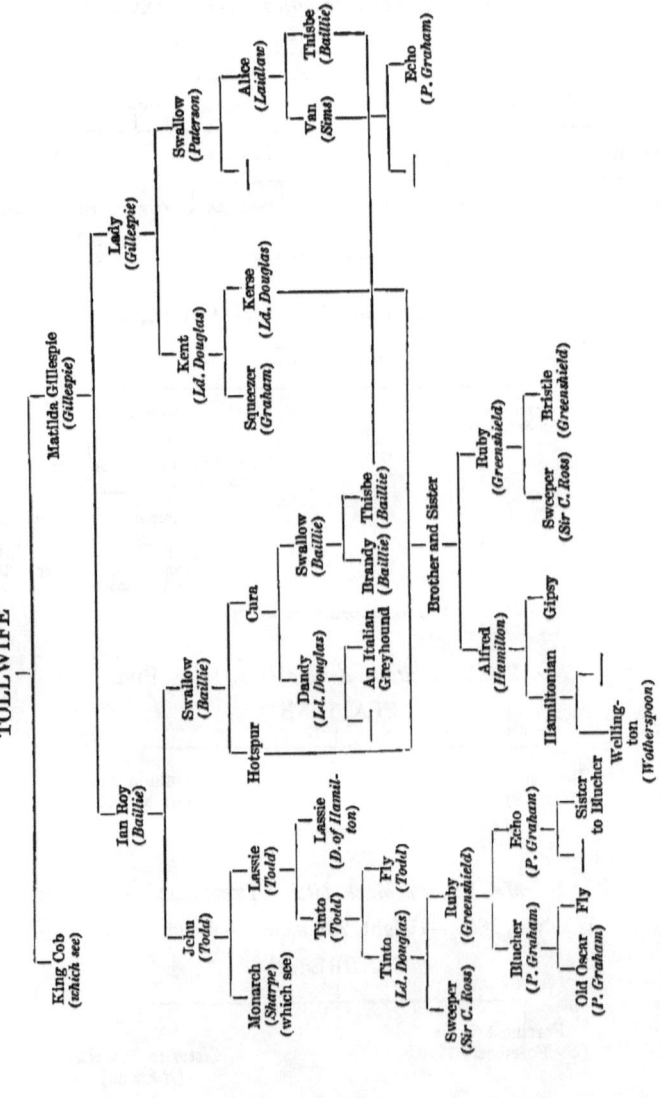

Mr. Jardine's black and white bitch 'TOLLWIFE.'

Note.—'Ian Roy' and 'Lady,' second cousins through 'Hotspur' and 'Kerse,' and third cousins once removed through 'Thisbe.'

APPENDIX. 389

PRODUCE.

1849, by 'Sam,' 'Ancrum,' ' Captain Cavers,' ' Cleik 'em in,' ' Kittie Brown.'
1850, by ,, ' Motley,' ' Money-Taker.'
1851, by ,, ' Miss Hannah,' ' Marmora,' ' Martinet.'
1852, by Malpas's ' Merry Lad,' ' Mighty Polite,' ' Miss Medley,' ' Mathex,' 'Mistake,' ' Malpas,' and ' Merry Andrew.'

Mr. Bagge's 'TWILIGHT.'

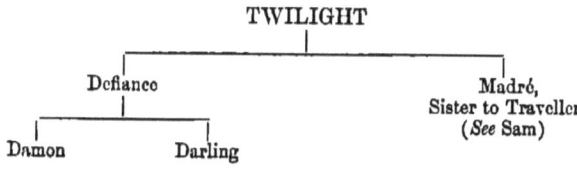

Mr. Bagge's ' TURQUOISE.'

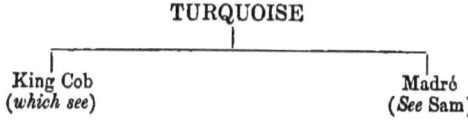

Mr. Temple's black bitch ' TITANIA.'
Whelped, 1849.—Height, 24½ inches.

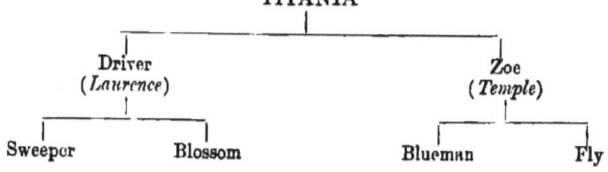

APPENDIX.

PERFORMANCES.

1843, Oct.—At Holywell, beaten in her third course, by 'Pastia Coular.'
  Nov.—Divided the Woodhouse Cup with 'Beeswing.'
  Dec.—At Southport, beaten in her third course, by 'Scrutiny.'
  Dec.—At Altcar, won the Croxteth Purse.
1844, Jan.—At Mold, beaten in second course, by 'Trajan.'
  Feb.—At Hardly, beaten by 'Beeswing.'
  Feb.—Beaten in her fourth course for the Waterloo Cup, by 'Dressmaker,' after undecided course.
  March.—At Mold, beaten in third course, by 'Sweep.'
1845, Jan.—Ran up for the Sefton Cup, 16 dogs; beaten by 'Rowena.'
  March.—Won Waterloo Cup.

PRODUCE.

1844, Oct.—'Topsail' and 'Thistle-down,' by 'Tom Tough.'
1845.—'Tom Bowling,' by 'Tom Tough.'
1846 and 1847.—She was put to 'Lissardo' (Mr. Lloyd), but the produce were large and lumbersome.
1848, Jan.—'Tribune' and 'Thalia,' by 'Scythian.'
  Nov.—'Trial,' by 'Counsellor.'
1850.—'Take,' 'Jet d'Eau,' and 'Pickwick,' by 'Lodore.'
1851.—'Turtle Dove,' 'Alice Tell,' and 'Oberon,' by 'Lodore.'

Captain Wyndham's black bitch 'WHIFF.'
Sister to 'Wench,' 'Westwind.'

Whelped, 1849.—Height, 24 inches.—Weight, 47 lbs.

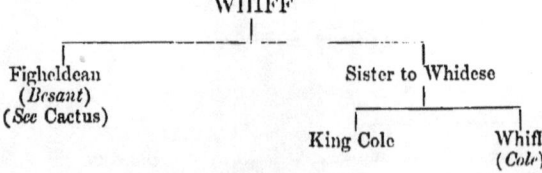

WHIFF
  |— Figheldean (*Besant*) (*See* Cactus)
  |— Sister to Whidese
      |— King Cole
      |— Whifl (*Cole*)

PERFORMANCES.

1850, Oct.—Won Stonehenge Bitch Puppy Stakes ; 4 dogs.
Oct.—Beaten by 'Egypt' in third course of Great Western, at Amesbury.
Dec.—Won Oaks, Deptford Inn ; 12 dogs.
1851, Feb.—Divided Ashdown Stakes, 24 dogs, with 'Manifesto.'
Feb.—Won Everleigh Cup; 16 dogs.
March.—Beaten by 'Leander,' first course of Great North and South Stakes, at Amesbury.
At same meeting, beaten by 'Baron,' in second course of Consolation Stakes, Amesbury.
Oct.—Beaten by 'Lizzie,' in third course, Druid Cup, at Amesbury.
Dec.—Ran up to 'Merry Lass,' in Deptford Inn Cup; 16 dogs.
1852, Jan.—Won Bush Inn Stakes, 8 dogs, at Ashdown Champion Meeting.
Dec.—Divided stake at Deptford Inn ; 8 dogs.
1853, Feb.—Divided stake at Amesbury ; 8 dogs.
Winning or dividing 31 courses and losing 5.

Mr. Webb's ' WICKED EYE.'
Sister to 'War Eagle,' (*which see*).
Dam of 'Blackflag' by 'Bluelight.'

PEDIGREES OF STALLION DOGS ALLUDED TO, OR ADVERTISED IN 1864.

Mr. J. L. Reed's black dog 'AJAX.'

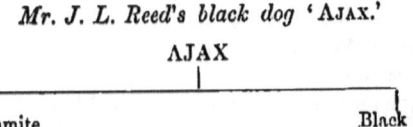

Mr. Wilson's 'ACROBAT.'

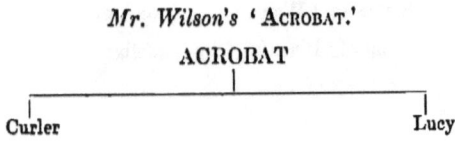

Mr. J. Jardine's black dog 'BARON.'

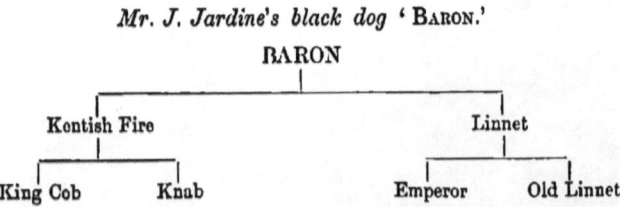

APPENDIX. 393

Mr. Brown's black dog 'BEDLAMITE.'
Brother to 'Bessy Bedlam,' 'Bedlam Lass,' 'Bright Eye,' 'Bird's Eye,'
and 'Bedlam Fury.'
Whelped, 1850.—Height, 26 inches.—Weight, about 58 lbs.

BEDLAMITE

```
                              BEDLAMITE
                                  |
          ┌───────────────────────┴───────────────────────┐
        Figaro                                      Bessy Bedlam
          |                                              |
  ┌───────┴───────┐                          ┌───────────┴───────────┐
King Cob       Frederica                  King Cob                Lively
(Daintree)      (Fyson)                   (Helmsley)            (Woodroffe)
                                              |
                                    ┌─────────┴─────────┐
                                  Smoker    Lady    Brother to    Lady
                                   (his)             Brigand    (Nixons)
                                                        |
                                              ┌─────────┴─────────┐
                                           Rubens   Eve    Tinker   Fan
                                              |                    (Parr)
                                         ┌────┴────┐
                                       Rocket   N. Violet
                                      (Bennett)      |
                                                ┌────┴────┐
                                              Brutus    Sister
                                                        to Nun
```

PERFORMANCES.

1851, Dec.—Won Cup at Hornby Park; 32 dogs.
1852, Jan.—Won Puppy Stakes at Ashdown Park; 24 dogs.
  Oct.—Won Druid Cup at Amesbury; 24 dogs.
  Nov.—Beaten in third course at Hornby by 'Larriston.'
    Winning 17 courses and losing 1.

Sire of 'Riot,' 'Ranter,' 'Gipsy Prince,' 'Gipsy Royal,' 'Blaeberry,' 'Jacobite,' 'Romping Girl,' 'Derry,' 'Seagull,' 'Rhapsody,' 'The Wizard,' 'Hopmarket,' 'Ajax,' and many other winners, or sires of winners.

Mr. Blanshard's black dog 'BELTED WILL.'

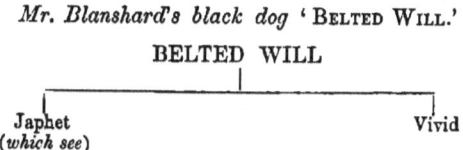

APPENDIX.

Mr. Brundritt's red and white dog 'BELLIGERENT.'
Brother to 'Emilia.'

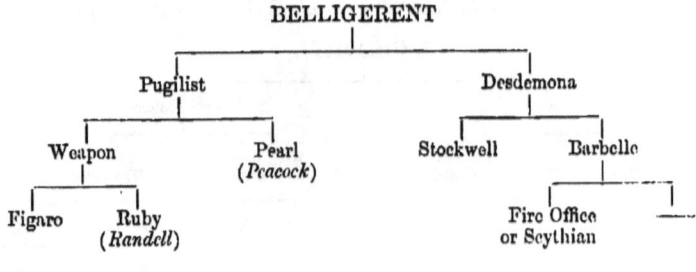

Mr. Blanshard's fawn dog 'BAFFLER.'

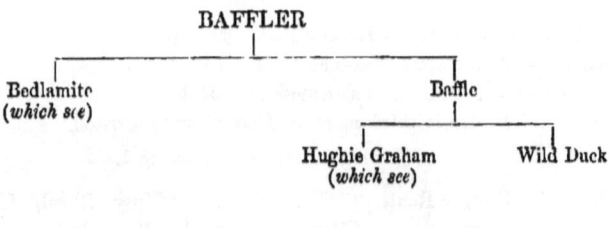

Mr. Hole's, late Mr. Briggs', black dog 'BARRATOR.'

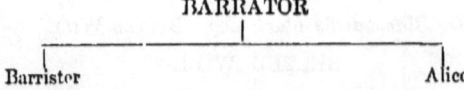

The pedigree of this dog has been traced back to 'King Cob,' but the lines are not very well authenticated.

APPENDIX. 395

Mr. Marfleet's, late Mr. Borrons', blue dog 'BEACON.'

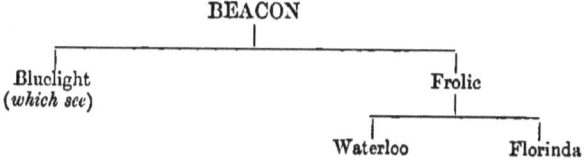

Sire of 'Canaradzo' and 'Roaring Meg,' and grandsire of 'King Death,' all winners of the Waterloo Cup, besides numberless other winners.

Mr. Bake's black dog 'BLACKLOCK' (*dead*).

Brother to 'Birdlime,' half-brother to 'Zurich.'

Whelped, 1841.—Height 26 inches.—Running weight 53 lbs.

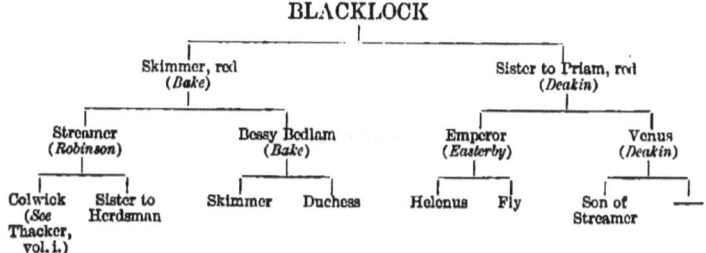

PERFORMANCES.

1842, Dec. 1.—Won Puppy Cup at Streatham; 16 dogs.
Dec. 21.—Won the All-Aged Stake at Fleetwood; 16 dogs.

APPENDIX.

1843, Feb. 1.—Won the All-Aged Broughton Cup; 16 dogs.

Feb. 16.—Ran up for the Puppy Cup at Lowther; beaten by 'Lady,' he breaking his leg in the deciding course.

Winning 15 courses, losing 1 from broken leg.

STOCK.

'Etonian,' 'Etona,' 'Enford Lass,' 'Eaglet,' 'Hylas,' 'Nunc aut nunquam,' &c.

Mr. Randell's, late Mr. Borron's, 'BLACKCLOUD.'

Brother to 'Beacon,' (*which see*).

Sire of 'Belle of the Village,' 'Rosy Morn,' 'Red Lion,' 'Hobbybird,' &c. &c.

Mr. Borron's blue dog 'BLUELIGHT.'

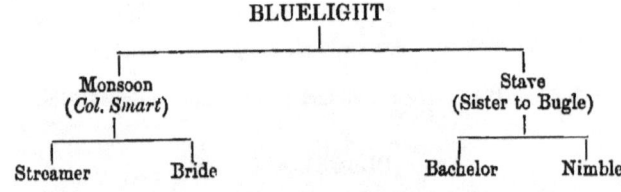

Mr. Gray's white and blue dog 'BLUE HAT.'

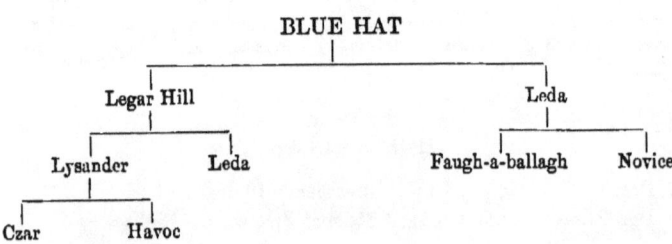

APPENDIX. 397

Mr. Marshall's, late Mr. Borron's, 'BRIGHT STEEL.'

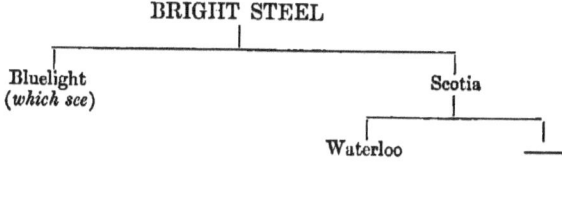

Mr. Blick's brindled dog 'BOUNCE.'

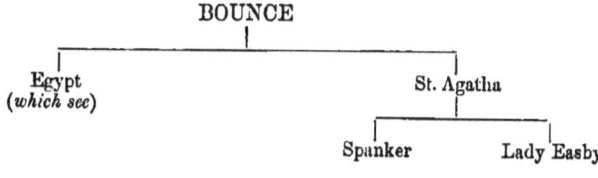

Captain Crichton's 'BARON GARNOCK.'

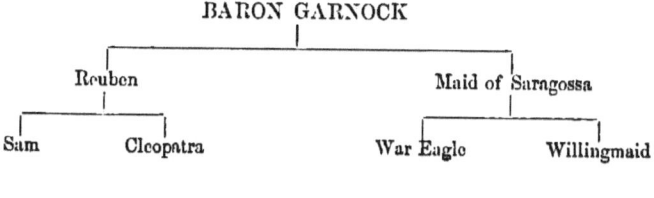

Mr. Jackson's red dog 'BRIDEGROOM.'

398   APPENDIX.

Mr. Blanshard's blue dog 'BUCEPHALUS.'

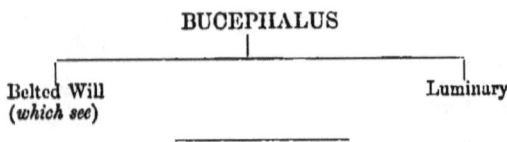

Mr. Borron's black dog 'BLACK FLAG.'

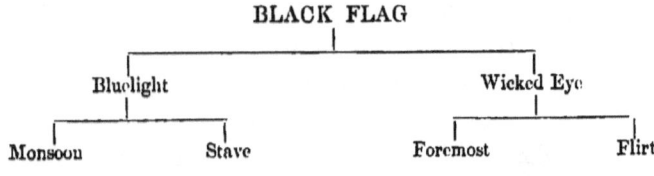

'BLACKADDER.'
'Brother to 'The Wizard,' (*which see*).

Mr. Blenkiron's 'BRITISH TAR.'

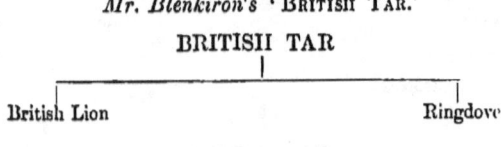

Mr. Smith's white and fawn dog 'BRITISH GRENADIER.'

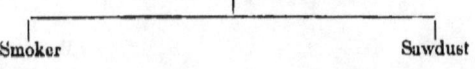

APPENDIX. 399

Mr. Goodaire's blue dog 'BUGLE.'
Brother to 'Canaradzo,' 'Sea Pink,' 'Sea Foam,' &c.

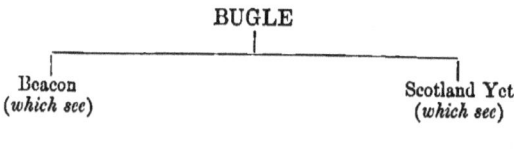

Colonel Bathurst's fawn dog 'THE BREWER.'
Brother to 'Effort' and 'Alboni.'

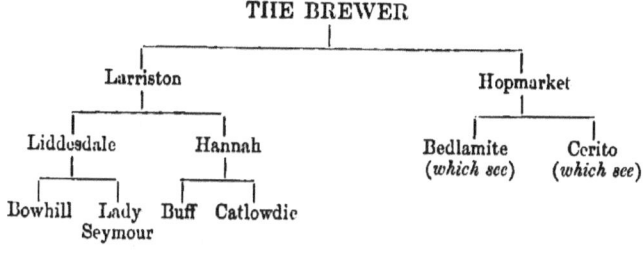

Mr. Unwin's black dog 'BIRD OF PREY.'

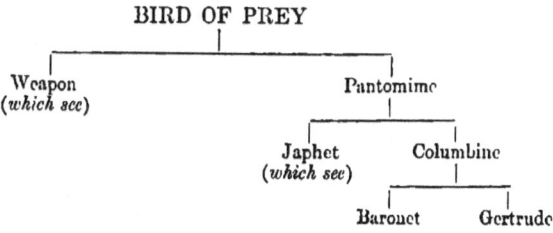

APPENDIX.

Mr. Noble's blue dog 'BANJO.'

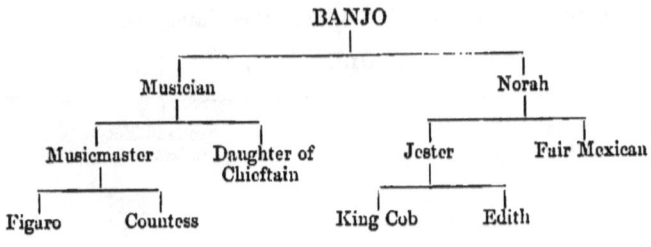

Mr. Campbell's white dog 'CANARADZO.'

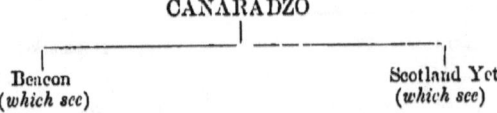

PERFORMANCES.

1859, Sept.—Divided St. Leger at Biggar with 'Terrona'; 57 dogs.
    Oct.—Beaten in fourth round of Caledonian St. Leger, by 'Lucknow.'
    Dec.—Beaten by 'Bold Enterprise' in second round of the Scarisbrook Puppy Stakes at Southport.

1860, Feb.—Beaten in second round of Waterloo Cup by 'Hidalgo.'
    Same meeting, beaten by 'Beranger' in first round of Waterloo Plate.
    April.—Won Western Stakes at the Caledonian Club Meeting; 32 dogs.
    Oct.—Ran up to 'Tipsy Cake' for the Vale of Clywd Cup; 32 dogs.
    Nov.—Beaten by 'Greta' in second round of Clifton Cup at the Ridgway Club Meeting.

1861, Feb.—Won the Waterloo Cup.

1862. —Beaten by 'Kingwater in third round of Waterloo Cup.

Winning 28½ courses, and losing 7.

Sire of 'King Death,' winner of the Waterloo Cup in 1864, 'Armstrong gun,' 'Skedaddler,' and many other winners.

APPENDIX.

Mr. East's black and white dog 'CANTAB.'

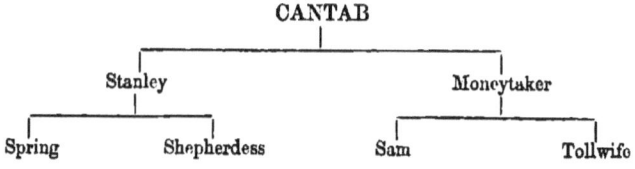

Mr. Dunlop's red and white dog 'CARDINAL YORK.'

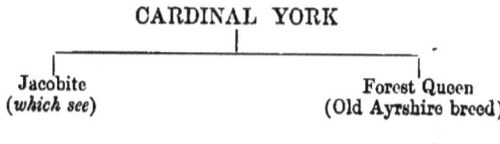

The Earl of Craven's blue dog 'COLCHICUM.'

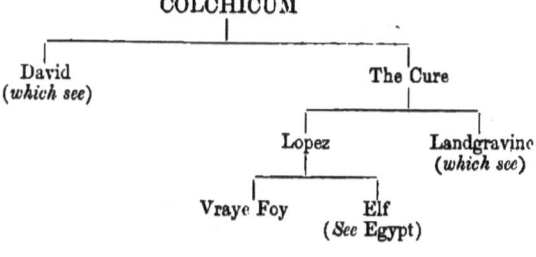

Mr. Gibson's white dog 'COOROORAN.'

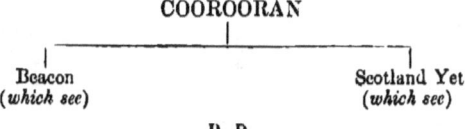

402 APPENDIX.

Mr. Loder's black dog 'CZAR.'
Brother to 'Forward,' 'Cannon Ball.'
Whelped, July 1848.—Running weight, 61½ lbs.—Height, 26½ inches.

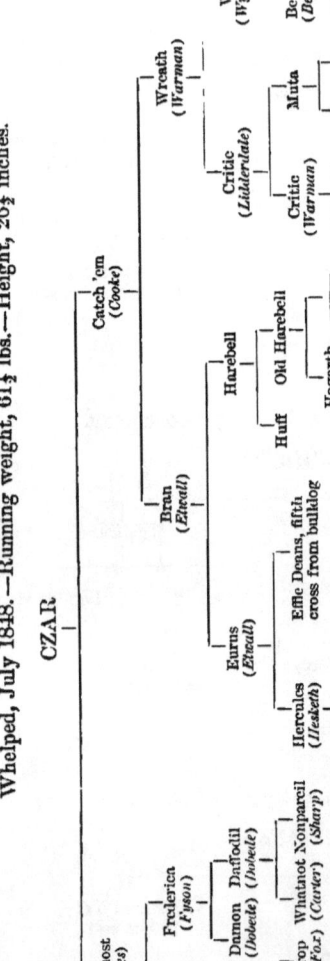

PERFORMANCES.

1847, Nov.—Won the Derby, 8 dogs, at Everleigh.
1848, Feb.—Won the Cup, 16 dogs, at Everleigh.
    Oct.—Ran up with 'Royalist' for the Druid Cup, at Amesbury.
    Dec.—Beaten in his first course for the Newmarket Champion Cup, by 'Lavender.'
1849, Dec.—Won the Bottisham Stakes; 8 dogs.
    Feb.—Beaten in first course for Waterloo Cup by 'Merry Lass.'
    Feb.—Ran up with 'Crenoline' for the Altcar Stakes.
    Oct.—Ran fourth for Druid Cup at Amesbury; beaten by 'Bridesmaid.'

Winning 20 courses, and losing 5.

APPENDIX.

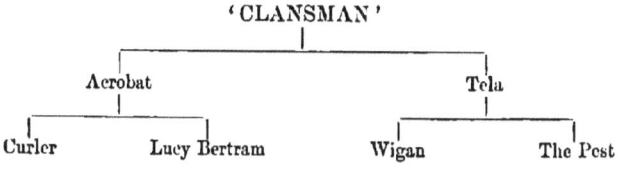

Sir James Boswell's red dog 'THE CURLER.'
Brother to 'Vraye Foy' (*which see*).

Mr. Long's red dog 'DAVID.'

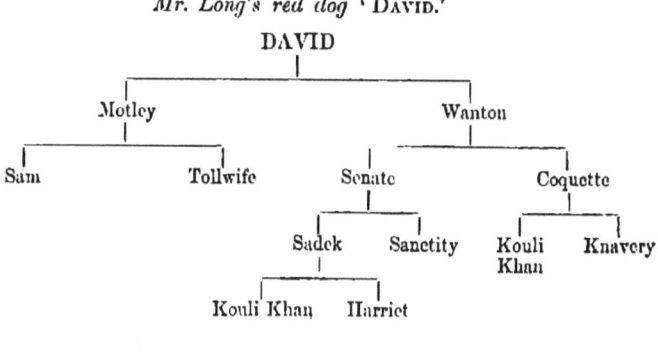

Mr. Deighton's black and white dog 'DER FREISCHUTZ.'

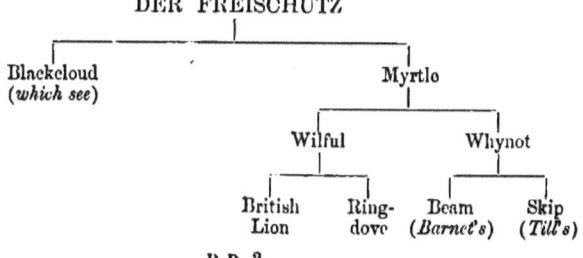

APPENDIX.

'DOCTOR FAUSTUS.'
Brother to 'Der Freischutz' (*which see*).

Mr. John Dunlop's black and white dog 'DARING.'

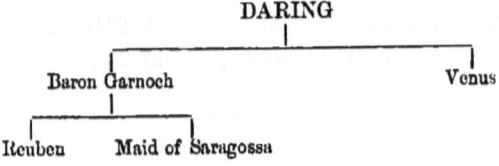

Mr. Grainger's, late Mr. Dobede's, 'DAMSON.'

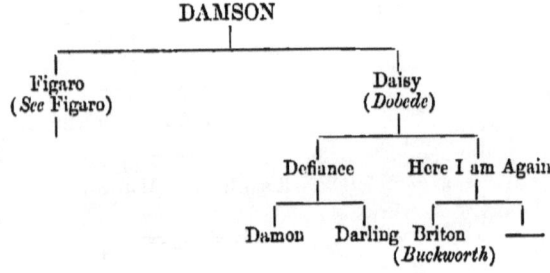

Mr. J. Moore's 'DERWENTWATER.'

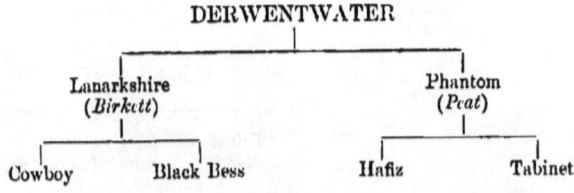

APPENDIX.

Mr. Wilson's 'ECCLEFECHAN.'

ECCLEFECHAN
- Tam Raeburn (*Lord Eglinton*)
- Bitch, by Waterloo (*Lord Eglinton*)

Mr. Eley's 'ESQUIRE,' *and Mr. George's* 'EXCHEQUER.'

ESQUIRE
- King Cob (*Daintree*)
- Edith
  - Fantail (*Fyson*)
  - Empress
    - Sambo
    - Belle

Mr. Etwall's 'EGYPT.'
Brother to 'Lopez.'

EGYPT
- Vraye Foy (*See* Vraye Foy)
- Elf (*Etwall*)
  - Westwind
    - Bran (*See* Czar)
    - Gaiety (*Ld. Stradbroke*)
    - Hilaris
      - England's Queen
        - Hornsea
          - Hilaris
          - f. b. (*Bellyse*)
        - Duck
          - Mountain
          - Dormouse
  - Snail (*Smith*)
    - Snail

APPENDIX.

Mr. *Noyes'* 'FOREMOST.'

Whelped, 1841.

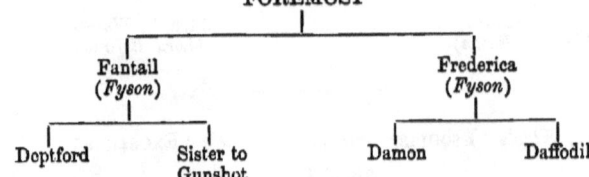

PERFORMANCES.

1842, Nov.—Beaten by 'Douglas,' in first course for Port Stakes, at Newmarket.

Dec.—Beaten by 'Prince' in first course for Rutland Stakes, at Newmarket.

1843, Feb.—Won Derby Stakes at Newmarket; 16 dogs.

Nov.—Beaten by 'Gipsy Queen' in first course for Newmarket Cup.

Nov.—Beaten by 'Duncan' in third course for Rutland Stakes at the same meeting.

Dec.—Beaten by 'Kizzie' in second course for All-Aged Stakes at Newmarket.

1844, Feb.—Beaten by 'Jet' in second course for Newmarket Cup.

Nov.—Beaten by 'Mintman' in second course of Port Stakes, at Newmarket.

1845, Feb.—Won the Newmarket Cup; 12 dogs.

Nov.—Beaten by 'Mintman' in first course for Port Stakes, at Newmarket.

Dec.—Beaten by 'Selborne' in second course of Chippenham Stakes at Newmarket.

Winning 14 courses, and losing 0.

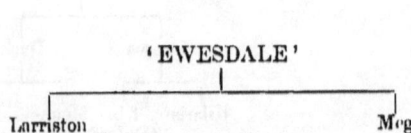

APPENDIX.

Mr. Armstrong's white and brindled dog 'DALGIG.'

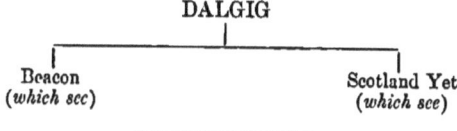

Mr. East's fawn dog 'EFFORT.'

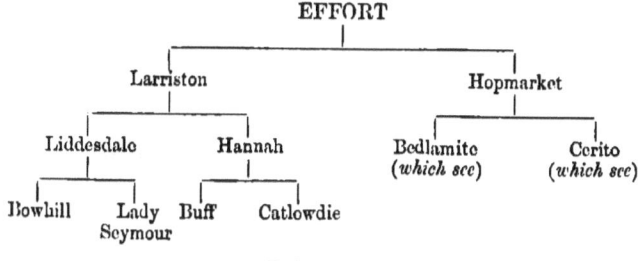

Mr. Simpson's fawn dog 'EDGAR.'

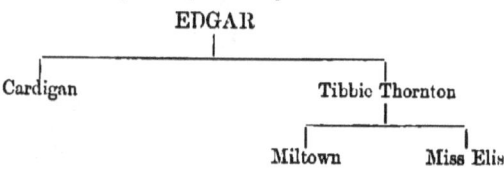

Mr. Faulkner's fawn dog 'FELIX.'

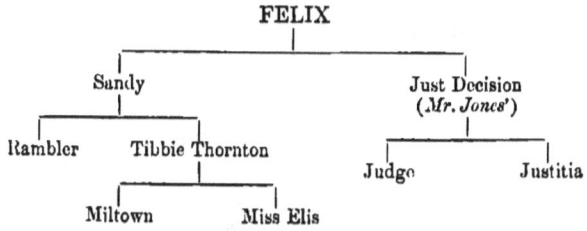

APPENDIX.

Mr. Goddard's 'FORWARD.'
Brother to 'Czar' (*which see*).

Mr. Jenner's 'FACTOTUM.'

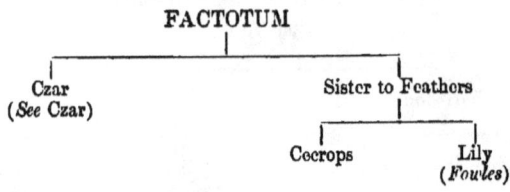

Captain Besant's red dog 'FIGHELDEAN.'
Brother to 'Cactus' and 'Royalist.'

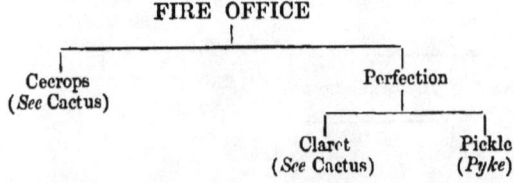

Mr. Fowles' 'FIRE OFFICE.'

```
               FIRE OFFICE
                    |
         _____|_____
        |                       |
     Cecrops                Perfection
    (See Cactus)                |
                        _____|_____
                       |               |
                     Claret          Pickle
                   (See Cactus)      (Pyke)
```

APPENDIX.

Mr. *Brown's* 'FIELD MARSHAL' (*late Fyson's*).

FIELD MARSHAL

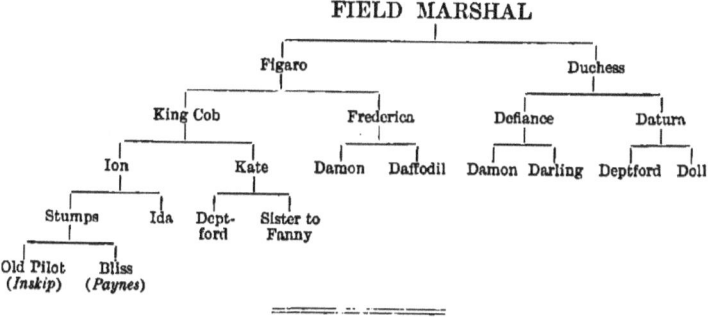

═══════════════

'FOREMOST,' *Jun.*

FOREMOST

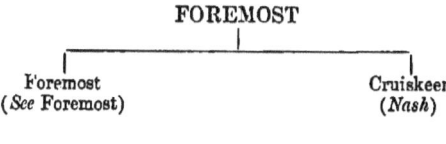

═══════════════

Mr. *Fyson's* 'FORERUNNER.'

FORERUNNER

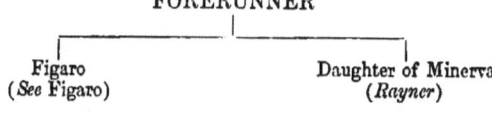

═══════════════

Mr. *J. Sharpe's* 'FORLORN HOPE.'

FORLORN HOPE

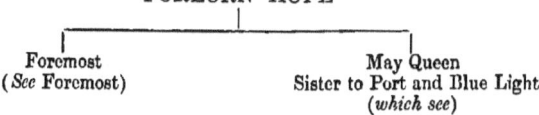

APPENDIX.

Mr. Bowman's 'FORESTER.'

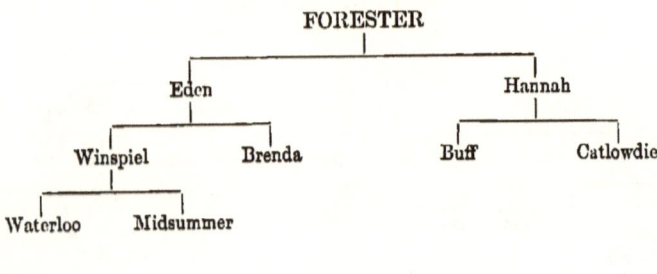

Mr. Fyson's black dog 'FIGARO.'
Brother to 'Dowager Queen' and 'Damask Rose.'
Whelped, 1844.—Height, 26½ inches.—Weight, 62 lbs.

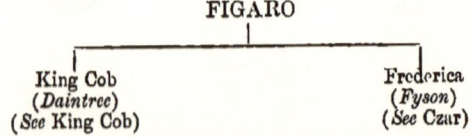

PERFORMANCES.

1845, Nov.—Won the All-Aged Cup, 16 dogs, at Newmarket Club.
    Dec.—Ran up with 'Seidlitz' for the Champion Puppy Stakes at Newmarket; 32 dogs.
1846, Feb.—Ran up with 'Miles' for the Newmarket Cup; 16 dogs.
    Nov.—Was beaten by 'Spinster' in second course for the Cup, at the Newmarket Club Meeting.
    Dec.—Beaten in second course for the All-Aged Cup in Champion Newmarket Meeting.
1847, Feb.—Again beaten in second course at the Picture Meeting, in Wiltshire.
    March.—Ran fourth for Waterloo Cup; beaten by 'Flirt.'

APPENDIX. 411

Nov.—Beaten in second course for the All-Aged Champion Cup at Newmarket.
1848.—Won the Port Stakes, 12 dogs, at Newmarket.
1849.—Won the Cup at Newmarket Club Meeting.
Thus winning 26 courses and losing 7.

STOCK.

'Bonny Lass,' 'Buzzard,' 'Damian,' 'Desperate,' 'Diamond,' 'Field Marshal,' 'Fortune Teller,' 'Merchant,' 'Barmaid,' 'Countess,' 'Mocking Bird,' 'Rhedecyna,' 'Trotzig,' 'Bedlamite,' 'Bedlam Bess,' 'Bedlam Lass,' 'Bird's Eye,' 'Bright Eye,' 'Bedlam Fury,' 'Falsetto,' 'Forerunner,' 'Hotspur,' 'Humming Bird,' 'Revolver,' (afterwards 'Weapon,') 'Six Shooter,' 'Evangeline,' 'Blanch Alpen,' and 'Lablache.'

Mr. Wood's black dog 'GENERAL HAVELOCK.'

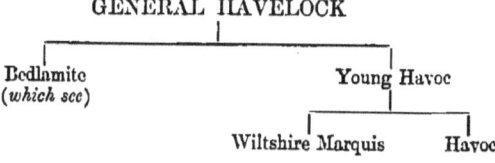

Lord Grey de Wilton's brindled and white dog 'GABRIEL.'

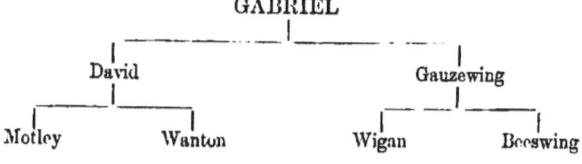

APPENDIX.

Mr. *Cunningham's* red dog 'GLADIATOR.'

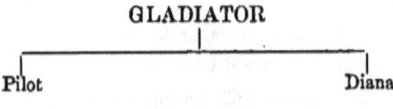

'GILBERT'

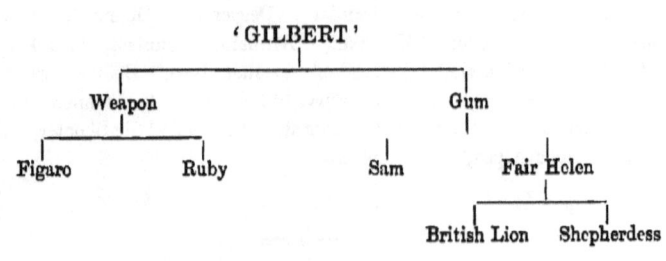

Mr. *Grainger's* red dog 'GHOORKAH.'

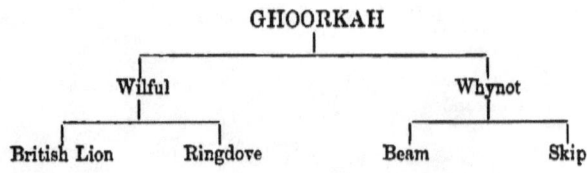

Mr. *W. Long's* 'GIPSY PRINCE.'
Brother to 'Riot' (*which see*).

Mr. *Gunn's* 'GIPSY ROYAL.'
Brother to 'Riot' (*which see*).

APPENDIX.

Mr. T. D. Hornby's 'HAYMAKER.'

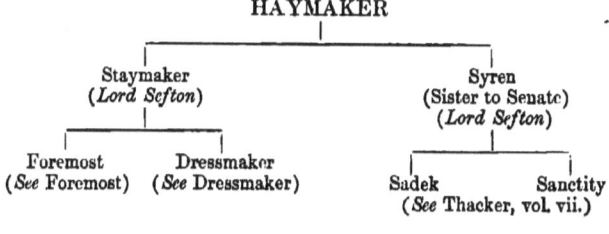

Mr. W. Sharpe's fawn dog 'HUGHIE GRAHAM.'
Brother to 'Bonnie Scotland,' 'Bell the Cat,' 'Queen of the Lothians,' 'Highland Queen,' and 'Lewie Gordon.'

Whelped, 1849.—Height, 26 inches.—Weight, 55 lbs.

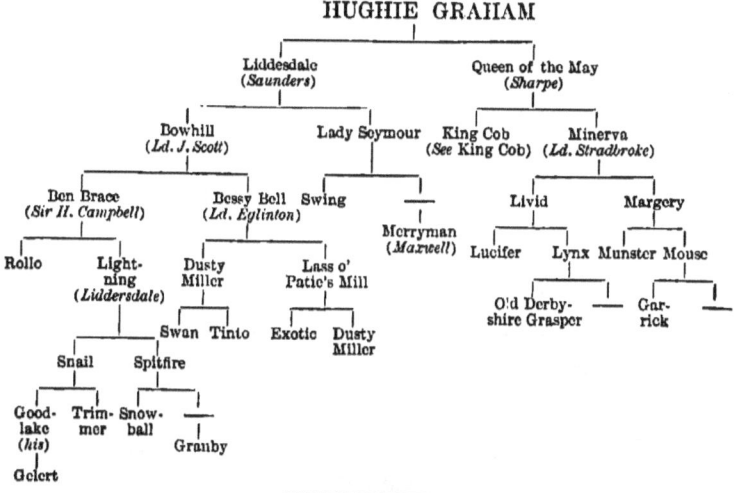

PERFORMANCES.

1850, Nov.—Beaten in second course for Newbattle Abbey Stakes, by 'Venus.'
Dec.—Won the Broughton Cup; 16 dogs.
1851, March.—Won the Waterloo Cup.

APPENDIX.

1852, Jan.—Divided the Clifton Cup, 16 dogs, with 'Larriston.'
  March.—Was beaten in the second course for the Waterloo Cup, by 'Larriston.'
      Winning 14½ courses, and losing 2.

STOCK.

The following bitches have been put to this dog in 1852-3:—
Mr. Sharpe's 'Wicked Eye;' Mr. Oates's 'Raffle;' Mr. Bake's 'Bride;' Mr. Leitche's 'Fly;' Mr. White's 'Maid of Team Valley;' Mr. Wilson's 'Lady;' Mr. Simpson's 'Security;' Mr. Ruddock's 'Red Red Rose;' Mr. Lister's 'Wanton;' Mr. Deane's 'The Nun;' Mr. Sharpe's 'The Rattlesnake;' Dr. Dickson of Forfar's bitch; Mr. Ben's 'Bashful;' Mr. Sharpe's 'Maid of Islay' (dead pups); Mr. Baillie's 'Victoria;' and Mr. Walker's 'Bella.'

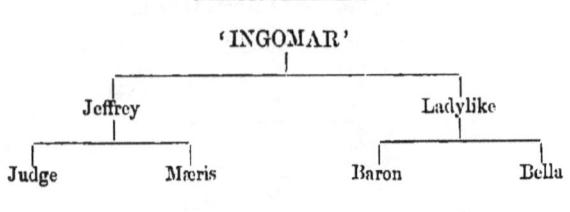

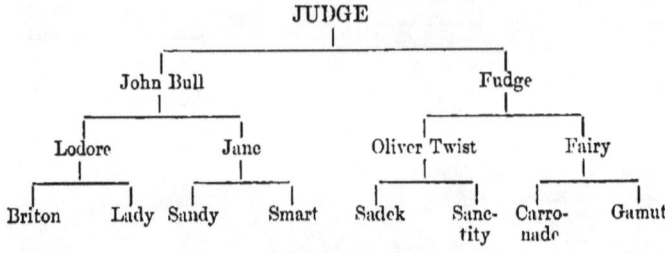

PERFORMANCES.

1853, Nov. 28.—Divided the Puppy Stakes, 8 dogs, with 'Bartolozzi,' at Workington.
1854, Feb. 28.—Won two courses for the Waterloo Cup, 32 dogs, at Altcar; beaten by 'Sackcloth,' the winner.

APPENDIX. 415

March 16.—Won Altcar Cup at Altcar, 16 dogs.
Nov. 9.—Won two courses for the Altcar Cup, 16 dogs, beaten by 'Junius' the winner.
Dec. 12.—Won the Cup at Bridekirk; 16 dogs.
1855, March 2.—Won the Waterloo Cup at Altcar; 32 dogs.
March 20.—Won three courses for the Great Champion Cup, 58 dogs, at Biggar; beaten by 'Bright Idea,' the winner after two undecided courses.
Oct. 20.—Won two courses for the Druid Cup at Amesbury, 24 dogs, and drawn lame after an undecided course with 'Jael,' the winner.
Nov. 8.—Beaten in his first course by 'Sackcloth' at Altcar.
1856, Feb. 28.—Ran up with 'Protest' for the Waterloo Cup at Altcar, 32 dogs, which he lost after two undecided courses.

Number of courses won, 28; lost 5.

Mr. Gibson's 'JACOBITE.'

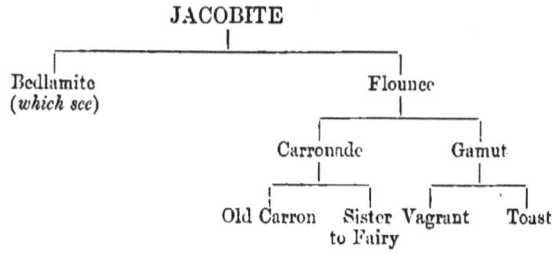

Mr. Jones' 'JUNTA.'

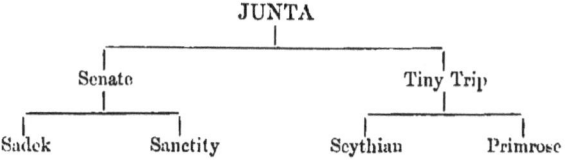

APPENDIX.

Mr. Wilson's 'JAMIE FOREST.'
Brother to 'Bravo,' 'Dick Thornton,' and 'Bonne.'

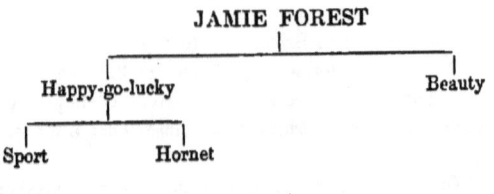

Mr. Smith's red dog 'JAPHET.'

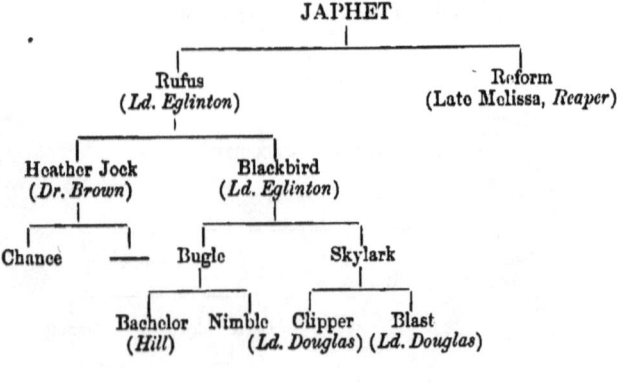

Mr. Smith's black dog 'JEFFREY.'

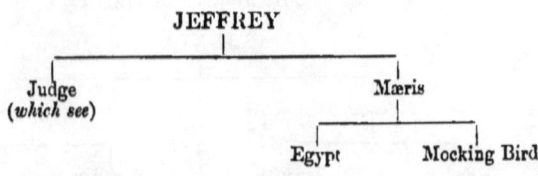

APPENDIX.

Captain Daintree's white and fawn dog 'KING COB' (*dead*).
Whelped, 1838.—Height, 26½ inches.

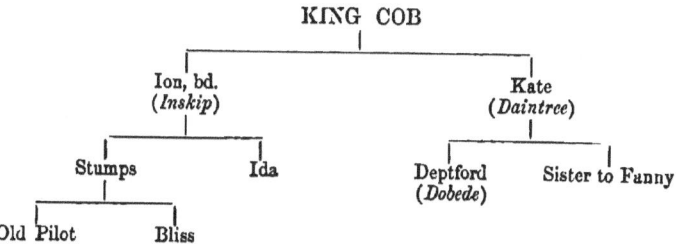

PERFORMANCES.

1840, Nov.—Won the Newmarket Cup; 16 dogs.
1841, Feb.—Won the St. Leger Stakes, 20 dogs, at Barton-on-Humber; and in Nov. was beaten in his second course for the Champion Cup at Newmarket.
1843.—Was beaten in his second course by 'Fairy' for the Antique Stakes at Newmarket.

Winning 11 courses, and losing 2.

WINNING STOCK.

'Kizzie,' 'Kotzebue,' 'Knabella,' 'Probity,' 'Figaro,' 'Damask Rose,' 'Miles,' 'Mercury,' 'Queen of the May,' 'Amina,' 'Turquoise,' 'Magician,' 'Bridesmaid,' 'Esquire,' 'Jester,' 'Exchequer,' 'Mainmast,' 'Maxse,' 'Great Western,' 'Jenny Lind,' 'Royal George,' 'Varna,' 'Kentish Fire,' &c.

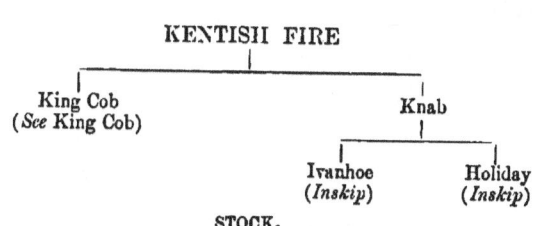

STOCK.

'British Lion,' 'Capacity,' 'Caprice,' 'Citadel,' and 'Lady Bird.'

418 APPENDIX.

Dr. Richardson's white and black dog 'KING DEATH.'

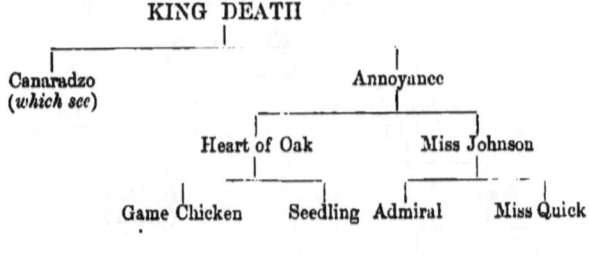

———

Mr. Jackson's fawn and white dog 'KINGWATER.'

———

Mr. R. Long's 'LABLACHE.'

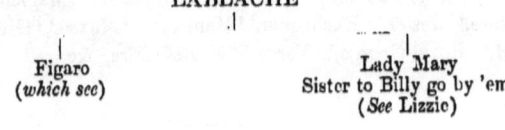

———

Mr. Lawrence's 'LOPEZ.'
Brother to 'Egypt,' (*which see*).

———

LET HIM BE EASY.
Brother to 'Sampler,' (*which see*).

APPENDIX. 419

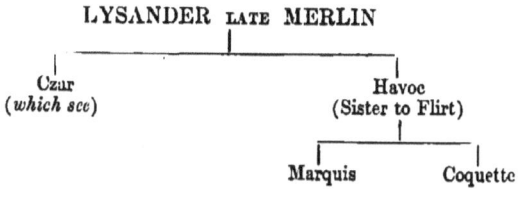

Mr. Missing's black dog 'LITTLE WONDER.'

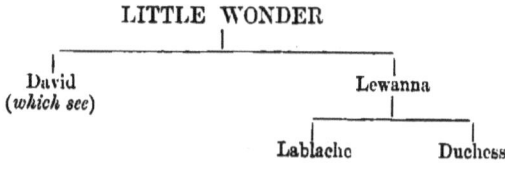

Mr. Bartholomew's black and white dog 'MUSICMASTER.'

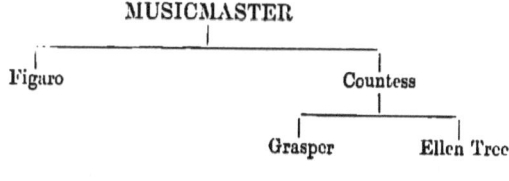

Mr. Clark's 'MONK OF THORNEY.'

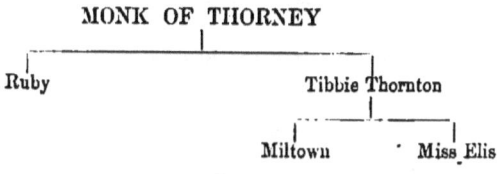

E E 2

420   APPENDIX.

Mr. Sharpe's fawn dog 'MONARCH.'
Whelped, 1835.—Height, 26 inches.

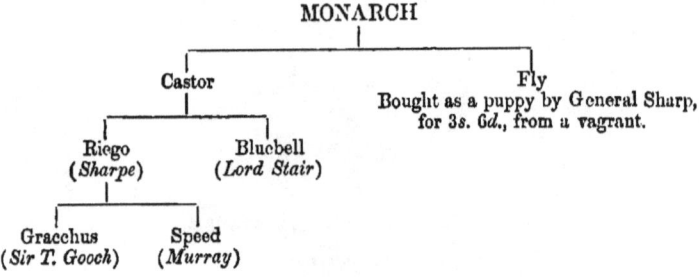

Won two or three stakes in 1838 and 1839.

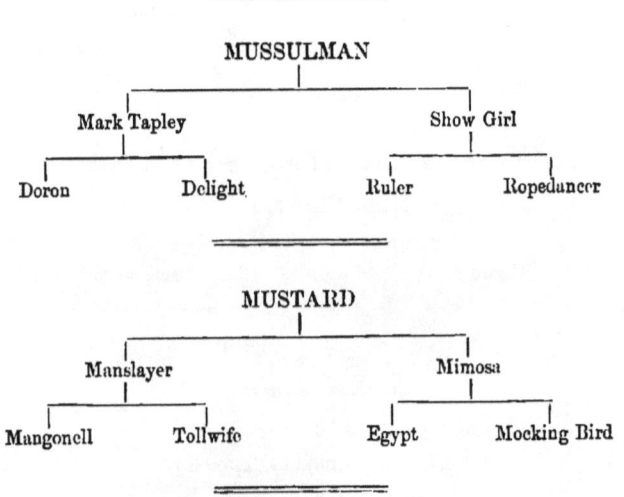

Mr. Myonett's red dog 'MONARCH.'

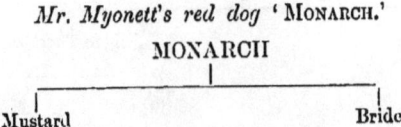

APPENDIX.

MASTER MOCKING BIRD
— Lopez
— Mocking Bird

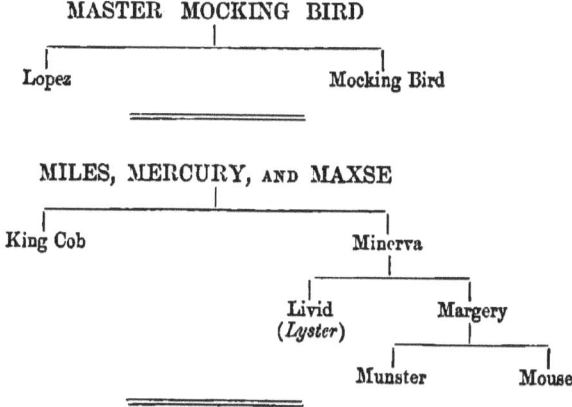

MILES, MERCURY, AND MAXSE
— King Cob
— Minerva
  — Livid (*Lyster*)
  — Margery
    — Munster
    — Mouse

Mr. Reed's black dog 'MECHANIC.'

MECHANIC
— Mathematics
— Mocking Bird

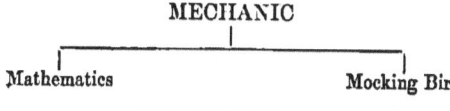

Mr. Gregson's red dog 'NEVILLE.'
Brother to 'St. Godric.'
Whelped, 1848.—Height, 25½ inches; Weight, about 60 lbs.

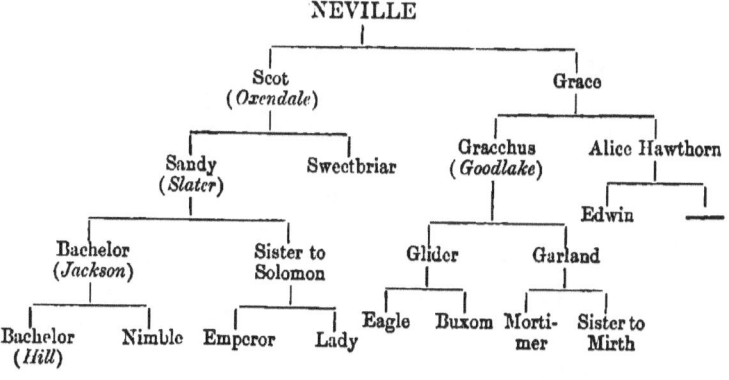

NEVILLE
— Scot (*Oxendale*)
  — Sandy (*Slater*)
    — Bachelor (*Jackson*)
      — Bachelor (*Hill*)
      — Nimble
    — Sister to Solomon
      — Emperor
      — Lady
  — Sweetbriar
— Grace
  — Gracchus (*Goodlake*)
    — Glider
      — Eagle
      — Buxom
    — Garland
      — Mortimer
      — Sister to Mirth
  — Alice Hawthorn
    — Edwin

PERFORMANCES.

1849.—Won St. Leger, Malleny; 92 dogs.
1850.—Ran up for Waterloo Cup.
        Divided Cup, Abingdon Open Meeting; 16 dogs.
        Nov.—Won an 8-dog Stake at Lytham.
1851.—Ran up for Waterloo Purse; 16 dogs.
1852.—Won the Waterloo Purse.

Mr. Gilbert's 'NORTH BRITON.'

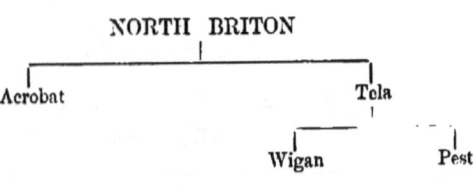

Mr. Reeve's 'PIRATE.'

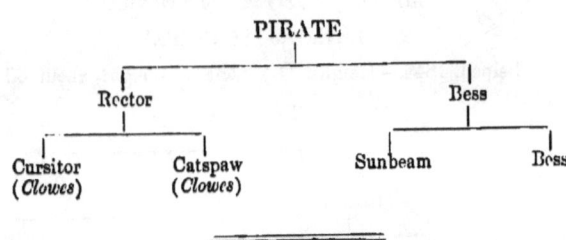

OTHELLO

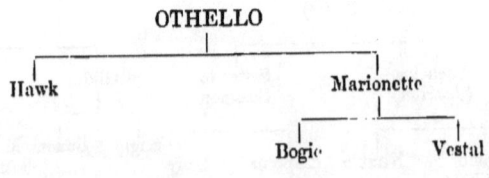

APPENDIX.

Mr. Till's red dog 'OAKBALL.'

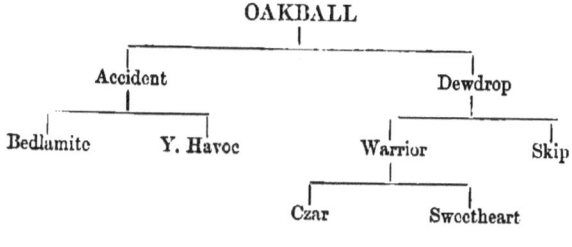

Mr. Price's brindled and white dog 'PATENT.'

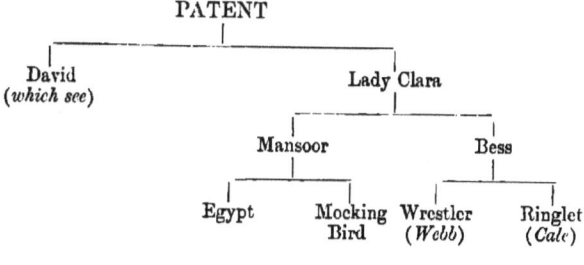

Mr. Purser's white dog 'PARAMOUNT.'

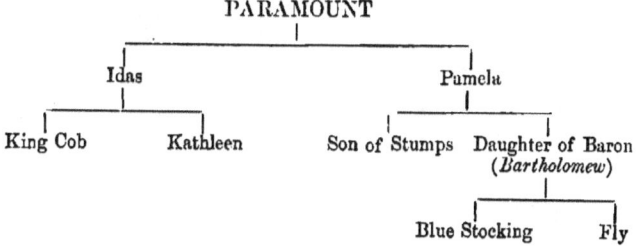

APPENDIX.

Mr. Dunlop's black and white dog 'PICTON.'
Brother to 'Cardinal York,' (*which see*).

Mr. Randell's black dog 'RANTER.'
Brother to 'Riot,' (*which see*)

Mr. Inskip's brindled dog 'RIPPER.'

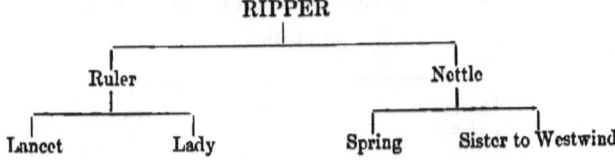

Mr. Loder's black and white dog 'RAILROAD.'
Brother to 'Rex.'

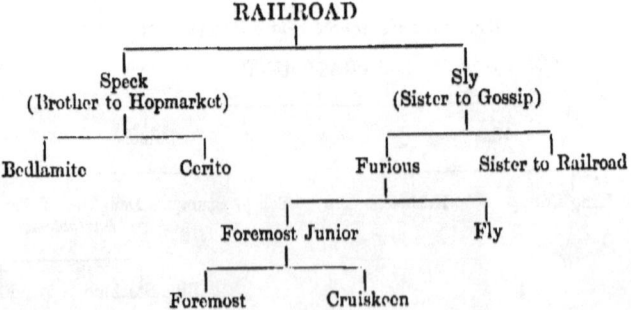

APPENDIX.

Mr. Hill's 'REBEL.'
Brother to 'Regan' and 'Ringleader.'

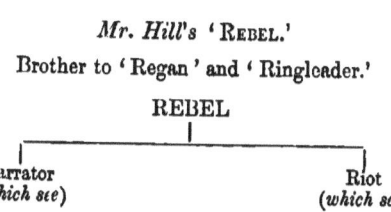

```
              REBEL
      _____|_____
      |               |
   Barrator          Riot
  (which see)      (which see)
```

Mr. William's red dog 'RED LION.'

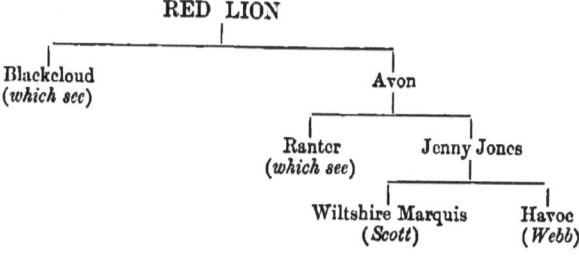

```
                RED LION
          _____|_____
          |                 |
      Blackcloud           Avon
      (which see)       ____|____
                        |       |
                     Ranter   Jenny Jones
                   (which see)    |
                              ____|____
                              |       |
                      Wiltshire Marquis  Havoc
                          (Scott)       (Webb)
```

Mr. Randell's black dog 'REGAN.'

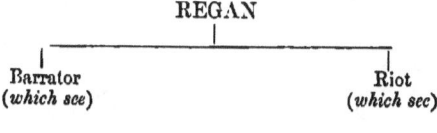

```
              REGAN
      _____|_____
      |               |
   Barrator          Riot
  (which see)      (which see)
```

Mr. Brocklebank's red dogs 'REFERREE' and 'RIENZI.'

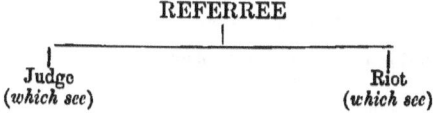

```
             REFERREE
      _____|_____
      |               |
    Judge            Riot
  (which see)     (which see)
```

APPENDIX.

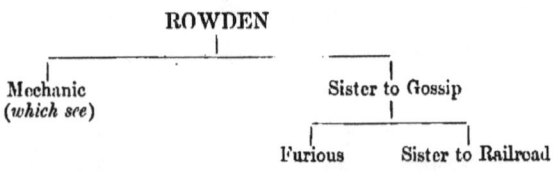

The Earl of Sefton's black dog 'SACKCLOTH.'

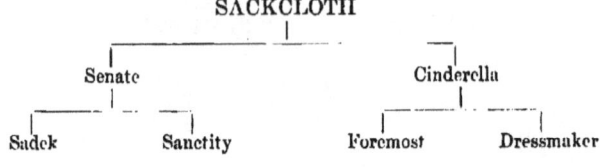

Mr. Gibson's black and white dog 'SAM.'
Brother to 'Sable.'

Whelped, 1847.—Height, 25 inches.—Weight, 58 lbs.

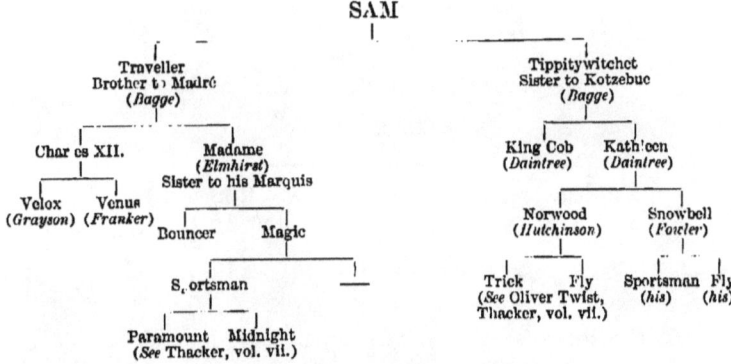

PERFORMANCES.

1848, Oct.—As Mr. Parkinson's, won the Stonehenge Puppy Stake at Amesbury.

Nov.—Was beaten in his third course for the Ashdown Park Derby, having cut and let down the toes of his hind foot. He was then bought by Mr. Gibson, and reserved for the stud.

STOCK.

'Sam Slick,' 'Sam Weller,' 'Cleik 'em in,' 'Kittie Brown,' 'Martinet,' 'Louis,' 'The Prize,' 'Regina,' 'Albert,' 'The Benedict,' 'The Nun,' 'Motley,' 'Nickname,' 'Ancrum,' 'Moneytaker,' 'Napoleon,' 'Bella,' 'Bidglee,' 'Miss Hannah,' 'Marmora,' 'Davie,' 'Ugly Buck,' 'Rosalie,' and 'Stella.'

Mr. Jones' 'SANDY.'
(*See* 'Felix.')

Mr. Spink's fawn dog 'SEA ROCK.'

SEA ROCK
|
Willow   Fanna

Mr. Spink's white dog 'SEA FOAM.'

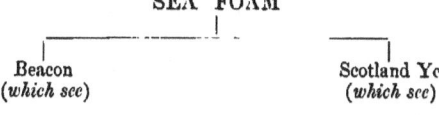

Mr. Spink's blue and white dog 'SEACOMBE.'

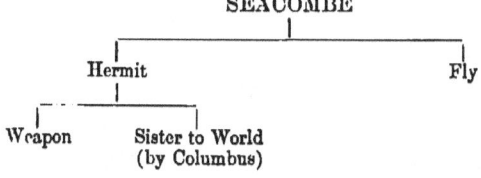

428 APPENDIX.

Mr. Spink's blue and white dog 'SEA KING.'

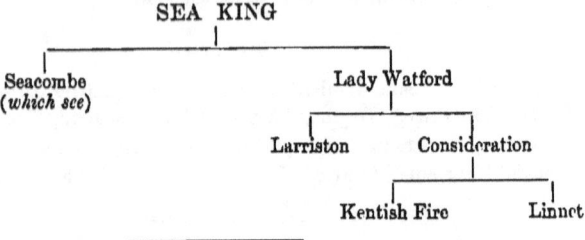

Mr. J. Jardine's black dog 'SELBY.'

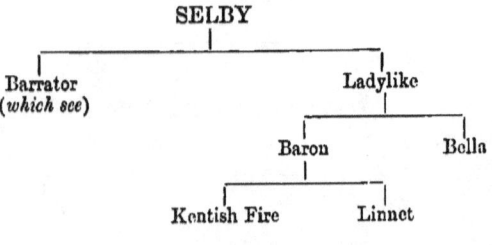

Captain Spencer's black dog 'SEAGULL.'
(Formerly 'Reveller.')

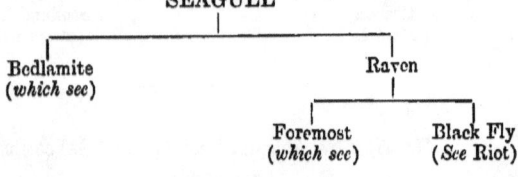

The Earl of Sefton's 'SKYSCRAPER.'

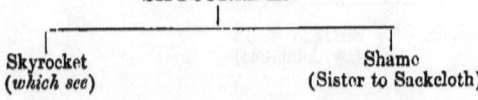

APPENDIX. 429

The Earl of Sefton's red dog 'SHILLELAGH.'

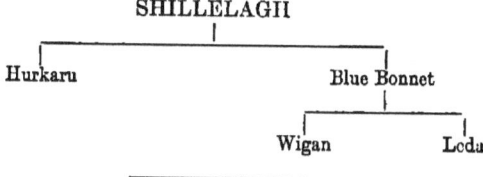

The Earl of Sefton's 'SKYROCKET.'

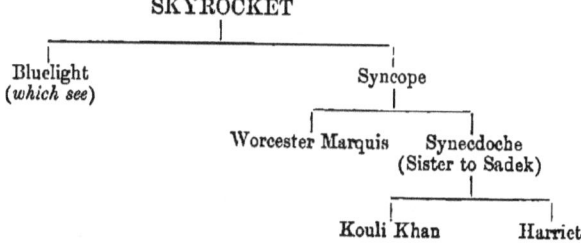

The Earl of Sefton's 'SHOOTING STAR.'

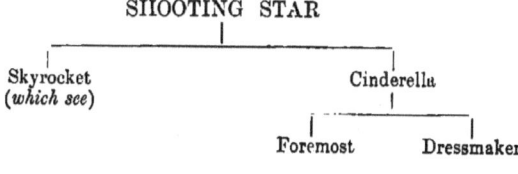

Mr. Steel's black dog 'SPENCER.'

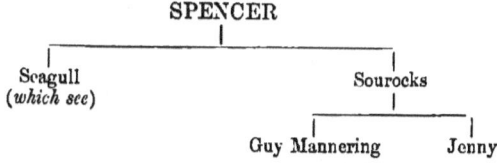

APPENDIX.

Mr. Gibson's fawn dog 'STANLEY.'

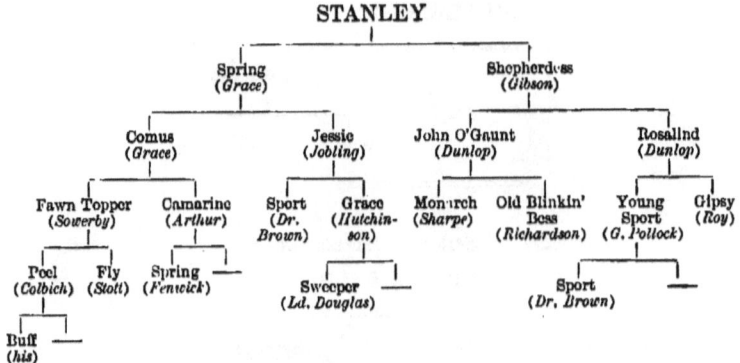

PERFORMANCES.

1851-2.—Won Dirleton St. Leger.
    Won Malleny St. Leger; 120 dogs.
    Beaten in third class of Waterloo Cup, by 'Cerito.'
1852-3, Oct.—Divided Roxburgh Stakes at the Border with Mr. Gibsons' 'Benedict.'
    Nov.—Was beaten in second course at Market Weighton, by 'Otho.'
    March 3.—Was beaten by 'Movement,' in third class of the Waterloo Cup.

The Earl of Sefton's 'SENATE.'
Brother to 'Oliver Twist.'

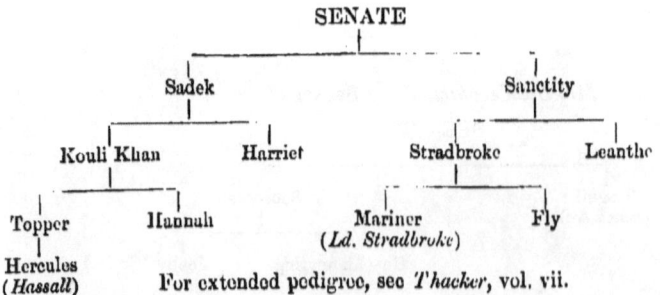

For extended pedigree, see *Thacker*, vol. vii.

APPENDIX. 431

PORT

Brother to 'Sam,' (*which see*).

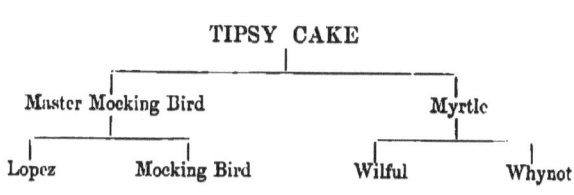

Sir James Boswell's red dog 'VRAYE FOY.'
Brother to 'Auchinleck,' 'The Curler,' 'Polka,' 'Sweetheart,' and 'Rosa.'
Whelped, 1845.—Height, 26 inches.—Weight, 63 lbs.

VRAYE FOY

```
                    |
    ┌───────────────┴───────────────┐
   Jason                          Rosebud
(Sir James Boswell)           (Sir James Boswell)
    |                               |
 ┌──┴────┐                   ┌──────┴──────┐
Walter  Risk              Majesty       Butterfly
(Sir J. Boswell) (his)    Brother to
                          Mariner
                          (Lord      Galloway  Snap
                          Stradbroke)
 ┌────┬──────┬──────┐         |
Monarch Betsy Deluge Butterfly
(Mr. W.Sharpe) Baker
(which see)
       ┌──┴──┐  ┌──┬────┬──────┐        ┌────┴────┐
    Majesty Meg Altcar Rapid Gallo- Snap Ambiguity   Mouse
   (as above) Mer- (Bor- (Raimes) way    (Gurney) (Lord Stradbroke)
              rilles ron)
                          |
                      Sister to Rattler and
   ┌────┬──────┐      Rainbow, great win-   Garrick      Start
 Sweeper Glenarmic    ners, and ninth from  (Gooch)      (his)
 (Marshall) (Lord E.) high-bred bull bitch
```

PERFORMANCES.

1846.—In October, divided the Puppy Stakes at Ardrossan with 'The Curler.'
Nov.—Was beaten in his first course by 'Auchinleck,' at Ardrossan.
1847.—In February, was beaten in his second course at Clydesdale, by 'Handi-
craft.'

Oct.—Was beaten in his second course for the Druid Cup, at Amesbury, by 'Gretna.'
In November, won the Ladies' Prize, 32 dogs, at the Greenway.
1848.—In March, ran fourth for the Waterloo Cup; beaten by 'Smut.'
1849.—In February, won the Ashdown Park Stakes; 8 dogs.

Winning 17½ courses, and losing 4.

STOCK.

'Lead the Way,' 'Lobster,' 'Lopez,' 'Egypt,' 'Lucio,' 'Cigarette,' 'Lucifer,' 'Lucy Ashton,' 'Lark,' 'Phenomenon,' 'Raffy,' &c.

Mr. Webb's black dog 'WAR EAGLE.'

Brother to 'Wrestler,' 'Wicked Eye' (*Mr. Sharpe's*), and 'Well I Never,' (*dead*).

Whelped, 1847.—Height, 25 inches.—Weight, 62 lbs.

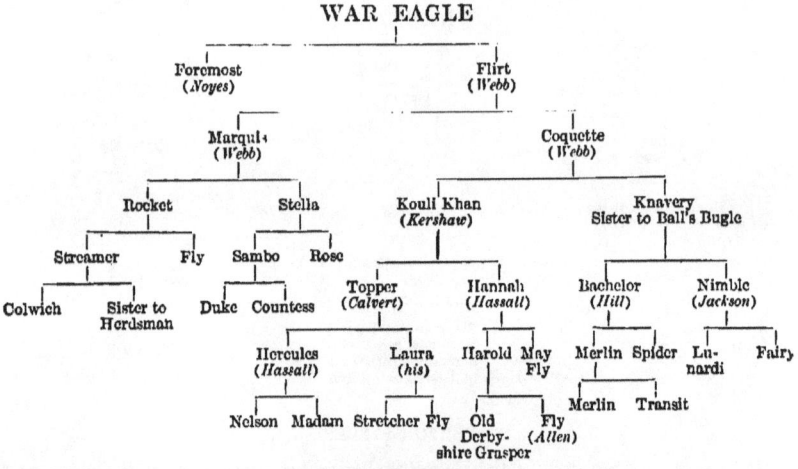

PERFORMANCES.

1848, Oct.—Divided the Biggar St. Leger with 'Wicked Eye;' 28 dogs.
Nov.—Won the All-Aged Cup at Barton-on-Humber; 16 dogs.

APPENDIX. 433

Dec.—Beaten by 'Anticipation,' in first course, Newmarket Puppy Stakes.
1849, March.—Ran fourth for Waterloo Cup; beaten by 'Forward.'
Nov.—Divided Barton-on-Humber St. Leger, 20 dogs, with 'Merry Lad' and 'Highland Laddie.'
Dec.—Won Sefton Cup, Altcar Open Meeting; 16 dogs.
1850, Feb.—Beaten by 'Frolic' in second course for Waterloo Cup.
March.—Beaten in second course for Sefton Cup, at Altcar, by 'Compact.'
Oct.—Ran third for the Druid Cup at Amesbury, beaten by 'Ebb.'
1851, Jan.—Won two courses in Broughton Champion Cup; and ran two undecided courses with 'Cerito,' afterwards drawn by agreement.
March.—Dislocated his knee in first course for Waterloo Cup, and has never since run.

Winning 26 courses, and losing 6.

Mr. Watton's fawn dog 'WOODMAN.'

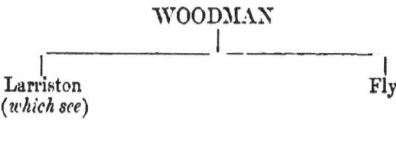

Mr. Hodson's black dog 'THE WIZARD.'

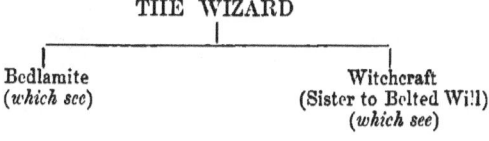

Mr. Webb's 'WRESTLER.'
Brother to 'War Eagle,' (*which see*).

F F

APPENDIX.

Mr. Wilson's black dog 'WEAPON.'
Formerly 'Revolver.'

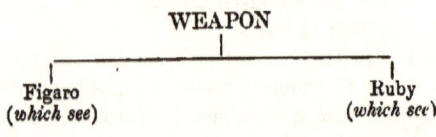

Lord Eglinton's 'WATERLOO.'
(*See* Randell's 'Ruby.')

Red dog 'WESTWIND.'
Brother to 'Whiff' and 'Wench.'

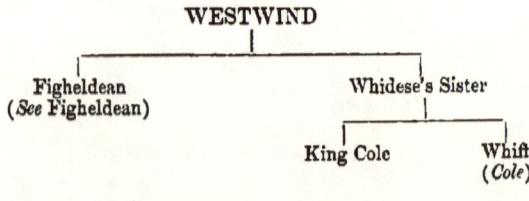

Mr. Hamilton's 'WIGAN.'

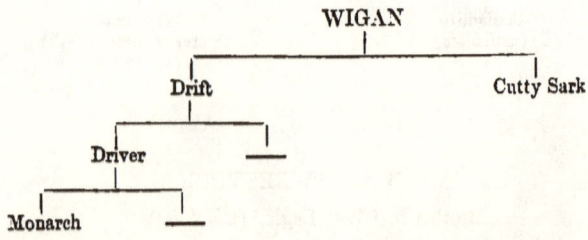

APPENDIX.

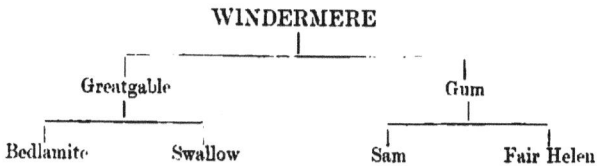

www.ingramcontent.com/pod-product-compliance
Lightning Source LLC
Chambersburg PA
CBHW022139300426
44115CB00006B/259